"This book is an important contribution to the field. I have been publishing articles using EFA for over 30 years, yet it provided me with new insights and information on EFA. More importantly, the material is easy to follow and accessible to researchers and graduate students new to EFA. I highly recommend it to anyone seeking to become competent in EFA."

Joseph J. Glutting, *University of Delaware, USA*

"This book provides a remarkably clear and detailed presentation of best practices in exploratory factor analysis (EFA) that will be of tremendous help to those first learning to understand and conduct EFA and also a great resource for those already using EFA or teaching its use. Its well organized and sequenced presentation of historical development and contemporary use, including annotated descriptions and illustrations, and sample data sets for practice, are invaluable for instruction or self-guided learning. As one who routinely conducts EFA using SPSS I have welcomed Dr. Watkins' creation and free distribution of standalone software to conduct various analyses related to EFA that are not available in SPSS (although they should be) and examples of their use (as well as other applications or SPSS syntax published in the literature) are indispensable resources. I cannot recommend this book more highly!"

Gary L. Canivez, *Eastern Illinois University, USA*

"*A Step-by-Step Guide to Exploratory Factor Analysis with SPSS* offers not only an explanation of how to use the SPSS syntax but also a clear overview of how to conduct an EFA. It is a valuable resource for students and researchers alike."

Stefan C. Dombrowski, *Rider University, USA*

"This is by far, the best book of its kind. Professor Watkins has an accessible and engaging writing style that nicely blends underlying theoretical assumptions of exploratory factor analysis with easy-to-follow, practical suggestions for the statistical calculations. This text will be a tremendous resource for beginning, intermediate, and advanced researchers. Highly recommended!"

Joseph C. Kush, *Duquesne University, USA*

A STEP-BY-STEP GUIDE TO EXPLORATORY FACTOR ANALYSIS WITH SPSS

This is a concise, easy-to-use, step-by-step guide for applied researchers conducting exploratory factor analysis (EFA) using **SPSS**.

In this book, Dr. Watkins systematically reviews each decision step in EFA with screen shots and code from **SPSS** and recommends evidence-based best-practice procedures. This is an eminently applied, practical approach with few or no formulas and is aimed at readers with little to no mathematical background. Dr. Watkins maintains an accessible tone throughout and uses minimal jargon to help facilitate grasp of the key issues users will face while applying EFA, along with how to implement, interpret, and report results. Copious scholarly references and quotations are included to support the reader in responding to editorial reviews.

This is a valuable resource for upper-level undergraduate and postgraduate students, as well as for more experienced researchers undertaking multivariate or structure equation modeling courses across the behavioral, medical, and social sciences.

Marley W. Watkins earned a Ph.D. in Educational Psychology and Measurements with a specialty in School Psychology from the University of Nebraska-Lincoln, USA. He is currently Research Professor in the Department of Educational Psychology at Baylor University, USA, and has authored more than 200 articles, books, and chapters and presented more than 150 papers at professional conferences.

A STEP-BY-STEP GUIDE TO EXPLORATORY FACTOR ANALYSIS WITH SPSS

Marley W. Watkins

Routledge
Taylor & Francis Group

NEW YORK AND LONDON

First published 2021
by Routledge
605 Third Avenue, New York, NY 10158

and by Routledge
2 Park Square, Milton Park, Abingdon, Oxon, OX14 4RN

Routledge is an imprint of the Taylor & Francis Group, an informa business

© 2021 Marley W. Watkins

Library of Congress Cataloging-in-Publication Data
Names: Watkins, Marley W., 1949– author.
Title: A step-by-step guide to exploratory factor analysis with SPSS /
    Marley W. Watkins.
Description: New York, NY : Routledge, 2021. | Includes
    bibliographical references and index. |
Identifiers: LCCN 2020056823 (print) | LCCN 2020056824 (ebook) |
    ISBN 9780367711115 (hardback) | ISBN 9780367710316 (paperback) |
    ISBN 9781003149347 (ebook)
Subjects: LCSH: Factor analysis—Computer programs. | SPSS
    (Computer file)
Classification: LCC QA278.5 .W383 2021 (print) | LCC QA278.5
    (ebook) | DDC 519.5/354—dc23
LC record available at https://lccn.loc.gov/2020056823
LC ebook record available at https://lccn.loc.gov/2020056824

ISBN: 978-0-367-71111-5 (hbk)
ISBN: 978-0-367-71031-6 (pbk)
ISBN: 978-1-003-14934-7 (ebk)

Typeset in Bembo
by Apex CoVantage, LLC

Access the Support Material: www.routledge.com/9780367710316

CONTENTS

FIGURES

PREFACE

Exploratory factor analysis (EFA) was developed more than 100 years ago (Spearman, 1904) and has been extensively applied in many scientific disciplines across the ensuing decades (Finch, 2020a). A *PsychInfo* database search of "exploratory factor analysis" found more than 14,000 citations for the years 2000–2020. However, EFA is a complex statistical tool that is all too easy to misapply, resulting in flawed results and potentially serious negative consequences (Preacher & MacCallum, 2003). Surveys of published research have consistently found that questionable or inappropriate EFA methods were applied (Conway & Huffcutt, 2003; Fabrigar et al., 1999; Ford et al., 1986; Gaskin & Happell, 2014; Henson & Roberts, 2006; Howard, 2016; Izquierdo et al., 2014; Lloret et al., 2017; McCroskey & Young, 1979; Norris & Lecavalier, 2010; Park et al., 2002; Plonsky & Gonulal, 2015; Roberson et al., 2014; Russell, 2002; Sakaluk & Short, 2017; Thurstone, 1937). The uniformity of these results across scientific disciplines (e.g., business, psychology, nursing, disability studies) and 80 years is striking.

Many graduate courses in multivariate statistics in business, education, and the social sciences provide relatively little coverage of EFA (Mvududu & Sink, 2013). A non-random online search for syllabi found, for example, that a graduate course in multivariate statistics at Oklahoma State University devoted three weeks to a combination of principal components analysis, EFA, and confirmatory factor analysis (CFA), whereas a multivariate course at the Graduate School of Business at Columbia University allocated two weeks to cover all forms of factor analysis. In recent decades, courses in structural equation modeling (SEM) have become popular and might include EFA as an introduction to CFA. For instance, an SEM course at the University of Nebraska devoted less than one week to coverage of EFA, whereas a similar course at the University of Oregon failed to include any mention of EFA. Of course, there is no assurance that all, or most, students are exposed to even the minimal content found in these courses. A survey of colleges of education found that doctoral programs typically required only four methods courses of which the majority were basic (Leech & Goodwin, 2008). Likewise, surveys of curriculum requirements in psychology have revealed that a full course in factor analysis was offered in only 18% of doctoral psychology programs, whereas around 25% offered no training at all (Aiken et al., 2008). As summarized by Henson et al. (2010), "the general level of training is inadequate for many, even basic, research purposes" (p. 238).

Researchers must make several thoughtful and evidence-based methodological decisions while conducting an EFA (Henson & Roberts, 2006). There are a number of options available for each decision, some better than others (Lloret et al., 2017). Poor decisions can produce "distorted and potentially meaningless solutions" (Ford et al., 1986, p. 307) that can negatively affect the development and refinement of theories and measurement instruments (Bandalos & Gerstner, 2016; Fabrigar & Wegener, 2012; Henson & Roberts, 2006; Izquierdo et al., 2014; Lloret et al., 2017) and thereby "create an illusion of scientific certainty and a false sense of objectivity" (Wang et al., 2013, p. 719). From a broader perspective, "understanding factor analysis is key to understanding much published research" (Finch, 2020a, p. 1), and "proficiency in quantitative methods is important in providing a necessary foundation for what many have conceptualized as scientifically based research" (Henson et al., 2010, p. 229).

In short, researchers tend to receive little formal training in EFA and, as a result, habitually rely on suboptimal EFA methods. Unfortunately, researchers are unlikely to make better methodological choices as they gain experience because the professional literature is littered with poor-quality EFA reports that model questionable EFA methods (Plonsky & Gonulal, 2015). Additionally, researchers tend to utilize software with unsound default options for EFA (Carroll, 1978, 1983; Izquierdo et al., 2014; Lloret et al., 2017; Osborne, 2014; Widaman, 2012).

Conway and Huffcutt (2003) proposed several potential solutions to improve EFA practice. One suggestion was for

> well-written books of the type that researchers are likely to turn to when conducting EFA (e.g., books on using specific software packages). These articles and books need to clearly spell out the appropriate use of EFA as well as different EFA choices and their implications and urge readers to think carefully about their decisions rather than accepting default options.
>
> *(p. 166)*

Following that suggestion, this book systematically reviews each decision step in EFA and recommends evidence-based methodological procedures that are "markedly better than others" (Fabrigar et al., 1999, p. 294) along with the SPSS (IBM, 2020) software commands needed to implement each recommended procedure. As such, this is an eminently applied, practical approach with few or no formulas. Rather, this book is intended to provide readers with a conceptual grasp of the main issues along with precise implementation instructions to supplement the more mathematical approach found in many multivariate and SEM books and courses. Copious scholarly references and quotations are included to provide the reader with additional resources that might be needed to respond to editorial reviews. This approach should be valuable for students as well as for more experienced researchers who wish to implement EFA in an evidence-based, best-practice, scientifically defensible manner.

1

INTRODUCTION

Historical Foundations

The idea that unobservable phenomena underlie observed measurements is very old and pervasive. In fact, it may be a basic scientific principle (Hägglund, 2001). Philosophers and scientists such as Plato, Descartes, Bacon, Locke, Hume, Quetelet, Galton, Pearson, and Mill articulated these philosophical and mathematical foundations. However, it was Spearman (1904) who explicated a mathematical model of the relations between observed measures and latent or unmeasured variables (Mulaik, 1987).

Spearman (1904) described his mathematical model as a " 'correlational psychology' for the purpose of positively determining all psychical tendencies, and in particular those which connect together the so-called 'mental tests' with psychical activities of greater generality and interest" (p. 205). That is, to analyze the correlations between mental tests in support of his theory of intelligence. Spearman posited a general intelligence (labeled *g*) that was responsible for the positive relationships (i.e., correlations) he found among mental tests. Given that this general intelligence could not account for the totality of the test intercorrelations, he assumed that a second factor specific to each test was also involved. "Thus was born Spearman's 'two-factor' theory which supposed that the observed value of each variable could be accounted for by something common to all variables (the general, or common, factor) and the residual (the specific factor)" (Bartholomew, 1995, p. 212). Spearman also assumed that mental test scores were measured with some degree of error that could be approximated by the correlation of two repeated measurements (i.e., test-retest reliability).

Exploratory factor analysis (EFA) methods were further debated and refined over the ensuing decades with seminal books appearing in the middle of the century (Burt, 1940; Cattell, 1952; Holzinger & Harman, 1941; Thomson, 1950; Thurstone, 1935, 1947; Vernon, 1961). These scholars found Spearman's

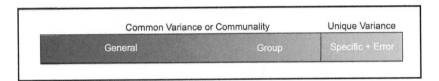

FIGURE 1.1 Variance components

two-factor theory over simple and proposed group factors in addition to general and specific factors. Thus, the observed value of each variable could be accounted for by something common to all measured variables (general factor), plus something common to some but not all measured variables (group factors), plus something unique to each variable (specific factor), plus error. Common variance, or the sum of variance due to both general and group factors, is called communality. The combination of specific variance and error variance is called uniqueness (Watkins, 2017). As portrayed in Figure 1.1, this is the common factor model: total variance = common variance + unique variance (Reise et al., 2018).

The contributions of Thurstone (1931, 1935, 1940, 1947) were particularly important in the development of EFA. He studied intelligence or ability and applied factor analysis to many datasets and continued the basic assumption that "a variety of phenomena within the domain are related and that they are determined, at least in part, by a relatively small number of functional unities, or factors" (1940, p. 189). Thurstone believed that "a test score can be expressed, in first approximation, as a linear function of a number of factors" (1935, p. vii) rather than by general and specific factors. Thus, he analyzed the correlation matrix to find multiple common factors and separate them from specific factors and error. To do so, Thurstone developed factorial methods and formalized his ideas in terms of matrix algebra. Using this methodology, Thurstone identified seven intercorrelated factors that he named primary mental abilities. Eventually, he recognized that the correlations between these primary mental ability factors could also be factor analyzed and would produce a second-order general factor. Currently, a model with general, group, and specific factors that identifies a hierarchy of abilities ranging in breadth from general to broad to narrow is ascendant (Carroll, 1993).

A variety of books on factor analysis have been published. Some presented new methods or improved older methods (Cattell, 1978; Harman, 1976; Lawley & Maxwell, 1963). Others compiled the existing evidence on factor analysis and presented the results for researchers and methodologists (Child, 2006; Comrey & Lee, 1992; Fabrigar & Wegener, 2012; Finch, 2020a; Garson, 2013; Gorsuch, 1983; Kline, 1994; Mulaik, 2010; Osborne, 2014; Osborne & Banjanovic, 2016; Pett et al., 2003; Rummel, 1970; Thompson, 2004; Walkey & Welch, 2010). In addition, there has been a veritable explosion of book chapters and journal articles explicitly designed to present best practices in EFA (e.g., Bandalos, 2018;

Beaujean, 2013; Benson & Nasser, 1998; Briggs & Cheek, 1986; Budaev, 2010; Carroll, 1985, 1995a; Comrey, 1988; Cudeck, 2000; DeVellis, 2017; Fabrigar et al., 1999; Ferrando & Lorenzo-Seva, 2018; Floyd & Widaman, 1995; Goldberg & Velicer, 2006; Hair et al., 2019; Hoelzle & Meyer, 2013; Lester & Bishop, 2000; Nunnally & Bernstein, 1994; Osborne et al., 2007; Preacher & MacCallum, 2003; Schmitt, 2011; Tabachnick & Fidell, 2019; Watkins, 2018; Widaman, 2012; Williams et al., 2010).

Conceptual Foundations

As previously noted, EFA is based on the concept that unobserved or latent variables underlie the variation of scores on observed or measured variables (Bollen, 2002). Alternative conceptualizations have been described by Epskamp et al. (2018). A correlation coefficient between two variables might exist due to: (a) a random relationship between those two variables, (b) one variable causing the other, or (c) some third variable being the common cause of both. Relying on the third possibility, EFA assumes that the correlations (covariance) between observed variables can be explained by a smaller number of latent variables or factors (Mulaik, 2018). "A factor is an unobservable variable that influences more than one observed measure and which accounts for the correlations among these observed measures" (Brown, 2013, p. 257).

Theoretically, variable intercorrelations should be zero after the influence of the factors has been removed. This does not happen in reality because no model is perfect, and a multitude of minor influences are present in practice. Nevertheless, it is the ideal. As described by Tinsley and Tinsley (1987), EFA

> is an analytic technique that permits the reduction of a large number of interrelated variables to a smaller number of latent or hidden dimensions. The goal of factor analysis is to achieve parsimony by using the smallest number of explanatory concepts to explain the maximum amount of common variance in a correlation matrix.
>
> *(p. 414)*

The simplest illustration of common variance is the bivariate correlation (r) between two continuous variables represented by the circles labeled A and B in Figure 1.2. The correlation between variables A and B represents the proportion of variance they share, which is area A•B. The amount of overlap between two variables can be computed by squaring their correlation coefficient. Thus, if $r = .50$, then the two variables share 25% of their variance.

With three variables, the shared variance of all three is represented by area A•B•C in Figure 1.3. This represents the general factor. The proportion of error variance is not portrayed in these illustrations, but it could be estimated by 1 minus the reliability coefficient of the total ABC score.

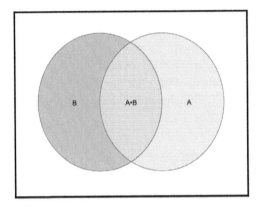

FIGURE 1.2 Common variance with the correlation of two variables

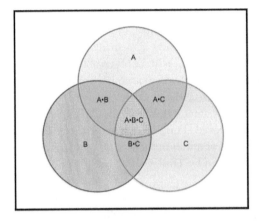

FIGURE 1.3 Common variance with the correlation of three variables

With multiple variables, the correlation structure of the data is summarized by EFA. As illustrated in Figure 1.4, there are 1 to n participants with scores on 1 to x variables (V1 to Vx) that are condensed into a V1 to Vx correlation matrix that will, in turn, be summarized by a factor matrix with 1 to y factors (Goldberg & Velicer, 2006).

EFA is one of several multivariate statistical methods. Other members of the multivariate "family" include multiple regression analysis, principal components analysis, confirmatory factor analysis, and structural equation modeling. In fact, EFA can be conceptualized as a multivariate multiple regression method where the factor serves as a predictor and the measured variables serve as criteria. EFA can be used for theory and instrument development as well as assessment of the

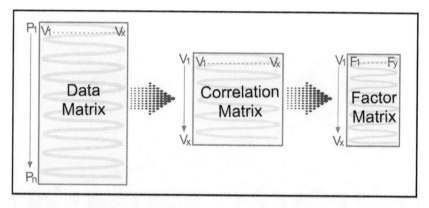

FIGURE 1.4 Summarize data into correlation and factor matrices

construct validity of existing instruments (e.g., Benson, 1998; Briggs & Cheek, 1986; Carroll, 1993; Comrey, 1988; DeVellis, 2017; Haig, 2018; Messick, 1995; Peterson, 2017; Rummel, 1967; Thompson, 2004). For example, EFA was instrumental in the development of modern models of intelligence (Carroll, 1993) and personality (Cattell, 1946; Digman, 1990) and has been extensively applied for the assessment of evidence for the construct validity of numerous tests (Benson, 1998; Briggs & Cheek, 1986; Canivez et al., 2016; Watkins et al., 2002).

Readers should review the following statistical concepts to ensure they possess the requisite knowledge for understanding EFA methods: reliability (internal consistency, alpha, test-rest, and alternate forms), true score (classical) test theory, validity (types of validity evidence), descriptive statistics (mean, mode, skew, kurtosis, standard deviation, and variance), Pearsonian correlations (product moment, phi, and point-biserial), polychoric correlation, tetrachoric correlation, partial correlation, multiple correlation, multiple regression, sample, population, multicollinearity, level of measurement (nominal, ordinal, interval, and ratio), confidence interval, and standard error of measurement. Readers can consult the textbooks written by Bandalos (2018) and Tabachnick and Fidell (2019) for exhaustive reviews of measurement and statistical concepts.

Graphical Displays and Vocabulary

Given the complexity of EFA, it is useful to display EFA models in path diagram form (Mueller & Hancock, 2019). This facilitates a quick grasp of the entire model and allows standardization of presentations. These graphs will visually

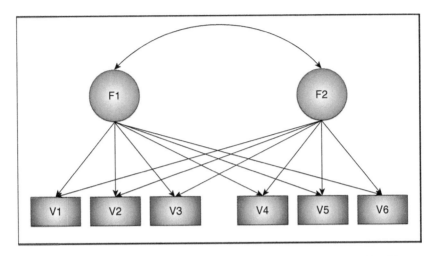

FIGURE 1.5   Simple EFA model with six measured variables and two correlated factors

illustrate the distinctions between latent variables (factors) and observed (measured) variables.

To this point, latent variables and factors have been used synonymously. Many other synonyms may be found in the professional literature, including unmeasured variables, unobserved variables, synthetic variables, constructs, true scores, hypothetical variables, and hypothetical constructs. Likewise, observed and measured variables have been used interchangeably, but terms such as manifest variables and indicator variables are also found in the professional literature. For this book, the terms factors and measured variables will be used to ensure consistency.

A simple EFA model with two factors and six measured variables is presented in Figure 1.5. In path diagrams, ellipses represent factors, and rectangles represent measured variables. Directional relationships between variables are indicated by single-headed arrows and non-directional (correlational) relationships by double-headed arrows. Although not included in this model, the strength of each relationship can be displayed on each directional and non-directional line. In this model, each factor directly influences all six measured variables, and the two factors are correlated. Given correlated factors at a single level, this is an oblique, first-order, or correlated factors model. It represents an unrestricted solution because every factor is allowed to influence every measured variable. Path diagrams may also display error terms for measured variables, variances, etc. Although errors and variances should not be forgotten, they tend to visually clutter path diagrams and will not be displayed. Additional information about path diagrams has been provided by DeVellis (2017).

Path diagrams can also be used to conceptually illustrate the components of variance of an EFA model (Figure 1.6) with one general factor and four measured variables.

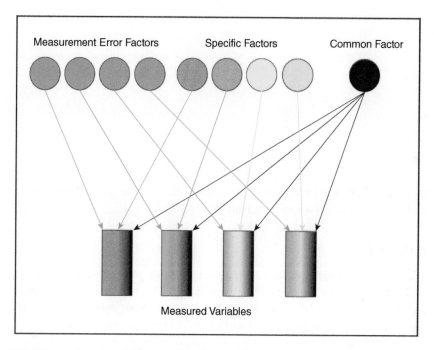

FIGURE 1.6   Conceptual illustration of the components of variance of an EFA model

2

DATA

Six datasets are used in this book to illustrate the steps in EFA. They can be downloaded from www.routledge.com/9780367710316.

Dataset 1

The first dataset contains scores from eight tests developed to measure cognitive ability that was administered to 152 participants. This dataset is in spreadsheet format, and the file is labeled iq.xlsx. These scores are from continuous variables with a mean of 100 and standard deviation of 15 in the general population.

It was anticipated that four tests would measure verbal ability (vocab1, similar1, veranal2, and vocab2) and four tests would measure nonverbal ability (designs1, matrix1, matrix2, and designs2). Brief descriptions of the eight measured variables in this iq dataset are presented in Figure 2.1.

The Pearson correlation matrix generated from the iq data is provided in Figure 2.2.

Dataset 2

A modification of the iq dataset was used to illustrate the procedures that can be employed with missing data. That file, iqmiss.xlsx, contains the same eight variables as Dataset 1, but missing values are indicated by values of −999.

Dataset 3

The third dataset is used to illustrate EFA with categorical variables. Each variable is one item from a self-concept scale. This dataset (sdq.xlsx) is in spreadsheet

Variable Name	Description
vocab1	Provide correct definition of words
designs1	Recreate square designs with colored blocks
similar1	Describe how two words are similar
matrix1	Complete matrix designs
veranal2	Explain verbal analogies
vocab2	Recognize correct definition of words
matrix2	Recognize correct completion of matrix designs
designs2	Recreate geometric designs with puzzle pieces

FIGURE 2.1   Description of the variables in the iq dataset

	vocab1	designs1	similar1	matrix1	verana2	vocab2	matrix2	designs2
vocab1	1.00	0.58	0.79	0.62	0.69	0.82	0.56	0.51
designs1	0.58	1.00	0.57	0.65	0.51	0.54	0.59	0.66
similar1	0.79	0.57	1.00	0.60	0.70	0.74	0.58	0.55
matrix1	0.62	0.65	0.60	1.00	0.53	0.57	0.71	0.62
verana2	0.69	0.51	0.70	0.53	1.00	0.71	0.65	0.51
vocab2	0.82	0.54	0.74	0.57	0.71	1.00	0.58	0.53
matrix2	0.56	0.59	0.58	0.71	0.65	0.58	1.00	0.62
designs2	0.51	0.66	0.55	0.62	0.51	0.53	0.62	1.00

FIGURE 2.2   Pearson correlation matrix for the iq dataset

format and contains 30 variables that were administered to 425 high school students. Responses to each item ranged from 1 (*False*) to 3 (*More True Than False*) to 6 (*True*). Thus, the data are ordinal, not continuous. All negatively valanced items were reverse scored before entry and are identified by an "r" appended to the item number in the dataset.

These 30 items (color-coded in Figure 2.3) are hypothesized to measure three aspects of self-concept: mathematical in red with 10 items, verbal in green with 10 items, and general in blue with 10 items (Marsh, 1990). Reliability estimates in the .80 to .90 range have been reported for these dimensions of self-concept (Gilman et al., 1999; Marsh, 1990).

Dataset 4

The fourth dataset (HolzingerSwineford.xlsx) contains nine mental-ability scales that were administered to 301 middle school students (Figure 2.4). This is an abbreviated version of the classic Holzinger and Swineford (1939) dataset that is used to illustrate higher-order and bifactor models.

No	Description	No	Description
1.	Math is my best subject	16.	Do badly on math tests
2.	Overall, I'm proud	17.	Not much to be proud of
3.	Hopeless in English class	18.	English is one of my best subjects
4.	Need help in math	19.	Good grades in math
5.	Overall, I'm no good	20.	Do things as well as most
6.	Look forward to English class	21.	I hate reading
7.	Look forward to math class	22.	Never want another math course
8.	Most things I do well	23.	My life is not very useful
9.	Do badly on reading tests	24.	Good grades in English
10.	Trouble understanding math	25.	Always done well in math
11.	Nothing ever turns out right	26.	Can do almost anything if I try
12.	English class is easy	27.	Trouble with writing
13.	I enjoy studying math	28.	Hate math
14.	Most things turn out well	29.	Overall, I'm a failure
15.	Not good at reading	30.	Learn quickly in English class

FIGURE 2.3   Description of the variables in the sdq dataset

Variable	Description
visper	Visual perception
cubes	Cubes
lozenges	Lozenges
paracomp	Paragraph comprehension
sencomp	Sentence comprehension
wordmean	Word meaning
speedadd	Speeded addition
speeddot	Speeded counting of dots
speedcap	Speeded discrim of capital letters

FIGURE 2.4   Description of the variables in the Holzinger–Swineford dataset

These nine scales were designed to measure three types of mental ability: spatial ability (visper, cubes, and lozenges), verbal ability (paracomp, sencomp, and wordmean), and mental speed (speedadd, speeddot, and speedcap).

Dataset 5

The fifth dataset is the first practice exercise. This dataset (Rmotivate.xlsx) is also in spreadsheet format and contains 20 variables. Each variable is one item from a reading motivation scale that was administered to 500 students in Grades 2–6 (100 at each grade level). Responses to each item ranged from 1 to 4 to represent

No.	Description	No.	Description
1.	My friends think I am	11.	I have trouble with reading
2.	Read a book	12.	Reading well is
3.	Reading skill	13.	I can answer teacher questions
4.	My friends think reading is	14.	I think reading is boring/interesting
5.	Can figure out unknown	15.	For me, reading is easy/hard
6.	Tell friends about books	16.	Will spend time reading when adult
7.	Understand what I read	17.	I understand reading assignments
8.	People who read are	18.	Would like more reading time
9.	As a reader, I am	19.	When reading aloud
10.	I think libraries are	20.	Would like books as presents

FIGURE 2.5 Description of the variables in the Rmotivate practice exercise dataset

increasingly positive opinions. For example, "My friends think I am: (1) a poor reader, (2) an OK reader, (3) a good reader, (4) a very good reader." Thus, the data are ordinal with four categories, not continuous. All negatively valanced items were reverse scored before entry.

These 20 items are hypothesized to reflect two aspects of reading motivation: reading self-concept (odd items) and value of reading (even items). Reliability estimates of .87 have been reported for each these dimensions of reading motivation (Watkins & Browning, 2015).

A Microsoft Excel file titled RmotivateCorr.xlsx is also available for download. It contains Pearson coefficients computed with SPSS in the upper diagonal and polychoric coefficients computed with Stata in the lower diagonal.

Dataset 6

The sixth dataset is used for the second practice exercise. This dataset is also in spreadsheet format and contains 10 variables. Each variable is one item from a scale designed to tap the symptoms of attention-deficit hyperactivity disorder (ADHD) that was completed by 500 young adults. Respondents reported the frequency of each behavior on a four-point scale: 0 (*Never or Rarely*), 1 (*Sometimes*), 2 (*Often*), and 3 (*Very Often*). Thus, the data are ordered categories and not continuous.

These 10 items are hypothesized to reflect two behavioral aspects of ADHD: attention problems and over-activity/impulsivity problems. It was assumed that the first five items would tap the attention problems dimension, whereas the final five items would tap the over-activity/impulsivity dimension. Similar scales with

Item	Description
instruct	Follows instructions
effort	Sustains mental effort
organize	Organization problems
forget	Forgetful
attention	Sustains attention
go	Constantly on the go
talks	Talks excessively
fidgets	Fidgets
turns	Has difficulty waiting turn
runs	Runs about

FIGURE 2.6   Description of the variables in the ADHD practice exercise dataset

	instruct	effort	organize	forget	attention	go	talks	fidgets	turns	runs
instruct	1.00	.60	.61	.49	.57	.35	.35	.33	.42	.40
effort	.71	1.00	.56	.50	.59	.37	.33	.33	.40	.38
organize	.71	.64	1.00	.53	.54	.36	.38	.31	.46	.40
forget	.58	.58	.61	1.00	.47	.40	.33	.38	.38	.36
attention	.70	.68	.63	.53	1.00	.51	.40	.49	.48	.50
go	.42	.43	.41	.45	.60	1.00	.51	.67	.49	.54
talks	.44	.38	.43	.37	.48	.70	1.00	.52	.50	.44
fidgets	.43	.38	.37	.44	.58	.74	.52	1.00	.43	.48
turns	.50	.49	.54	.44	.56	.61	.63	.55	1.00	.45
runs	.51	.46	.50	.44	.61	.68	.58	.60	.59	1.00

FIGURE 2.7   Pearson (upper) and polychoric (lower) correlation matrices for the ADHD practice exercise dataset

15 to 20 items have typically found internal consistency reliability coefficients of around .85 to .90 for these factors (Nichols et al., 2017).

Pearson coefficients computed with SPSS in the upper diagonal and polychoric coefficients computed with Stata in the lower diagonal for the ADHD data are presented in Figure 2.7.

Correlations have been reported to two decimal places because statistical simulations have shown that "it never makes sense, unless one has a sample size greater than 100,000, to report results beyond the first two leading digits" (Bedeian et al., 2009, p. 693).

3

SPSS SOFTWARE

There are many commercial software packages that can be used to conduct exploratory factor analysis. SPSS, SAS, and Stata are the most popular. A review of statistical software used in academic articles found that SPSS was cited most frequently, followed by **R**, SAS, and Stata (see http://r4stats.com/articles/popularity). SPSS is frequently licensed by colleges and universities, so it is widely available to faculty and students. Accordingly, SPSS will be employed in this book.

SPSS

The first version of SPSS was released in 1968 and the 27th version in 2020. SPSS is more properly titled IBM SPSS Statistics (IBM, 2020). IBM makes several versions of SPSS available: base, standard, professional, and premium. Additionally, there is a separate campus edition for licensure by colleges and universities. These versions differ in the number and type of statistical methods they include, but all versions are available for Windows and Macintosh operating systems. Consequently, users should check their version of SPSS to verify that it includes the statistical methods detailed in this book. This book will reflect the operation of SPSS 27.0.0 on a Macintosh computer and will use the generic title of SPSS regardless of version or operating system. There may be minor differences between operating systems, but results will generally be similar. Detailed information about the various SPSS options is available from IBM at www.ibm.com/products/spss-statistics.

Users of SPSS should download and install the software on their computers according to instructions from IBM and their sponsoring college, university, or employer. Once installed, SPSS can be launched like other programs. On first

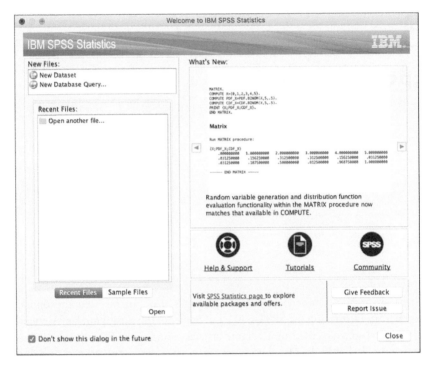

FIGURE 3.1   SPSS welcome window

activation, SPSS generates an introductory "welcome" window that provides access to SPSS support and tutorial web pages, a list of recent files, and the option to report issues to IBM. This opening window can be deactivated by clicking the bottom left ***Don't show this dialog in the future*** checkbox (Figure 3.1). This window is not needed because its functions are duplicated in the SPSS ***Help*** menu.

Data Editor Window

After deactivating the introductory window, SPSS will open a **Data Editor** window and display its main menu (Figure 3.2). SPSS windows are denoted by **bold** type in this book. Like other software, the size of the **Data Editor** window can be adjusted by clicking and dragging its boundaries. The **Data Editor** window is similar to an Excel spreadsheet, where rows and columns of data can be entered. Traditionally, rows are individual participants and columns are variables. The **Data Editor** window is used to input, view, and edit data. Generally, data is input via the keyboard or by loading or importing from a file.

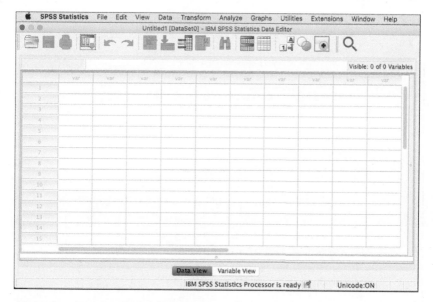

FIGURE 3.2   SPSS Data Editor window

Menus

As displayed in Figure 3.2, the SPSS menu bar contains *File*, *Edit*, *View*, *Data*, *Transform*, *Analyze*, *Graphs*, *Utilities*, *Extensions*, *Window*, and *Help* menus and a row of icons that are shortcuts to menu operations. SPSS menus will be used for a variety of purposes. When encountered, menus and their options are denoted by *bold italic* type in this book (e.g., **Data Editor** > *File* > *Import Data*).

Many aspects of the SPSS display can be modified by "Preferences" that are located in the usual Windows or Macintosh location (*SPSS Statistics* > *Preferences*). The default preferences are probably adequate for most users. However, you may not want the default output to be in scientific notation. That option can be deactivated by clicking on *SPSS Statistics* > *Preferences* > *General* > *No scientific notation for small numbers*.

Output Viewer Window

The **Output Viewer** window is used for SPSS output, both text and graphics. SPSS will automatically display the results of an analysis in the **Output Viewer** window as well as the SPSS command code used to generate that output if that preference has been enabled (Figure 3.3). The command code display can be suppressed via **Output Viewer** > *SPSS Statistics* > *Preferences* > *Log* > *Hidden*.

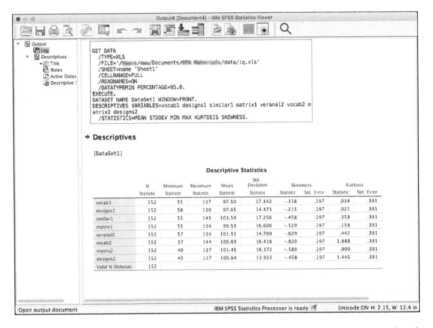

FIGURE 3.3   SPSS Output Viewer window with descriptive statistics command code and output

The **Output Viewer** window is separated into two resizable panes. The **Outline** pane on the left provides an overview of the operations that have been conducted, and the **Results** pane on the right contains the output text, graphics, and syntax code structured as a series of objects. An object may be as simple as a title or as complex as tables or graphs. In this example, an Excel data file has been imported and descriptive statistics generated for the eight variables in that data file. Output from the **Viewer** window can be selected, copied, and pasted into other documents. The **Output Viewer** window and all its contents can also be printed via **Output Viewer > File > Print**. Alternatively, selected objects can be printed by first selecting them and then invoking the **Print** option.

Syntax Window

The **Syntax** window is the source for command code that underlies the point-and-click menus. Essentially, SPSS incorporates a computer language that the user can access through command code. Thus, a wide variety of statistical methods can be directly programmed by knowledgeable users.

Like the **Output Viewer** window, the **Syntax** window is separated into two resizable panes. The left pane is a summary of syntax commands and the right pane contains the detailed list of commands, subcommands, and specifications. Both panes are surmounted by a row of icon shortcuts. As displayed in Figure 3.4, SPSS colors the command codes. That color scheme can be altered via **Viewer > SPSS Statistics > Preferences > Syntax Editor**.

SPSS command code has a mandatory structure. First, commands begin with a keyword that is often the name of the statistical method. In this case, the keyword is DESCRIPTIVES. Upper and lower case can be used for keywords, and keywords can be abbreviated to the first three letters. Thus, DES and DESCRIPT will both be read by SPSS as DESCRIPTIVES. Second, the keyword is followed by subcommands and additional specifications that are separated from each other by a forward slash (/). If one of the specifications is a list of variable names, they can be shortened by listing the first variable followed by the word "TO" and then the final variable. Even shorter would be to use the word "ALL" instead of a variable list. Finally, each keyword and its associated subcommands and specifications *must* end in a period. Comments can be included for explanatory text. The first line of a comment can begin with the keyword COMMENT or with an asterisk and must end with a period. Comment lines will be ignored by the syntax editor.

After command code is entered into the **Syntax** window, it must be executed. That can be accomplished by selecting the command code lines to be executed and then clicking the green triangle on the icon bar. Alternatively, SPSS creates a new menu option, **Run**, when the **Syntax** window is active that can be used to execute some (**Syntax > Run > Selection**) or all (**Syntax > Run > All**) of the command code in the **Syntax** window.

A new **Syntax** window can be opened and the command code entered via the keyboard, or SPSS can generate the **Syntax** window and command code from one of its **Analysis** windows.

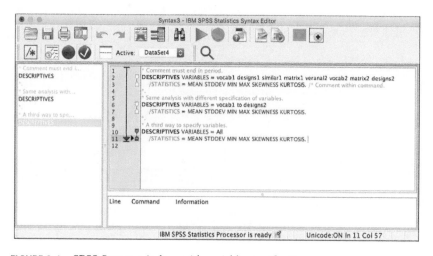

FIGURE 3.4   SPSS Syntax window with variable specification

The same analyses can be conducted via SPSS menu options. Figure 3.5 presents the menu options (*Analyze > Descriptive Statistics > Descriptives*) to begin this analysis.

In this example, The *Descriptives* option was selected from the *Analyze > Descriptive* Statistics menu (Figure 3.6). Like other methods, the user must specify which variables to include in the analysis by moving them from the small window on the left to the **Variable(s)** window on the right. That is done by selecting the variable(s) and clicking the blue arrow.

Once the variables have been moved (Figure 3.7), SPSS enables the *Paste* and *OK* buttons. The *Paste* button will create a new **Syntax** window that contains the *Descriptives* command code. Alternatively, the *OK* button will execute the *Descriptives* command and place the output in an **Output Viewer** window.

Command code may be easier and more accurate than the SPSS graphical user interface, at least in the long run. First, command code is relatively easy to type (or paste from a separate file or from an analysis window) whereas the

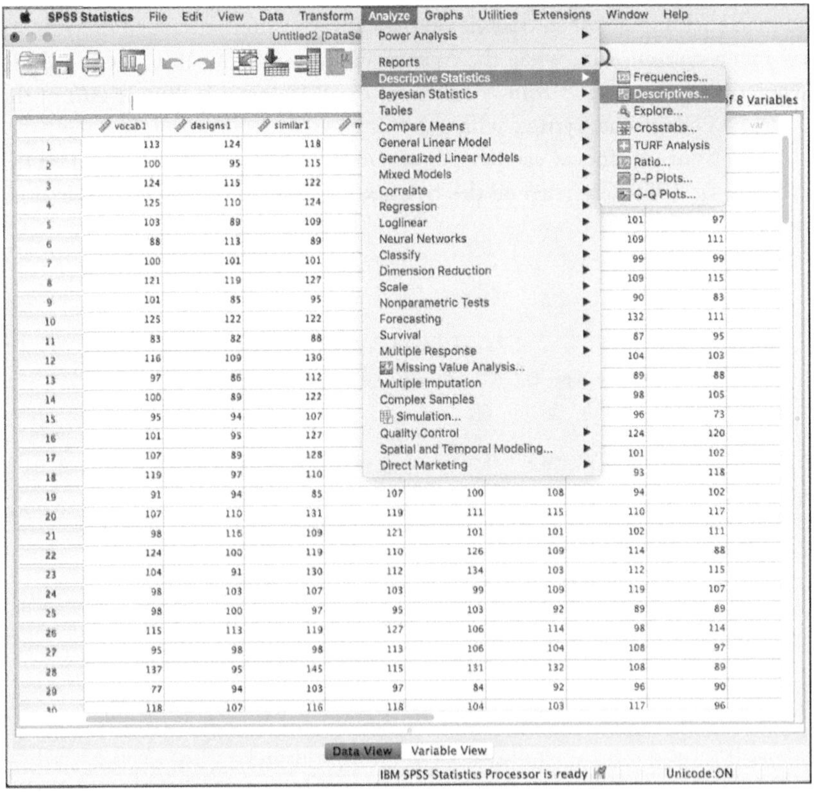

FIGURE 3.5 SPSS Analyze menu

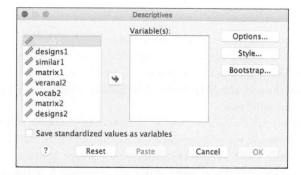

FIGURE 3.6   SPSS Descriptives: no variables selected

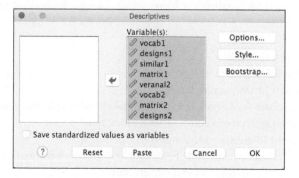

FIGURE 3.7   SPSS Descriptives: all variables selected

point-and-click method may require navigation through menu after menu. Second, command code can easily be edited and rerun if an error is found or if new participants are added to the data, whereas the point-and-click method will require navigation through all the menus once again. Third, the **Syntax** window commands can be saved in case there is a future question about the analyses. This record can facilitate scientific replication. Finally, some SPSS options may not be available in the menu system and can only be implemented via command code (Hayes, 2018). That being said, it may be more convenient to use menus for data input and manipulation and easier to use command code when conducting analyses. Both methods will be illustrated in this book to ensure that users have both options.

Files

To match its three types of windows, SPSS has three types of files. Files with an .sav suffix are data files, files with an .spv suffix are **Output Viewer** files that contain output text and graphics, and files with an .sps suffix are **Syntax** files.

Help

Information about the many procedures available within SPSS can be obtained via the *Help* menu. Details about specific statistical topics can be found via *Help > Topics*. SPSS documentation in.pdf format, including coverage of command syntax, is available through the *Help* menu. Additionally, a help icon **(?)** is included on many analysis windows.

Introductory texts that cover basic SPSS operation might be useful to more inexperienced users (Cronk, 2020; Green & Salkind, 2017; Reddy, 2020). Texts that provide details about SPSS data management (George & Mallery, 2020) and SPSS syntax are also available (Collier, 2010; te Grotenhuis & Visscher, 2014).

There is considerable online support for SPSS users. First, IBM provides extensive support, including video tutorials, manuals, blog posts, etc. at www.ibm.com/products/spss-statistics. Other online sources for general information about SPSS include:

www.spss-tutorials.com
https://stats.idre.ucla.edu/spss
https://guides.lib.uoguelph.ca/SPSS
www.westga.edu/academics/research/vrc/assets/docs/spss_basics.pdf
http://calcnet.mth.cmich.edu/org/spss/index.htm
https://latrobe.libguides.com/ibmspss
www.statisticshowto.com/probability-and-statistics/spss-tutorial-beginners
http://core.ecu.edu/psyc/wuenschk/spss.htm
https://sites.google.com/a/lakeheadu.ca/bweaver/Home/statistics/spss

Sources of information about SPSS syntax include:

http://spsstools.net/en
http://spsstools.net/en/macros/KO-spssmacros
www.ssc.wisc.edu/sscc/pubs/spss/Windows/SPSS_Syntax.html
www.unige.ch/ses/sococ/cl///spss/comlang/syntwindow.html?
www.ottersbek.de/software

4

IMPORTING AND SAVING DATA

Importing Data

SPSS can import data via its *File > Import Data* menu, including data in Excel, text, SAS, Stata, dBase, and other files. For the iq data in spreadsheet format, select *File > Import Data > Excel* and use the computer's operating system to find the Excel file.

Once the Excel file has been selected, SPSS will recognize the spreadsheet format, including the possibility that variable names occupy the first row of the file (Figure 4.1). A preview of the data is presented to ensure that the correct data and format have been selected. When satisfied, click the *OK* button on the bottom-right corner of the import screen (Figure 4.1).

The yellow file folder icon is a shortcut for opening files (Figure 4.2). When clicked, it uses the computer's operating system to locate data files. When a file is selected, SPSS immediately reads the data into its memory and opens an untitled **Data Editor** window (Figure 4.2). To ensure that the correct data have been imported, scroll through the data and verify that the number of participants and number of variables correspond to the known dimensions of the iq data file (i.e., 152 participants and 8 variables).

Details about the variables can be viewed by selecting the *Variable View* button at the bottom of the **Data Editor** window (Figure 4.3). This view verifies that there are 8 variables of numeric type with no missing value indicators. These characteristics can be edited by clicking on the appropriate cell. It is important that variables are categorized correctly as to type (numeric, string, dollar, etc.) and level of measurement (scale, ordinal, nominal) because assumptions about measurement level may be foundational for some analyses. Measures at the scale level are continuous numbers, measures at the ordinal level are ordered numbers, and

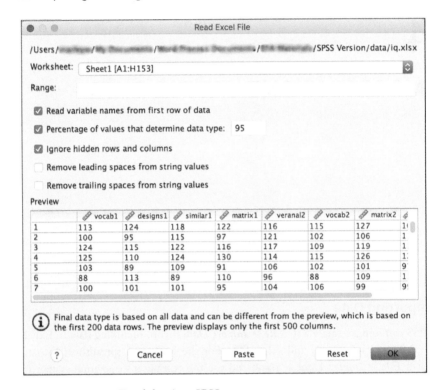

FIGURE 4.1 Import Excel data into SPSS

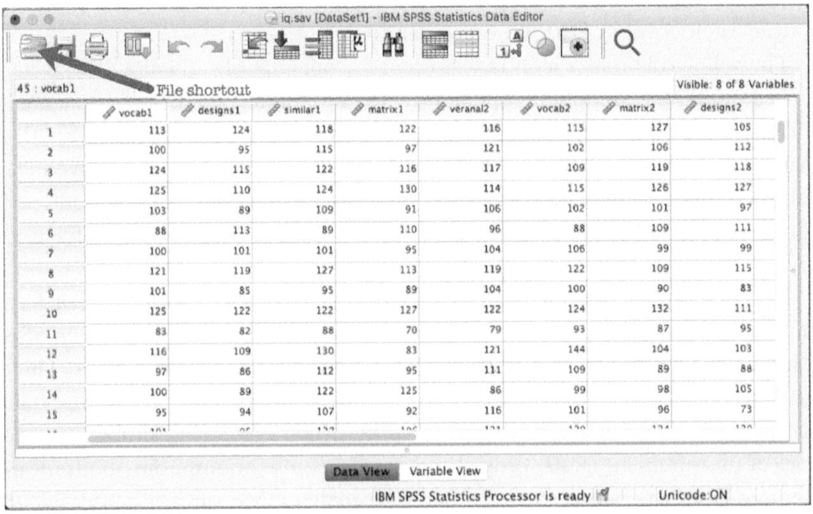

FIGURE 4.2 Data View option of Data Editor window with file shortcut icon

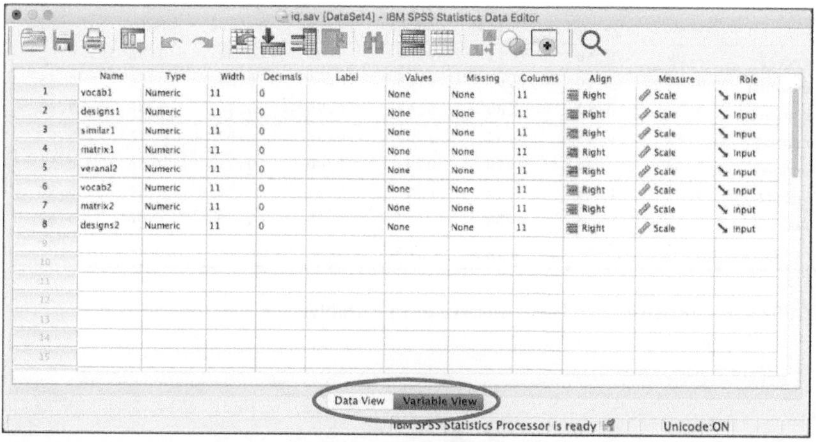

FIGURE 4.3   Variable View option of Data Editor window

measures at the nominal level are only labels and have no quantitative value (e.g., 0 and 1 to represent male and female). Data and variable views can be selected by selecting the corresponding button at the at the bottom of the **Data Editor** window.

Importing a Correlation Matrix

Raw data are not always available. For example, journal articles may provide the correlation matrix but not the raw data. Correlation matrices can be input for later use in EFA or other analyses.

For example, the correlation matrix of the iq data (Figure 4.4) might be input instead of the iq raw data. Unfortunately, there is no point-and-click menu option for importing correlation matrices. Rather, command code via a **Syntax** window must be employed.

The full correlation matrix has been entered via command code in a **Syntax** window in Figure 4.5. It will generally be easier to input only the UPPER or LOWER diagonal of the matrix using the "FORMAT" command to specify the type of matrix to read. In any case, subsequent statistical analyses based on the correlation matrix must be executed with command code and not via menus.

Saving Data

It might be useful to save the imported iq data as a native SPSS data file so the importation process will not have to be repeated. That is accomplished via *File > Save As*. Provide a name (iq) and disk location to complete this operation. SPSS will automatically recognize that data are being saved and will use the proper file

	vocab1	designs1	similar1	matrix1	verana2	vocab2	matrix2	designs2
vocab1	1.00	0.58	0.79	0.62	0.69	0.82	0.56	0.51
designs1	0.58	1.00	0.57	0.65	0.51	0.54	0.59	0.66
similar1	0.79	0.57	1.00	0.60	0.70	0.74	0.58	0.55
matrix1	0.62	0.65	0.60	1.00	0.53	0.57	0.71	0.62
verana2	0.69	0.51	0.70	0.53	1.00	0.71	0.65	0.51
vocab2	0.82	0.54	0.74	0.57	0.71	1.00	0.58	0.53
matrix2	0.56	0.59	0.58	0.71	0.65	0.58	1.00	0.62
designs2	0.51	0.66	0.55	0.62	0.51	0.53	0.62	1.00

FIGURE 4.4 Pearson correlation matrix of iq variables

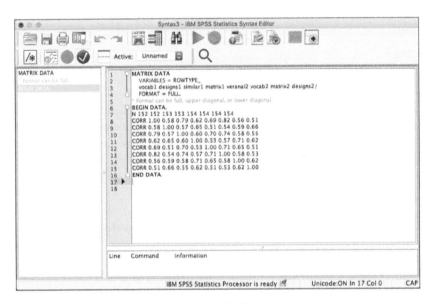

FIGURE 4.5 Import correlation matrix via the Syntax window

format (.sav). Alternatively, the data could have been exported in Excel, text, SAS, Stata, or another format via *File > Export*. To open the new SPSS data file, simply click the file icon shortcut and navigate to the iq .sav file.

Saving Output

As illustrated in Figure 3.3, results of analyses are displayed in the **Output Viewer** window. Results can be selected and copied from that pane and then pasted into Word or other programs via *Edit > Copy* or *Edit > Copy Special*. Alternatively, all objects in the **Output Viewer** window can be saved using the *File > Save*

As menu. SPSS automatically recognizes the type of file and will automatically append .spv to the file name.

Saving Command Code

As with data and output, the contents of the **Syntax** window can be saved via the *File > Save As* menu. SPSS automatically recognizes that this is a syntax file and appends .sps to the file name.

Data Management

As may be apparent, an extended session with SPSS can result in an extremely long list of objects in the **Output Viewer** window. Objects can be deleted by selecting them one by one or as a group and pressing the DELETE key. The entire window can be deleted by closing it, using methods provided within the operating system. Objects on the *Results* pane of an **Output Viewer** window can be hidden to reduce clutter. Just select the desired object and then *View > Hide*. The object has not been deleted, simply hidden from view. It remains visible in the *Outline* pane and can be made visible in the *Results* pane by selecting it in the *Outline* pane and selecting *View > Show*. Additionally, a record of all SPSS operations is automatically stored in a "hidden" file. Called the session journal, the operation of this file can be specified via *SPSS Statistics > Preferences > File Locations > Session Journal menus.*

SPSS includes a robust ensemble of data management options that are directly available through command code or via the *Data* and *Transform* menus. Cronk (2020), George and Mallery (2020), and Reddy (2020) provide detailed guidance on data management.

5

DECISION STEPS IN EXPLORATORY FACTOR ANALYSIS

Researchers must make several thoughtful and evidence-based methodological decisions while conducting an exploratory factor analysis (EFA; Henson & Roberts, 2006). There are a number of options available for each decision, some better than others (Lloret et al., 2017).

Those decisions (steps in the EFA process) are charted in Figure 5.1. Note that each decision might be sufficient for movement to the next step, or it might necessitate a return to a previous step. This visual presentation emphasizes the exploratory nature of EFA and the knowledge that the evidence for some decisions is uncertain or dependent upon prior results.

There are numerous decision steps, and each step contains several complex components. Accordingly, users are encouraged to print Figure 5.2 and use it as a checklist as they conduct an EFA. That practice will ensure consistent implication of evidence-based, best-practice decisions (Watkins, 2009).

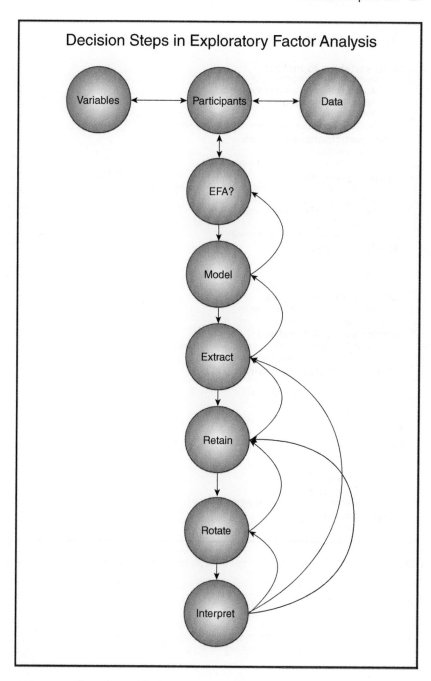

FIGURE 5.1 Flow chart of decision steps in exploratory factor analysis

Decision Steps in Exploratory Factor Analysis

What variables to include
☐ Number of variables per factor
☐ Adequate representation of the domain
☐ Avoid low communality
☐ Avoid low reliability
☐ Variables cannot be dependent upon each other

What participants to include
☐ Number of participants
☐ Adequate representation of the population

Is data appropriate
☐ Accuracy (out of range values, plausible summary values)
☐ Missing data (amount and distribution)
☐ Univariate and multivariate outliers
☐ Linearity
☐ Univariate and multivariate normality

Is EFA appropriate?
☐ Bartlett's test of sphericity
☐ Kaiser–Meyer–Olkin test of sampling adequacy
☐ Correlation matrix

Model of factor analysis
☐ Principal components analysis
☐ Common factor analysis

Factor extraction method
☐ Weak factors/Nonnormal: Least-squares, Principal Axis
☐ Multivariate normal: Maximum Likelihood

How many factors to retain
☐ Parallel analysis
☐ Minimum average partials (MAP)
☐ Visual scree
☐ Theoretical convergence and parsimony
☐ Others

Rotate factors
☐ Orthogonal: Varimax
☐ Oblique: Oblimin, Promax

Interpret results
☐ Simple structure
☐ Theoretical convergence and parsimony

Report results
☐ All decision steps

FIGURE 5.2   Checklist of decision steps in exploratory factor analysis

6

STEP 1

Variables to Include

The choice of variables to include in an exploratory factor analysis (EFA) is important because "if the indicators are not selected well, the recovered structure will be misleading and biased" (Little et al., 1999, p. 209). Consequently, the measured variables must be selected after careful consideration of the domain of interest (Cattell, 1978; Widaman, 2012). Some domains will be relatively narrow (e.g., depression) whereas others will be broad (e.g., psychopathology). Nevertheless, variables that assess all important aspects of the domain of interest should be sampled (Carroll, 1985; Wegener & Fabrigar, 2000).

Psychometric Properties

The psychometric properties of the measured variables must also be carefully considered. When EFA is conducted on measured variables with low communalities (those that do not share much common variance), substantial distortion can result. One obvious reason for low communality is poor reliability. Scores can vary due to true responses of the examinees or due to error. The reliability coefficient estimates the proportion of true score variance. For example, a reliability coefficient of .40 indicates 40% true score variance and 60% error. Error variance, by definition, cannot be explained by factors. Because of this, variables with low reliability will have little in common with other variables and should be avoided in EFA (Fabrigar et al., 1999). Therefore, the reliability of measured variables should be considered when selecting them for inclusion in an EFA (Feldt & Brennan, 1993; Watkins, 2017). "If $r_{xx} < .50$, then most of the total variance is due to measurement error. Indicators with such low score reliabilities should be excluded from the analysis" (Kline, 2013, p. 173). Nevertheless, decisions about variables to include in EFA must also consider the possibility that systematic error might have artificially inflated reliability estimates at the expense of validity (see Clifton, 2020 for a discussion of this phenomenon).

A second psychometric reason that a variable might have a low communality is that it is reliable but unrelated to the domain of interest and thus shares little common variance with the variables that tap that domain. Thus, the validity of measured variables must also be respected (Messick, 1995). This is related to reliability in that reliability is necessary but not sufficient for validity. Validity suggests that the relationship between the measured variables and factors should be congruent. Given that EFA assumes the factors influence the measured variables, what measured variables make sense given the domain of interest? For instance, if the domain of interest is assumed to be depression, it makes no sense to include variables that measure body mass, family income, and height because they are not reasonably influenced by depression. This is an example of construct irrelevance. Likewise, it makes little sense to include only addition and subtraction problems as variables if the domain of interest is arithmetic. That domain includes multiplication and division as well as addition and subtraction. This is an example of construct underrepresentation (Spurgeon, 2017). Readers should consult texts on measurement and scale development to gain a better understanding of these psychometric issues (Bandalos, 2018; Clifton, 2020; Cooper, 2019; DeVellis, 2017; Kline, 2000).

Marker Variables

It might be useful to include variables with known properties that have previously been studied (marker variables) in an EFA if the remainder of the measured variables are relatively unknown (Carroll, 1985; Comrey & Lee, 1992; Gorsuch, 1988; Nunnally & Bernstein, 1994; Tabachnick & Fidell, 2019; Zhang & Preacher, 2015). For example, vocabulary tests have long been used as measures of verbal ability, so a vocabulary test might be included in an EFA if several new tests that purport to measure verbal ability are analyzed.

Formative Versus Effect Indicators

In theory, there are situations where the measured variables are more properly treated as determinants rather than effects of latent variables (Edwards & Bagozzi, 2000). These are called *formative* indicators. That is, the causal direction goes from measured variables to the latent variable. For example, loss of job and divorce are measures of exposure to stress that might best be thought of as causal indicators. Each event creates stress rather than the reverse. Education, income, and occupational prestige may be causal indicators of socioeconomic status (SES). Clearly, more education and income and a high-prestige job cause higher SES; SES does not cause these indicators. Thus, losing one's job would lead to lower SES, but this lowered status would leave one's years of education unchanged. Eliminating one causal indicator (say, education) from the model changes the meaning of the SES scale because part of the SES construct is not represented. For most purposes, we will assume *effect* indicators and proceed accordingly, but the type of indicators should be carefully considered because application of EFA with formative indicators may produce severely biased results (Rhemtulla et al., 2020).

Number of Variables

Two measured variables are sometimes used to identify a factor. However, at least three variables are necessary for identification (Goldberg & Velicer, 2006; Mulaik, 2010; Streiner, 1994). Imagine that the sphere pictured in Figure 6.1 represents multidimensional space. The star is the construct centroid. If there are only two variables (A and B), drawing a line between them (to simplistically represent a perfect linear relationship) does not encompass the construct centroid. However, adding variable C and its relationship with the other measured variables does enclose the construct centroid. Thus, factors formed by only two variables are underdetermined and may be unstable (Goldberg & Velicer, 2006; Hahs-Vaughn, 2017).

Given this information, how many variables should be included in an EFA? Too few variables per factor "becomes not only an issue of model identification and replication, but also a matter of construct underrepresentation" (Schmitt et al., 2018, p. 350). The number of measured variables will also impact the sample size decision. The requisite number of variables is also influenced by the reliability and validity of the measured variables. Fewer variables might be needed

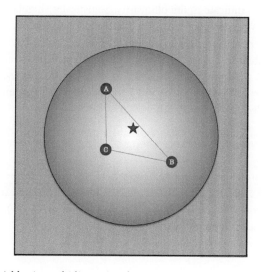

FIGURE 6.1   Variables in multidimensional space

if they exhibit high reliability and validity. For example, subscales from individually administered tests of cognitive ability typically meet this definition, and only three to four per factor might be needed. It is generally recommended that at least three to six reliable variables representing each common factor be included in an analysis (Carroll, 1985; Comrey & Lee, 1992; Fabrigar & Wegener, 2012; Fabrigar et al., 1999; Goldberg & Velicer, 2006; Gorsuch, 1988; Hair et al., 2019; Hancock & Schoonen, 2015; Kline, 2013; McCoach et al., 2013; McDonald, 1985; Mulaik, 2010; Streiner, 1994; Tabachnick & Fidell, 2019). In contrast, individual items on both ability and personality tests are generally of low reliability, so many more might be needed to adequately represent the domain of interest. Kline (1994) recommended that at least 10 items should be included for finalizing a test and many more if the test is in the development stage.

Statistical Issues

There are several situations where the choice of variables can create statistical problems that preclude EFA: if there are more variables than participants; if the number of participants with scores on each variable are not equal, which could be caused by pairwise deletion of missing data; or if there are linear dependencies among the variables, for example, variables that are composites of other variables. "Singularity" is the term used when measured variables are linearly dependent on each other. Other examples of inappropriate variables are "right" and "wrong" and ipsative scores. Short of singularity, a statistical problem akin to dividing by zero in arithmetic can appear with extreme multicollinearity, that is, when correlations among the measured variables are too high (Lorenzo-Seva & Ferrando, 2020). Tabachnick and Fidell (2019) suggested that correlations above .90 among measured variables indicate multicollinearity. Statistically, singularity prevents the matrix operations needed for EFA to be performed, and multicollinearity causes those matrix operations to produce unstable results. Finally, EFA is not possible if a variable exhibits zero variance. Technically, these situations can cause the statistical analysis to produce the equivalent of a negative variance called a nonpositive definite matrix. Wothke (1993) and Lorenzo-Seva and Ferrando (2020) have provided a detailed description of these issues.

Report

The eight measured variables in this study were developed to measure cognitive ability. Based on typical ability tests, these variables are expected to exhibit good psychometric properties. As suggested by Fabrigar et al. (1999), four variables were hypothesized to represent each factor.

7

STEP 2

Participants

Characteristics of Participants

First, which participants? This is primarily a matter of logic and common sense. To which population are the results to generalize? Sample from that population. Does the sample make sense given the factors you are attempting to measure?

Child (2006) warned against using samples collected from different populations to compute correlations because factors that are specific to a population might be obscured when pooled. Tabachnick and Fidell (2019) and Comrey and Lee (1992) also warned about pooling the results of several samples or the same sample measured across time. Sampling procedures are acceptable, but there must be a clear understanding of sample–population differences (Widaman, 2012).

Additionally, negligent responses from unmotivated participants may introduce bias. Woods (2006) found that factor analysis results were affected when more than 10% of the participants responded carelessly. Thus, the validity of participants' responses must be considered.

Number of Participants

Beyond which participants to include in an EFA, it is also important to know how many participants to include. Correlation coefficients tend to be less reliable when estimated from small samples. For example, with a true population correlation of zero and a sample size of 100, about 95% of the correlations will fall between $-.20$ and $+.20$. In contrast, about 95% of the correlations will fall between $-.09$ and $+.09$ when the sample size is 500. One simulation study found that 1,000 participants were needed to estimate correlation coefficients within

± .05, and 250 participants were needed for "reasonable trade-offs between accuracy and confidence" (Schönbrodt & Perugini, 2013, p. 611).

Guidelines for estimating the number of participants required for an EFA have focused on the: (a) absolute number of participants, (b) ratio of participants to measured variables, (c) quality of the measured variables, and (d) ratio of measured variables to factors. In the first case, Comrey and Lee (1992) suggested that 100 participants is poor, 200 is fair, 300 is good, 500 is very good, and 1,000 or more is excellent. Regarding the participant to variable ratio, both Child (2006) and Gorsuch (1983) recommended five participants per measured variable with a minimum of 100 participants. Other measurement experts have suggested a 10:1 or 20:1 ratio of participants to measured variables (Benson & Nasser, 1998; Hair et al., 2019; Osborne & Banjanovic, 2016). Unfortunately, "these guidelines all share three characteristics: (1) no agreement among different authorities, (2) no rigorous theoretical basis provided, and (3) no empirical basis for the rules" (Velicer & Fava, 1998, p. 232).

In contrast, sample-size guidelines based on the quality of measured variables and the variable-to-factor ratio have often been based on statistical simulation studies where the number of variables, number of participants, number of variables per factor (factor overdetermination), and the percent of variance accounted for by the factors (communality) were systematically modified and evaluated (Guadagnoli & Velicer, 1988; Hogarty et al., 2005; MacCallum et al., 1999, 2001; Mundfrom et al., 2005; Velicer & Fava, 1998; Wolf et al., 2013). These simulation studies have used dissimilar numbers of factors, variables, variance estimates, EFA methods, etc., so their results are not always compatible. However, factor overdetermination (i.e., the number of measured variables per factor) and communality were consistently found to be important determinants of sample size. Greater factor overdetermination and communality tended to require smaller sample sizes than the reverse. Further, sample size, factor overdetermination, and communality seemed to interact so that "strength on one of these variables could compensate for a weakness on another" (Velicer & Fava, 1998, p. 243). Given these results, try to include variables with high communalities (≥ .60; Gibson et al., 2020), overdetermined factors (> 3 variables per factor), and a parsimonious number of factors.

Although "it is impossible to derive a minimum sample size that is appropriate in all situations" (Reise et al., 2000, p. 290), the subjective guidelines for good factor recovery enumerated in Figure 7.1 are consistent with the tables provided by Mundfrom et al. (2005) and the results reported in other studies (Guadagnoli & Velicer, 1988; Hogarty et al., 2005; MacCallum et al., 1999, 2001; Velicer & Fava, 1998).

Two additional considerations in determining the appropriate sample size are type of data and amount of missing data. The recommendations in Figure 7.1 are based on data from continuous, normally distributed data. Dichotomous variables (two response options) are neither continuous nor normally distributed and will

Communality	Variables per Factor	Number of Factors	Number of Participants
	3	2	100
	3	3	170
	3	4	260
	3	5	300
	4	2	100
	4	3	120
≥ .60	4	4	170
	4	5	220
	5	3	100
	5	4	100
	5	5	130
	10	6	100
	3	2	160
	3	3	450
	3	4	500
	3	5	700
	4	3	130
.20 − .80	4	4	240
	4	5	320
	5	3	100
	5	4	110
	5	5	140
	10	6	100
	3	3	1,200
	3	4	1,200
	3	5	1,300
	4	3	230
≤ .20	4	4	250
	4	5	400
	5	3	150
	5	4	170
	5	5	180
	10	6	150

FIGURE 7.1   Sample size estimates based on communality and variable:factor ratio

require three to ten times more participants (Pearson & Mundfrom, 2010; Rouquette & Falissard, 2011).

Additionally, models with 10% missing data may require a 25% increase in sample size, and models with 20% missing data may need a 50% increase in sample size (Wolf et al., 2013). Regardless of type of data and missing values, more data is always better "because the probability of error is less, population estimates are more accurate, and the findings are more generalizable" (Reio & Shuck, 2015, p. 15).

For ordinal data, a simulation study by Rouquette and Falissard (2011) suggested that stable and accurate factor solutions can be obtained with: (a) 350 to

400 participants when there are 10 variables per factor; (b) 400 to 450 participants when there are seven or eight variables per factor; and (c) 500 to 600 participants when there are five or six variables per factor.

Report

The participants in this study were children in Grades 2–6 who were referred for assessment for consideration of special educational accommodations. The average communality of variables similar to those in this study is $\geq$ .60 (Dombrowski et al., 2018). Additionally, these cognitive variables were relatively reliable ($\alpha \geq$ .80) and normally distributed. Given the communality, number of factors, and number of variables, 100 participants would be needed for good factor recovery. Thus, the current sample of 152 participants appears to be adequate for EFA.

8

STEP 3

Data Screening

Effective data screening involves inspection of both statistics and graphics (Hoelzle & Meyer, 2013; Malone & Lubansky, 2012). Either alone is insufficient. This was famously demonstrated by Anscombe (1973), who created four x-y datasets with relatively equivalent summary statistics.

A quick scan of those data seems to indicate relatively normal distributions with no obvious problem (Figure 8.1).

However, there is danger in relying on summary statistics alone. When this "Anscombe quartet" is graphed as in Figure 8.2, the real relationships in the data emerge. Specifically, the x1-y1 data appear to follow a roughly linear relationship with some variability, the x2-y2 data display a curvilinear rather than a linear relationship, the x3-y3 data depict a linear relationship except for one large outlier, and the x4-y4 data show x remaining constant except for one (off the chart) outlier.

Assumptions

All multivariate statistics are based on assumptions that will bias results if they are violated. The assumptions of exploratory factor analysis (EFA) are mostly conceptual: It is assumed that some underlying structure exists, that the relationship between measured variables and the underlying common factors are linear, and that the linear relationships are invariant across participants (Fabrigar & Wegener, 2012; Hair et al., 2019).

However, EFA is dependent on Pearson product–moment correlations that make statistical assumptions. Specifically, it is assumed that a linear relationship exists between the variables and that there is an underlying normal distribution (Hahs-Vaughn, 2017). To meet these assumptions, variables must be measured

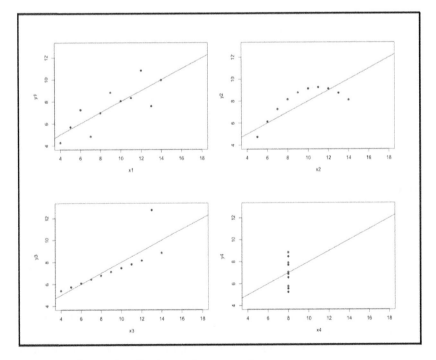

Output [ ] - IBM SPSS Statistics Viewer

Descriptive Statistics

	Mean	Std. Deviation	Analysis N
x1	9.00	3.317	11
y1	7.5009	2.03157	11
x2	9.00	3.317	11
y2	7.5009	2.03166	11
x3	9.00	3.317	11
y3	7.5000	2.03042	11
x4	9.00	3.317	11
y4	7.5009	2.03058	11

Correlation Matrix

		x1	y1	x2	y2	x3	y3	x4	y4
Correlation	x1	1.000	.816	1.000	.816	1.000	.816	-.500	-.314
	y1	.816	1.000	.816	.750	.816	.469	-.529	-.489
	x2	1.000	.816	1.000	.816	1.000	.816	-.500	-.314
	y2	.816	.750	.816	1.000	.816	.588	-.718	-.478
	x3	1.000	.816	1.000	.816	1.000	.816	-.500	-.314
	y3	.816	.469	.816	.588	.816	1.000	-.345	-.155
	x4	-.500	-.529	-.500	-.718	-.500	-.345	1.000	.817
	y4	-.314	-.489	-.314	-.478	-.314	-.155	.817	1.000

IBM SPSS Statistics Processor is ready   Unicode:ON H: 1.38, W: 11.85 in

FIGURE 8.1   Descriptive statistics and correlation matrix for Anscombe quartet data

FIGURE 8.2   Scatterplots for Anscombe quartet data

on a continuous scale (Bandalos, 2018; Puth et al., 2015; Walsh, 1996). Violation of the assumptions that underlie the Pearson product–moment correlation may bias EFA results. As suggested by Carroll (1961), "there is no particular point in making a factor analysis of a matrix of raw correlation coefficients when these coefficients represent manifest relationships which mask and distort latent relationships" (p. 356).

More broadly, anything that influences the correlation matrix can potentially affect EFA results (Carroll, 1985; Onwuegbuzie & Daniel, 2002). As noted by Warner (2007), "because the input to factor analysis is a matrix of correlations, any problems that make Pearson *r* misleading as a description of the strength of the relationship between pairs of variables will also lead to problems in factor analysis" (p. 765). Accordingly, the data must be carefully screened before conducting an EFA to ensure that some untoward influence has not biased the results (Flora et al., 2012; Goodwin & Leech, 2006; Hair et al., 2019; Walsh, 1996). Potential influences include restricted score range, linearity, data distributions, outliers, and missing data. "Consideration and resolution of these issues before the main analysis are fundamental to an honest analysis of the data" (Tabachnick & Fidell, 2019, p. 52).

SPSS offers a routine that combines statistics and graphics to explore data (*Analyze > Descriptive Statistics > Explore*), but it may be more instructive and systematic to manually generate and examine output. Thus, each aspect of the data that might affect EFA results is subsequently explored.

Restricted Score Range

The range of scores on the measured variables must be considered. If the sample is more homogeneous than the population, restriction of range in the measured variables can result and thereby attenuate correlations among the variables. At the extreme, a measured variable with zero variance will cause statistical estimation problems and inadmissible EFA results (Lorenzo-Seva & Ferrando, 2020; Wothke, 1993). Less extreme attenuation can result in biased EFA estimates. For example, using quantitative and verbal test scores from the 1949 applicant pool of the U.S. Coast Guard Academy, the quantitative and verbal test score correlations dropped from .50 for all 2,253 applicants to only .12 for the 128 students who entered the Academy (French et al., 1952). In such cases, a "factor cannot emerge with any clarity" (Kline, 1991, p. 16).

Linearity

Pearson coefficients are measures of the linear relationship between two variables. That is, their relationship is best approximated by a straight line. Curvilinear or nonlinear relationships will not be accurately estimated by Pearson coefficients. Although subjective, visual inspection of scatterplots can be used to assess linearity.

SPSS offers a wide variety of graphics, including scatterplots. Its **Graphs >**
Chart Builder menu option allows the user to construct a graph from the ground
up in great detail. Although powerful, its complexity is not needed for the basic
graphs in this book.

Therefore, navigate the SPSS menus **Graphs > Legacy Dialogs > Scatter/Dot >**
Simple Scatter to obtain a scatterplot of two variables. The resulting scatterplot
will be displayed in an **Output Viewer** window, as demonstrated in Figure 8.3.

The scatterplot can be edited by right clicking the graph and selecting the **Edit**
Content > In Separate Window options. Alternatively, this can be done via the menu
choices **Edit > Edit Content > In Separate Window**. Either method generates a
Chart Editor window with an editable scatterplot, a new set of menus (**File, Edit,**
View, Options, Elements, Help), and several rows of shortcut icons (Figure 8.4).
Every property of the scatterplot can be edited via these options. For example, the
color palette was changed from blue to red, the inner grid lines were removed, the
markers were changed to diamonds instead of circles, and a linear line of best fit was
imposed.

It may be more efficient to review a scatterplot matrix rather than individual
scatterplots. Selecting **Graphs > Legacy Dialogs > Scatter/Dot > Matrix Scatter**
will generate a scatterplot matrix in an **Output Viewer** window. The SPSS default
scatterplot matrix is not as intelligible as might be desired, so, as with the simple scatterplot, the scatterplot matrix can be edited by right clicking the graph and selecting
the **Edit Content > In Separate Window** options or by choosing menus **Edit > Edit**
Content > In Separate Window. The scatterplot matrix is somewhat more legible

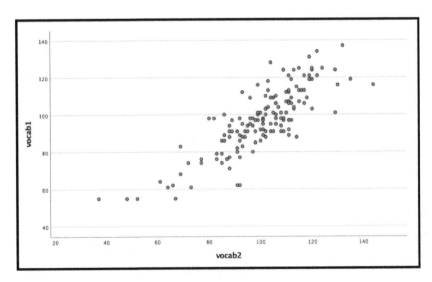

FIGURE 8.3　Scatterplot for two iq data variables

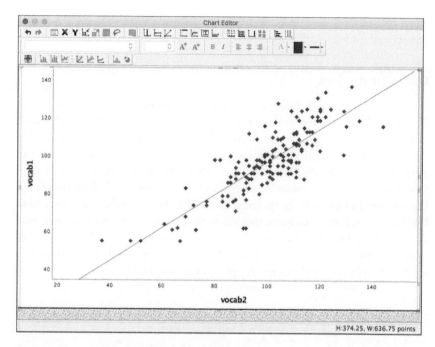

FIGURE 8.4 Scatterplot in SPSS Chart Editor

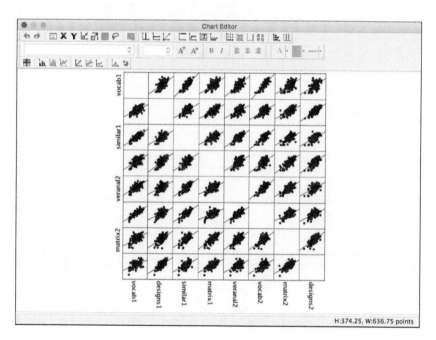

FIGURE 8.5 Scatterplot matrix in SPSS Chart Editor

when best-fit lines were added and the markers made smaller (Figure 8.5). After reviewing the scatterplots, it appears the iq variables are linearly related.

Data Distributions

Pearson correlation coefficients (r) theoretically range from -1.00 to $+1.00$. However, that is only possible when the two variables have exactly the same distribution. If, for example, one variable is normally distributed and the other distribution is skewed, the maximum value of the Pearson correlation is less than 1.00. The more the distribution shapes differ, the greater the restriction of r. Consequently, it is important to understand the distributional characteristics of the measured variables to be included in an EFA. For example, it has long been known that dichotomous items that are skewed in opposite directions may produce what are known as difficulty factors when submitted to EFA (Bernstein & Teng, 1989; Greer et al., 2006). That is, a factor may appear that is an artifact of variable distributions rather than the effect of their content.

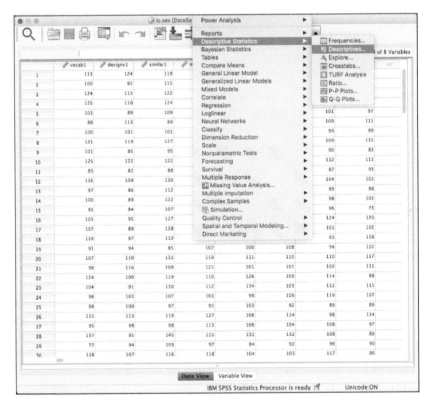

FIGURE 8.6   Menu access to descriptive statistics

Descriptive statistics that describe the variable distributions can be generated via **Analyze > Descriptive Statistics > Descriptives** as displayed in Figure 8.6.

The **Descriptives** menu option generates a new **Descriptives** window where all six variables can be selected and moved to the **Variables(s)** window on the right to include them in the requested analyses. The **Options** button opens the **Descriptives: Options** window and displays the descriptive statistics that are available in SPSS (Figure 8.7).

These selections generate a descriptive statistics object (table) in an **Output Viewer** window, as shown in Figure 8.8. Skew > 2.0 or kurtosis > 7.0 would indicate severe univariate nonnormality (Curran et al., 1996). These univariate statistics seem to indicate that all eight measured variables are relatively normally distributed (skew < 1.0 and kurtosis < 2.0), so there should not be much concern about correlations being restricted due to variable distributions. Skew (departures from symmetry) and kurtosis (distributions with heavier or lighter tails and higher or flatter peaks) of all variables seem to be close to normal (normal distributions have expected values of zero).

Graphs can be useful for visual verification of this conclusion. A boxplot that displays the distributional statistics of the measured variables can be generated

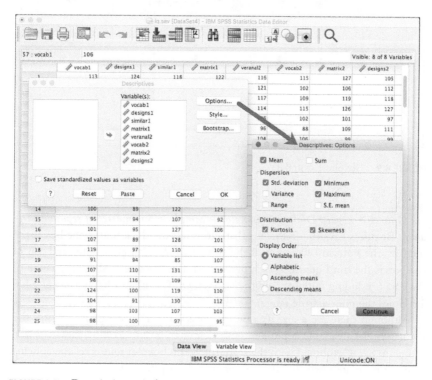

FIGURE 8.7   Descriptives window

Descriptive Statistics

	N	Minimum	Maximum	Mean	Std. Deviation	Skewness		Kurtosis	
	Statistic	Statistic	Statistic	Statistic	Statistic	Statistic	Std. Error	Statistic	Std. Error
vocab1	152	55	137	97.50	17.342	-.318	.197	.034	.391
designs1	152	58	130	97.65	14.473	-.215	.197	.021	.391
similar1	152	55	145	103.59	17.256	-.458	.197	.358	.391
matrix1	152	55	134	99.53	16.606	-.529	.197	.158	.391
veranal2	152	57	134	101.51	14.769	-.629	.197	.442	.391
vocab2	152	37	144	100.63	16.416	-.820	.197	1.888	.391
matrix2	152	49	137	101.45	16.172	-.580	.197	.900	.391
designs2	152	45	137	100.64	13.922	-.458	.197	1.445	.391
Valid N (listwise)	152								

FIGURE 8.8 Descriptive statistics output for iq data

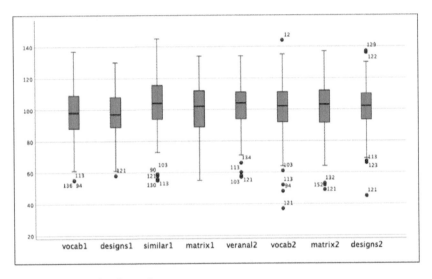

FIGURE 8.9 Boxplot for iq data

via **Graphs > Legacy Dialogs > Boxplot > Simple > Summaries of separate variables**. Boxplots have the following characteristics: the thick line in the box is the median, the bottom of the box is the first quartile (25th percentile), the top of the box is the third quartile (75th percentile), the "whiskers" show the range of the data (excluding outliers), and the circles identify outliers (defined as any value 1.5 times the interquartile range).

Although there are a few data points outside the 1.5 interquartile range, the median of each variable appears roughly centered in the variable boxes displayed in Figure 8.9. Combined with the scatterplot, this boxplot reinforces the conclusion of univariate normality drawn from the descriptive statistics.

A group of measured variables might exhibit univariate normality and yet be multivariate nonnormal. That is, the joint distribution of all the variables might be nonnormal. SPSS does not include a test of multivariate normality. DeCarlo (1997) contributed SPSS command code to compute multivariate normality indices, but that code is complex and many not operate on some computers. Alternatively, an online calculator at https://webpower.psychstat.org/models/kurtosis/ can accept an SPSS data file (.sav) as input and is easy to operate. This calculator does not provide a reference, but it seems to be using an implementation of Mardia's multivariate tests (1970).

When the iq data was submitted to this online calculator (as shown in Figure 8.10), multivariate skew was 6.28 ($p < .01$) and multivariate kurtosis was 84.12 ($p < .05$). Nonnormality, especially kurtosis, can bias Pearson correlation estimates and thereby bias EFA results (Cain et al., 2017; DeCarlo, 1997; Greer et al., 2006).

The extent to which variables can be nonnormal and not substantially affect EFA results has been addressed by several researchers. Curran et al. (1996) opined

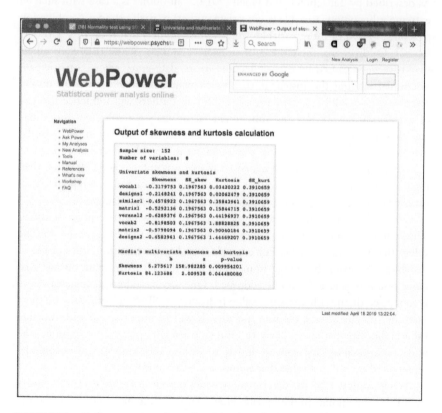

FIGURE 8.10   Online computation of multivariate skewness and kurtosis

that univariate skew should not exceed 2.0 and univariate kurtosis should not exceed 7.0. Other measurement specialists have agreed with those guidelines (Bandalos, 2018; Fabrigar et al., 1999; Wegener & Fabrigar, 2000). In terms of multinormality, statistically significant multivariate kurtosis values > 3.0 to 5.0 might bias factor analysis results (Bentler, 2005; Finney & DiStefano, 2013; Mueller & Hancock, 2019). Spearman or other types of correlation coefficients might be more accurate in those instances (Bishara & Hittner, 2015; Onwueg-buzie & Daniel, 2002; Puth et al., 2015). Given these univariate guidelines, it seems unlikely that the distributional characteristics of the iq will bias Pearson correlation estimates. On the other hand, the multivariate kurtosis is elevated but only marginally significant ($p = .045$), which is weak statistical evidence (Anderson, 2020) that does not approach the .005 threshold recommended by some statisticians (Benjamin & Berger, 2019).

Outliers

As described by Tabachnick and Fidell (2019), "an outlier is a case with such an extreme value on one variable (a univariate outlier) or such a strange combination of scores on two or more variables (multivariate outlier) that it distorts statistics" (p. 62). Outliers are, therefore, questionable members of the dataset. Outliers may have been caused by data-collection errors, data-entry errors, a participant not understanding the instructions, a participant deliberately entering invalid responses, or a valid but extreme value. Not all outliers will influence the size of correlation coefficients and subsequent factor analysis results, but some may have a major effect (Liu et al., 2012). For example, the correlation between the matrix1 and designs1 variables in the iq dataset is .65. That correlation drops to .10 when the final value in the matrix1 variable was entered as −999 rather than the correct value of 80. A data point like this might be caused by a typographical error or by considering a missing data indicator to be a real data point.

Obviously, some outliers can be detected by reviewing descriptive statistics. The minimum and maximum values might reveal data that exceeds the possible values that the data can take. For example, it is known that the values of the iq variables can reasonably range from around 40 to 160. Any value outside that range is improbable and must be addressed. One way to address such illegal values is to replace them with a missing value indicator. In SPSS, missing data are indicated by any character(s) the user specifies. It will be important to select missing value indicators that are unlikely to represent real data points. For example, the iq data is known to vary from around 40 to around 160, so missing data could be represented by −999, a value that is impossible in the real data.

As demonstrated by the descriptive statistics output in Figure 8.11, there were no missing data points in the iq data. However, the minimum value of 37 for the vocab2 variable may be too low to be a valid entry. The boxplot in Figure 8.9 revealed that case 121 exhibited that low vocab2 score. The average score for the

Descriptive Statistics

	N Statistic	Minimum Statistic	Maximum Statistic	Mean Statistic	Std. Deviation Statistic	Skewness Statistic	Skewness Std. Error	Kurtosis Statistic	Kurtosis Std. Error
vocab1	152	55	137	97.50	17.342	-.318	.197	.034	.391
designs1	152	58	130	97.65	14.473	-.215	.197	.021	.391
similar1	152	55	145	103.59	17.256	-.458	.197	.358	.391
matrix1	152	55	134	99.53	16.606	-.529	.197	.158	.391
veranal2	152	57	134	101.51	14.769	-.629	.197	.442	.391
vocab2	152	37	144	100.63	16.416	-.820	.197	1.888	.391
matrix2	152	49	137	101.45	16.172	-.580	.197	.900	.391
designs2	152	45	137	100.64	13.922	-.458	.197	1.445	.391
Valid N (listwise)	152								

FIGURE 8.11   Descriptive statistics output of iq data for detecting outliers and missing data

seven other variables for case 121 is 54. Although the low vocab2 score is consistent with these other scores, it could be replaced with a new value via the **Data Editor**. For now, the data file will be left unchanged.

Other outliers might be detected with plots as illustrated with the boxplot in Figure 8.9. That plot clearly reveals data points that are more than 1.5 times the interquartile range. That might be a somewhat liberal standard given that some experts suggest that 2.2 times the interquartile range be used (Streiner, 2018). Nevertheless, a review of those cases shows that those values are within plausible ranges and their cause is not clear. Additionally, they are univariate outliers, and EFA is a multivariate procedure that necessitates that the multidimensional position of each data point be considered.

The Mahalanobis distance (D^2) is a measure of the distance of each data point from the mean of all data points in multidimensional space. Higher D^2 values represent observations further removed from the general distribution of observations in multidimensional space, and high values are potential multivariate outliers.

There is no direct command in SPSS to compute D^2 values. Rather, an indirect method must be used. First, create a new variable in the **Data Editor** called id via *Transform > Compute Variable*. These options generate the **Compute Variable** window (Figure 8.12) where the new variable is named and filled with values. A unique id number for each might be useful, so name the *Target Variable* "id" and give it the *Numeric Expression* of "$casenum."

After clicking OK, the new id variable is generated and inserted at the end of the variable list in the **Data Editor**. SPSS used the default variable format of two decimal places in creating the id variable. To edit that format, click the *Variable View* option at the bottom of the **Data Editor** window and change the value of the id–Decimals cell to zero. To view that change, click the *Data View* option at the bottom of the **Data Editor** window (Figure 8.13). Given that the id data will be useful in future analyses, save it via *File > Save*.

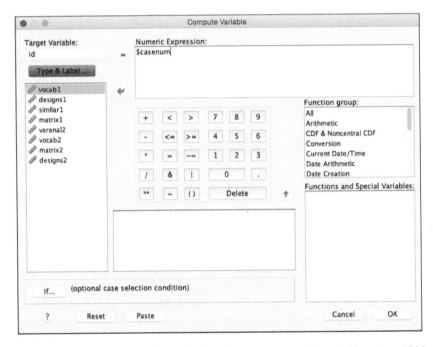

FIGURE 8.12 Compute Variable window for creating an id variable using SPSS $casenum

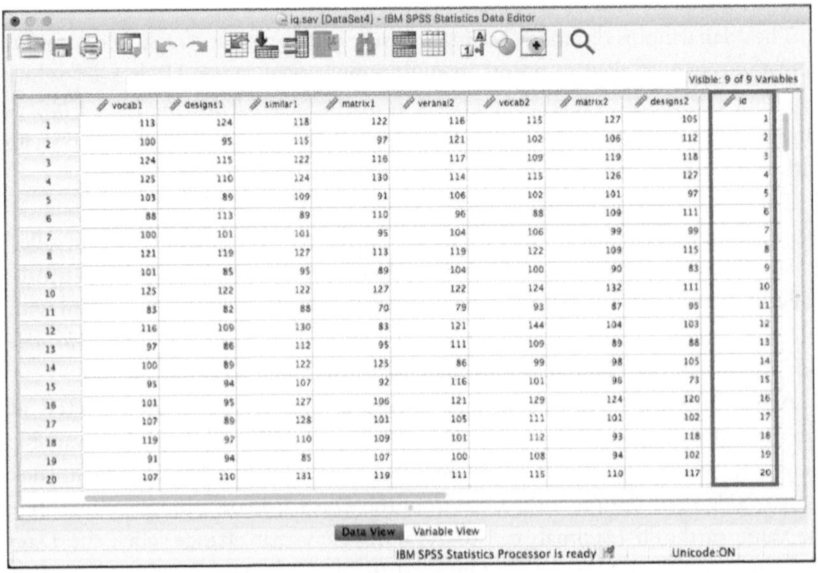

FIGURE 8.13 Data Editor window with newly created id variable

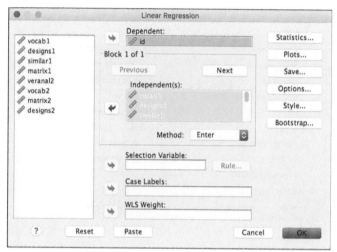

FIGURE 8.14   Linear Regression window for computing Mahalanobis distance using the id variable

SPSS computes D^2 values through its *Analyze > Regression > Linear* menus, which will open a **Linear Regression** window (Figure 8.14). After selecting the id variable as the dependent variable and the eight iq variables (vocab1–designs2) as independent variables, click the *Save* option, which will open a **Linear Regression: Save** window.

This window offers many options, but the Mahalanobis distance is the only one needed (Figure 8.15). Check that box and then click the *Continue* button to return to the **Linear Regression** window and then click the **OK** button to generate D^2 values. The **Data Editor** window will now display a new variable labeled MAH_1 at the end of the variable list.

To more easily identify the most extreme D^2 values, sort the MAH_1 values via the *Data > Sort Cases* menu options (Figure 8.16). Move the MAH_1 variable into the *Sort by* window, enable the *Descending* radio button, and click **OK**.

These manipulations allow Figure 8.17 to reveal that case 121 has the largest D^2 value, case 142 the next largest, etc. D^2 values can be tested for statistical significance, but "it is suggested that conservative levels of significance (e.g., .005 or .001) be used as the threshold value for designation as an outlier" (Hair et al., 2019, p. 89). SPSS can compute the chi-square probability level of each D^2 value, or they can be obtained from printed tables or online calculators.

To use SPSS to compute probability values, a new variable must be created (Figure 8.18). As with the new id variable, the *Transform > Compute Variable* menu options will generate a **Compute Variable** window where the new

FIGURE 8.15 Linear Regression: Save window for computing Mahalanobis distance

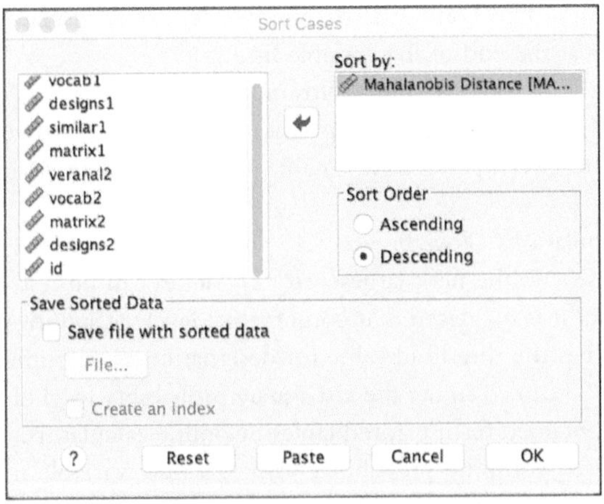

FIGURE 8.16 Sort Cases window for descending sort of Mahalanobis distance values

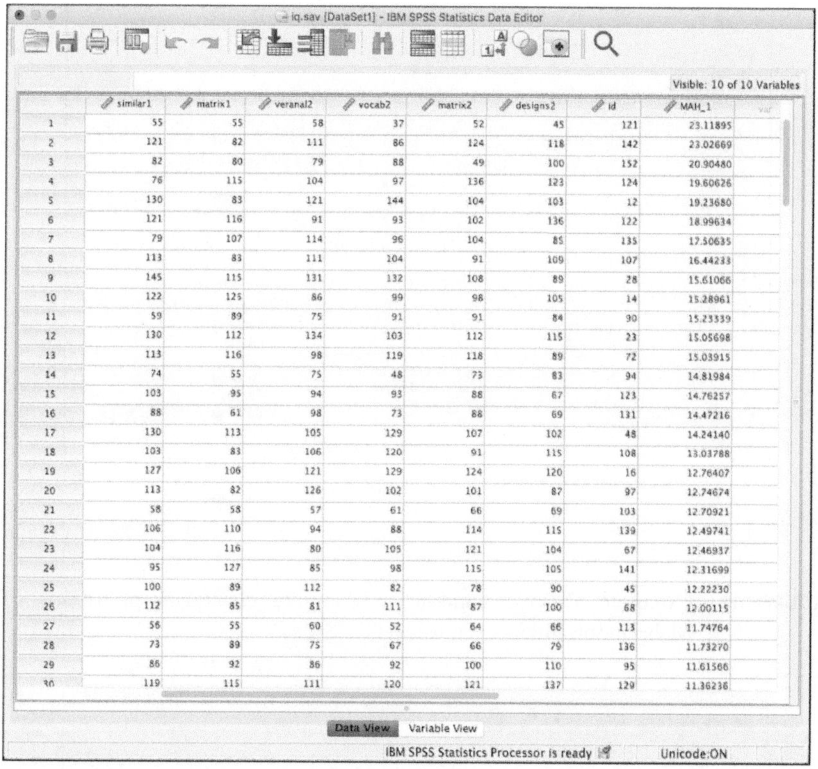

iq.sav [DataSet1] - IBM SPSS Statistics Data Editor

Visible: 10 of 10 Variables

	similar1	matrix1	veranal2	vocab2	matrix2	designs2	id	MAH_1	var
1	55	55	58	37	52	45	121	23.11895	
2	121	82	111	86	124	118	142	23.02669	
3	82	80	79	88	49	100	152	20.90480	
4	76	115	104	97	136	123	124	19.60626	
5	130	83	121	144	104	103	12	19.23680	
6	121	116	91	93	102	136	122	18.99634	
7	79	107	114	96	104	85	135	17.50635	
8	113	83	111	104	91	109	107	16.44233	
9	145	115	131	132	108	89	28	15.61066	
10	122	125	86	99	98	105	14	15.28961	
11	59	89	75	91	91	84	90	15.23339	
12	130	112	134	103	112	115	23	15.05698	
13	113	116	98	119	118	89	72	15.03915	
14	74	55	75	48	73	83	94	14.81984	
15	103	95	94	93	88	67	123	14.76257	
16	88	61	98	73	88	69	131	14.47216	
17	130	113	105	129	107	102	48	14.24140	
18	103	83	106	120	91	115	108	13.03788	
19	127	106	121	129	124	120	16	12.76407	
20	113	82	126	102	101	87	97	12.74674	
21	58	58	57	61	66	69	103	12.70921	
22	106	110	94	88	114	115	139	12.49741	
23	104	116	80	105	121	104	67	12.46937	
24	95	127	85	98	115	105	141	12.31699	
25	100	89	112	82	78	90	45	12.22230	
26	112	85	81	111	87	100	68	12.00115	
27	56	55	60	52	64	66	113	11.74764	
28	73	89	75	67	66	79	136	11.73270	
29	86	92	86	92	100	110	95	11.61566	
30	119	115	111	120	121	137	129	11.36236	

Data View | Variable View

IBM SPSS Statistics Processor is ready | Unicode:ON

FIGURE 8.17 Data Editor window with newly created Mahalanobis distance variable (MAH_1)

variable is named and filled with values. Name the new variable "probM." Complete the Numeric Expression field by typing "1 -" and then clicking on the chi-square distribution functions. That will generate "CDF.CHISQ(X1,X2)." Replace X1 with the MAH_1 variable and X2 with the number of iq variables, thus: 1 - CDF.CHISQ(MAH_1,8).

Given the small probability values, go to the ***Variable View*** option of the **Data Editor** window and allow the probM variable to display four decimal places. Using $p < .001$ as the threshold, none of the cases are potential outliers (Figure 8.19). At the .005 level, cases 121 and 142 are potential outliers. An examination of case 121 shows that it contains the previously identified aberrant value of 37 for the vocab2 variable. However, all the variable values for this case are very low (45 to 58) and consistent with impaired intellectual functioning. Given this consistency, there is no good reason to delete or modify the value of this case. Case 142 is not as easily understood. Some of its values are lower than

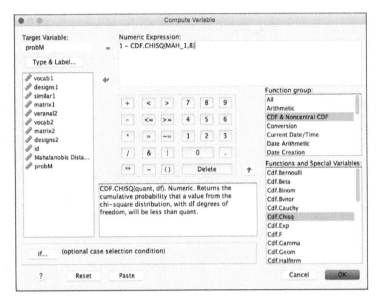

FIGURE 8.18 Compute Variable window to compute chi-square probability of Mahalanobis distance values

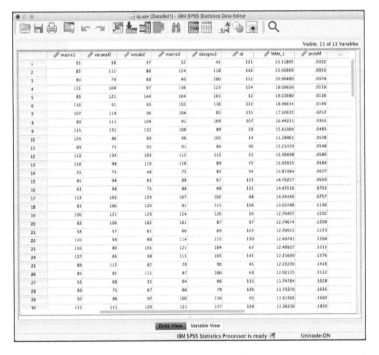

FIGURE 8.19 Data Editor window with Mahalanobis distance (MAH_1) and probability (probM) variables

average (e.g., 85), and others are higher than average (e.g., 127). There is no obvious explanation for why these values are discrepant.

It is important to articulate an outlier policy prior to data analysis (Leys et al., 2018). Not to do so makes the researcher vulnerable to interpreting this ambiguous information inconsistent with best statistical practice (Simmons et al., 2011). Although there is considerable debate among statisticians as to the advisability of deleting outliers, Goodwin and Leech (2006) suggested that

> the researcher should first check for data collection or data entry errors. If there were no errors of this type and there is no obvious explanation for the outlier—the outlier cannot be explained by a third variable affecting the person's score—the outlier should not be removed.
>
> *(p. 260)*

Hair et al. (2019) expressed similar sentiments about outliers: "they should be retained unless demonstrable proof indicates that they are truly aberrant and not representative of any observations in the population" (p. 91). Alternative suggestions for identifying and reducing the effect of outliers have been offered (e.g., Tabachnick & Fidell, 2019). Regardless, extreme values might drastically influence EFA results, so it is incumbent upon the researcher to perform a sensitivity analysis. That is, conduct EFAs with and without outlier data to verify that the results are robust (Bandalos & Finney, 2019; Leys et al., 2018; Tabachnick & Fidell, 2019; Thompson, 2004).

Missing Data

Ideally, there will be no missing data. In practice, there often are: people sometimes skip items on tests or surveys, are absent on exam day, etc. First described by Rubin (1976), it is now well accepted that the treatment of missing data is contingent on the mechanism that caused the data to be missing. Data that is missing completely at random (MCAR) is entirely unsystematic and not related

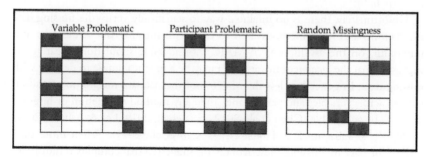

FIGURE 8.20   Missing data patterns

to any other value on any measured variable. For example, a person may accidently skip one question on a test. Data missing at random (MAR), contrary to its label, is not missing at random. Rather, it is a situation where the missingness can be fully accounted for by the remainder of the data. For instance, nonresponse to self-esteem questions might be related to other questions, such as gender and age. Finally, missing not at random (MNAR) applies when the missing data is related to the reason it is missing. For example, an anxious person might not respond to survey questions dealing with anxiety.

It is useful to look for patterns at both variable and participant levels when considering missing data (Fernstad, 2019). For example, the first variable in the left panel in Figure 8.20 seems to be problematic, whereas the final participant is problematic in the middle panel. The third panel depicts relatively random missingness. Generally, randomly scattered missing data is less problematic than other patterns (Tabachnick & Fidell, 2019).

Researchers tend to rely on two general approaches to dealing with missing data: discard a portion of the data or replace missing values with estimated or imputed values. When discarding data, the entire case can be discarded if one or more of its data values are missing (listwise deletion). Alternatively, only the actual missing values can be discarded (pairwise deletion). Most statistical programs offer these two missing data methods. Both methods will reduce power and may result in statistical estimation problems and biased parameter estimates (Zygmont & Smith, 2014). However, pairwise deletion is especially prone to statistical problems that create inadmissible EFA results (Lorenzo-Seva & Ferrando, 2020; Wothke, 1993).

A wide variety of methods have been developed to estimate or impute missing data values (Hair et al., 2019; Roth, 1994; Tabachnick & Fidell, 2019) that range from simple (replace missing values with the mean value of that variable) to more complex (predict the missing data value using non-missing values via regression analysis) to extremely complex (multiple imputation and maximum likelihood estimation). Baraldi and Enders (2013) suggested that "researchers must formulate logical arguments that support a particular missing data mechanism and choose an analysis method that is most defensible, given their assumptions about missingness" (p. 639).

Unfortunately, there is no infallible way to statistically verify the missing data mechanism, and most methods used to deal with missing data values rely, at a minimum, on the assumption of MAR. Considerable simulation research has suggested that the *amount* of missing data may be a practical guide to dealing with missing data. In general, if less than 5–10% of the data are missing in a random pattern across variables and participants, then any method of deletion or imputation will be acceptable (Chen et al., 2012; Hair et al., 2019; Lee & Ashton, 2007; Roth, 1994; Tabachnick & Fidell, 2019; Xiao et al., 2019). When more than 10% of the data are missing, Newman (2014) suggested that complex multivariate techniques, such as multiple imputation or maximum likelihood estimation, be used. As with outliers, extensive missing data requires a sensitivity analysis where the EFA results from different methods of dealing with missing data are compared for robustness (Goldberg & Velicer, 2006; Hair et al., 2019; Tabachnick & Fidell, 2019). Additionally, the amount and location of missing data at variable and participant levels should be transparently reported.

Missing data in SPSS. Often, missing data are recognized during data entry, and indicator values are deliberately assigned. For example, −9 assigned to missing values without apparent cause, −99 to missing values where the survey respondent refused to answer, and −999 when the question did not apply. Sometimes, those missing value indicators are assigned, but SPSS was not informed that those values are not real but are only indicators of missingness.

The iq dataset does not contain any missing data, but a version of that dataset was created with 10 random missing values (all indicated with −999) and imported via the menu sequence of *File > Import Dataset > From Excel > iqmiss.xlsx* to demonstrate missing data in SPSS.

It is important that data be carefully screened to verify that missing values are appropriately indicated and handled. The *Variable View* option on the **Data Editor** window displays all the variables with the missing data indicator(s) SPSS recognizes for each variable. Unfortunately, missing data indicators were not specified for this data, as reflected in the "None" entries under the *Missing* column in Figure 8.21. Therefore, SPSS will consider −999 to be valid iq values and use them in subsequent computations.

As demonstrated in Figure 8.22, values of −999 have been assumed to be real and were used in the computation of descriptive statistics, which are incorrect.

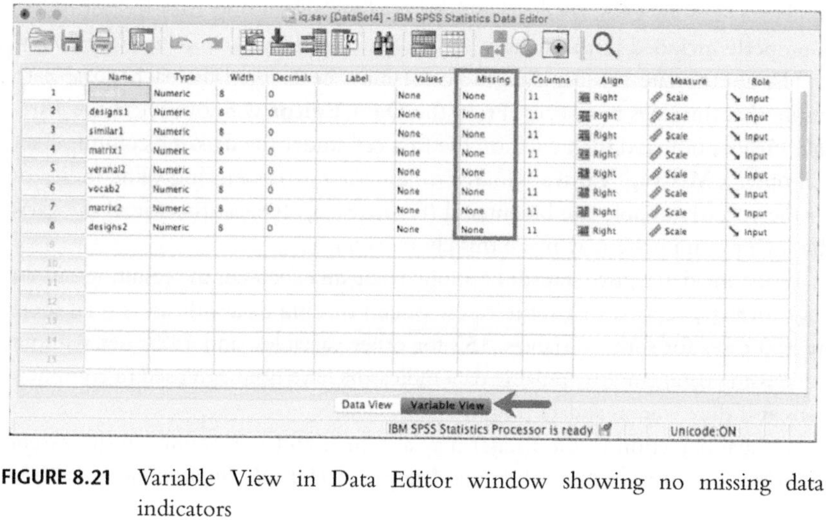

FIGURE 8.21   Variable View in Data Editor window showing no missing data indicators

Descriptive Statistics

	N	Minimum	Maximum	Mean	Std. Deviation
vocab1	152	-999	137	83.19	126.556
designs1	152	-999	130	83.30	126.194
similar1	152	55	145	103.59	17.256
matrix1	152	-999	134	84.93	126.648
veranal2	152	-999	134	94.17	90.461
vocab2	152	37	144	100.63	16.416
matrix2	152	-999	137	87.11	126.856
designs2	152	-999	137	93.37	90.268
Valid N (listwise)	152				

FIGURE 8.22 Descriptive statistics output with missing data indicators mistakenly considered to be real data

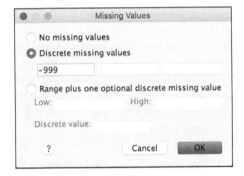

FIGURE 8.23 Assigning missing data indicators to variables in Missing Values window

Similar erroneous EFA results could be obtained if missing data indicators are improperly included in the analysis.

The appropriate missing data indicator must be entered for each variable to ensure that this does not occur. From the **Data Editor** window, select the *Variable View* option and then click on the first cell under the *Missing* column. This will open a **Missing Values** window where the correct missing value indicator for the vocab1 variable can be entered (Figure 8.23). Repeat this for all the variables. Copy and paste may make this chore easier.

When the descriptive statistics options are again executed, the resulting output now correctly reports that some cases contain missing data indicators (i.e., there are 150 cases for some variables, 152 for other variables, and 142 cases without any missing data), and the missing data indicators have not been used in computations as if they were real data (Figure 8.24).

A visual depiction of the dataset may also be useful in recognizing the extent and pattern of missing data values via *Analyze > Multiple Imputation > Analyze*

Descriptive Statistics

	N	Minimum	Maximum	Mean	Std. Deviation
vocab1	150	55	137	97.62	17.375
designs1	150	58	130	97.73	14.350
similar1	152	55	145	103.59	17.256
matrix1	150	55	134	99.38	16.560
veranal2	151	57	134	101.41	14.770
vocab2	152	37	144	100.63	16.416
matrix2	150	49	137	101.59	16.231
designs2	151	45	137	100.60	13.959
Valid N (listwise)	142				

FIGURE 8.24 Descriptive statistics for iqmiss data after assigning missing data indicators

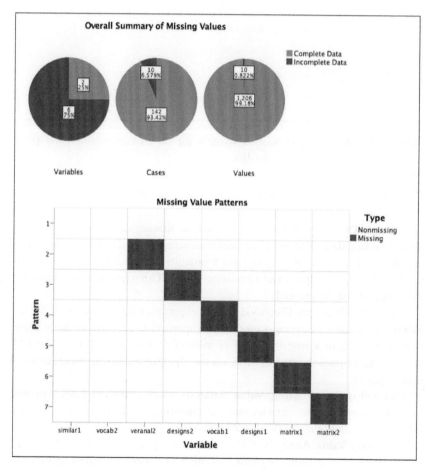

FIGURE 8.25 Missingness map for iqmiss data

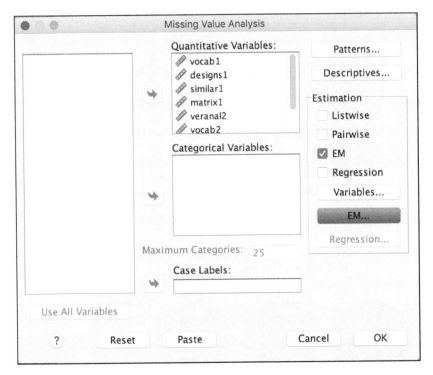

FIGURE 8.26   Missing Value Analysis window for expectation-maximization (EM) imputation of iqmiss data

Patterns. Move all eight variables into the *Analyze Across Variables* field and check all three of the check boxes.

As displayed in Figure 8.25, six variables are missing data, and two variables are not missing data. However, 142 cases were complete and only 10 (6.6%) contained missing data. With 152 cases and 8 variables, there are 1,216 data cells. Of those, 1,206 were complete and 10 missing (0.8%). This trivial amount of missing data can probably be ignored.

Currently, maximum likelihood (called expectation-maximization [EM] by SPSS) and multiple imputation are the most appropriate methods to apply when there is more than a trivial amount of missing data (Enders, 2017). The EM method can be implemented in SPSS via the *Analyze > Missing Value Analysis* menu options.

This will open a **Missing Value Analysis** window (Figure 8.26). For this example, move all eight variables into the *Quantitative Variables* field, click the *EM* checkbox, and then click the *EM* button.

A **Missing Value Analysis: EM** window will open (Figure 8.27). The *Normal* radio button, the *Save completed data* checkbox, and the *Create a new dataset* radio button can be selected, and the dataset name (iqEM) can be entered. Click

FIGURE 8.27 Missing Value Analysis: EM window to specify EM missing value imputation

Descriptive Statistics

	N	Minimum	Maximum	Mean	Std. Deviation
vocab1	152	55	137	97.55	17.303
designs1	152	58	130	97.67	14.300
similar1	152	55	145	103.59	17.256
matrix1	152	55	134	99.41	16.658
veranal2	152	57	134	101.40	14.722
vocab2	152	37	144	100.63	16.416
matrix2	152	49	137	101.45	16.245
designs2	152	45	137	100.65	13.924
Valid N (listwise)	152				

FIGURE 8.28 Descriptive statistics output of iqmiss data after EM imputation

the *Continue* button on the **Missing Value Analysis: EM** window and the **OK** button on the **Missing Value Analysis** window. A new dataset has been created that can be accessed via *Window > iqEM*. Notice that there are no longer any −999 values in that dataset.

Compare the descriptive statistics from this imputed dataset (Figure 8.28) to the original dataset without missing data previously presented in Figure 8.8. Of course, these values will be slightly different for each EM imputation.

SPSS also provides simple listwise and pairwise missing data replacement as well as the more complex regression replacement method via its *Analyze > Missing Value Analysis* menus. The very complex multiple imputation method can be executed via the *Analyze > Multiple Imputation > Impute Missing Data Values* menu options. Tutorials on missing data and SPSS can be consulted if

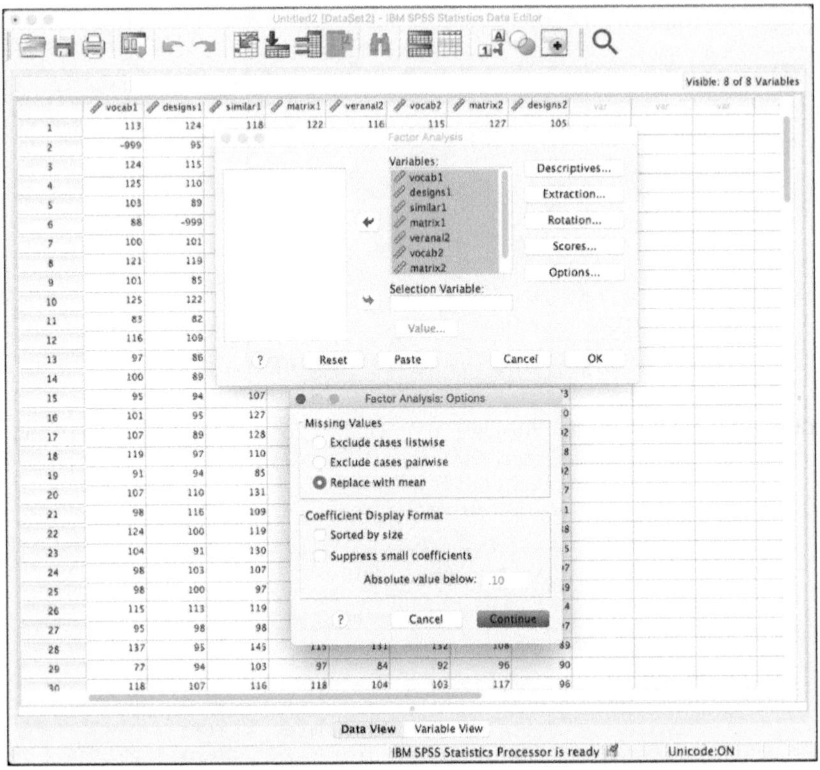

FIGURE 8.29 Replace missing values with mean via Factor Analysis: Options menu

	Mean	Std. Deviation[a]	Analysis N[a]	Missing N
Descriptive Statistics				
vocab1	97.62	17.259	152	2
designs1	97.73	14.255	152	2
similar1	103.59	17.256	152	0
matrix1	99.38	16.450	152	2
veranal2	101.41	14.721	152	1
vocab2	100.63	16.416	152	0
matrix2	101.59	16.123	152	2
designs2	100.60	13.913	152	1

a. For each variable, missing values are replaced with the variable mean.

FIGURE 8.30 Descriptive statistics output of iqmiss data after mean imputation

multiple imputation is needed (Heymans & Eekhout, 2019; Weaver & Maxwell, 2014).

If the missing value analysis procedures are not included in your version of SPSS, the EFA routine allows for exclusion of cases listwise or pairwise as well as mean imputation via *Analyze > Dimension Reduction > Factor > Options > Replace with mean*, as shown in Figure 8.29.

Mean imputation should be acceptable, given the small amount of missing data involved in this analysis (Chen et al., 2012; Hair et al., 2019; Lee & Ashton, 2007; Roth, 1994; Tabachnick & Fidell, 2019; Xiao et al., 2019). The descriptive statistics from this mean imputation, which are presented in Figure 8.30, can be compared to the full dataset in Figure 8.8 and the EM data in Figure 8.28 to confirm that conclusion.

Report

Scatterplots revealed that linear relationships exist between the variables. Measures of univariate and multivariate normality indicated a relatively normal data distribution (Curran et al., 1996; Finney & DiStefano, 2013; Mardia, 1970). There was no evidence that restriction of range or outliers substantially affected the scores, and there was no missing data. Therefore, a Pearson product–moment correlation matrix was submitted for EFA.

9

STEP 4

Is Exploratory Factor Analysis Appropriate?

Given that exploratory factor analysis (EFA) is based on the correlation matrix, it seems reasonable that the correlation matrix should contain enough covariance to justify conducting an EFA (Dziuban & Shirkey, 1974). First, the correlation matrix can be visually scanned to ensure that there are several coefficients $\geq .30$ (Hair et al., 2019; Tabachnick & Fidell, 2019).

Scanning a large matrix for coefficients $\geq .30$ can be laborious, but, as illustrated in Figure 9.1, it took only a single command code to produce a correlation matrix for the small iq dataset. A quick visual scan of this 8-by-8 matrix reveals many coefficients $\geq .30$. The smallest coefficient is .507 and the largest is .824.

The likelihood of a singularity or multicollinearity problem can be checked by ascertaining the determinant of the correlation matrix. If the determinant is greater than .00001, then multicollinearity is probably not a problem (Field et al., 2012).

As displayed in Figure 9.2, another command code can compute and display the determinant. A value of .002 indicates that multicollinearity is probably not a problem.

A second assessment of the appropriateness of the correlation matrix for EFA is provided by Bartlett's test of sphericity (1950), which tests the null hypothesis that the correlation matrix is an identify matrix (ones on the diagonal and zeros on the off-diagonal) in the population. That is, it is random. The desired outcome is rejection of the random matrix with a statistically significant chi-square test. Bartlett's test is sensitive to sample size and should be considered a minimal standard (Nunnally & Bernstein, 1994).

A final assessment of the appropriateness of the correlation matrix for EFA is offered by the Kaiser–Meyer–Olkin (KMO) measure of sampling adequacy (Kaiser, 1974). KMO values range from 0 to 1, only reaching 1 when each variable is

```
factor
/variables vocab1 to designs2
/print correlation.
```

Correlation Matrix

		vocab1	designs1	similar1	matrix1	veranal2	vocab2	matrix2	designs2
Correlation	vocab1	1.000	.576	.789	.618	.689	.824	.564	.507
	designs1	.576	1.000	.570	.650	.509	.539	.586	.662
	similar1	.789	.570	1.000	.598	.702	.735	.582	.550
	matrix1	.618	.650	.598	1.000	.533	.566	.715	.619
	veranal2	.689	.509	.702	.533	1.000	.706	.648	.514
	vocab2	.824	.539	.735	.566	.706	1.000	.577	.530
	matrix2	.564	.586	.582	.715	.648	.577	1.000	.624
	designs2	.507	.662	.550	.619	.514	.530	.624	1.000

FIGURE 9.1 Pearson correlation matrix for iq data with smallest (blue) and largest (red) coefficients

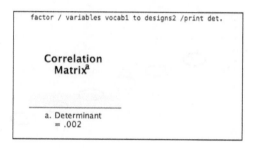

```
factor / variables vocab1 to designs2 /print det.
```

Correlation Matrix[a]

a. Determinant = .002

FIGURE 9.2 Determinant of iq correlation matrix

perfectly predicted by the other variables. A KMO value is a ratio of the sum of squared correlations to the sum of squared correlations plus the sum of squared partial correlations. Essentially, partial correlations will be small and KMO values large if the items share common variance. Kaiser (1974) suggested that KMO values < .50 are unacceptable, but other measurement specialists have recommended a minimum value of .60 (Mvududu & Sink, 2013; Watson, 2017) for acceptability, with values ≥ .70 preferred (Hoelzle & Meyer, 2013). KMO values for each variable as well as the total sample should be reviewed. If no KMO values can be computed or if they fall outside the theoretical range of 0 to 1, the correlation matrix may not be positive definite and should be reviewed for accuracy and appropriateness (Lorenzo-Seva & Ferrando, 2020).

In SPSS, Bartlett's test and the KMO index can be computed with a single command code (Figure 9.3). Bartlett's test of sphericity is statistically significant ($p <$ .001), and the KMO value of .903 is high. SPSS reported a significance value of .000, but that does not mean that p is zero, only that it is significant to three decimal places.

```
factor / variables vocab1 to designs2 /print KMO.
```

KMO and Bartlett's Test

Kaiser-Meyer-Olkin Measure of Sampling Adequacy.		.903
Bartlett's Test of Sphericity	Approx. Chi-Square	887.074
	df	28
	Sig.	.000

FIGURE 9.3 KMO and Bartlett's test for iq data

```
factor / variables vocab1 to designs2 /print AIC.
```

Anti-image Matrices

		vocab1	designs1	similar1	matrix1	veranal2	vocab2	matrix2	designs2
Anti-image Covariance	vocab1	.230	-.036	-.098	-.053	-.032	-.129	.022	.032
	designs1	-.036	.440	-.021	-.093	-.001	.002	-.021	-.159
	similar1	-.098	-.021	.308	-.024	-.081	-.033	-.001	-.038
	matrix1	-.053	-.093	-.024	.367	.038	.009	-.154	-.057
	veranal2	-.032	-.001	-.081	.038	.370	-.070	-.120	-.009
	vocab2	-.129	.002	-.033	.009	-.070	.273	-.018	-.035
	matrix2	.022	-.021	-.001	-.154	-.120	-.018	.364	-.080
	designs2	.032	-.159	-.038	-.057	-.009	-.035	-.080	.451
Anti-image Correlation	vocab1	.866ᵃ	-.114	-.369	-.184	-.110	-.516	.074	.100
	designs1	-.114	.923ᵃ	-.058	-.233	-.003	.007	-.053	-.357
	similar1	-.369	-.058	.930ᵃ	-.071	-.239	-.114	-.004	-.101
	matrix1	-.184	-.233	-.071	.898ᵃ	.104	.029	-.421	-.139
	veranal2	-.110	-.003	-.239	.104	.919ᵃ	-.219	-.328	-.023
	vocab2	-.516	.007	-.114	.029	-.219	.896ᵃ	-.056	-.101
	matrix2	.074	-.053	-.004	-.421	-.328	-.056	.888ᵃ	-.197
	designs2	.100	-.357	-.101	-.139	-.023	-.101	-.197	.914ᵃ

a. Measures of Sampling Adequacy (MSA)

FIGURE 9.4 KMO values for each measured variable in iq data

The KMO value of .903 is an average for all the variables. It is possible that the average is acceptable, but the sampling adequacy of one or more variables might be unacceptable. The KMO value for each variable can be produced with another command, producing the KMO values for each variable in the diagonal of the anti-image correlation matrix (Figure 9.4). Those values range from .866 to .930, so the overall KMO value is a fair representation of the data.

Of course, the command code could have been combined to produce all these metrics: *factor/variables vocab1 to designs2/print correlation det KMO AIC*. Alternatively, the menu sequence of *Analyze > Dimension Reduction > Factor > Descriptives* opens a **Factor Analysis: Descriptives** window where the *coefficients, determinant, KMO and Bartlett's test*, and *anti-image* options can be selected (Figure 9.5).

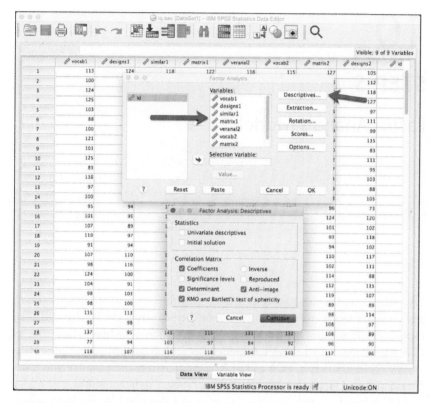

FIGURE 9.5   Correlation coefficients, determinant, KMO, and Bartlett's test via menu options

Report

A visual scan of the correlation matrix for the data revealed that all the coefficients were ≥ .30, but none exceeded .90 (Tabachnick & Fidell, 2019). Bartlett's test of sphericity (1950) rejected the hypothesis that the correlation matrix was an identity matrix (chi-square of 887.1 with 28 degrees of freedom). The KMO measure of sampling adequacy was acceptable, with values of .90 for the total model and .87 to .93 for each of the measured variables (Kaiser, 1974). Altogether, these measures indicate that the correlation matrix is appropriate for EFA (Hair et al., 2019; Tabachnick & Fidell, 2019).

10

STEP 5

Factor Analysis Model

Two major models must be considered: principal components analysis (PCA) and common factor analysis. Only common factor analysis can be classified as an exploratory factor analysis (EFA) model. Researchers sometimes claim that an EFA was conducted when a PCA model was actually applied (Osborne & Banjanovic, 2016). However, PCA and EFA have different purposes and might, given the number and type of measured variables, produce different results.

EFA is based on the common factor model described in the Introduction (Fabrigar & Wegener, 2012) and is pictured in Figure 10.1. The purpose of EFA is to explain as well as possible the correlations among measured variables. In EFA, measured variables are thought to correlate with each other due to underlying latent constructs called factors. The direction of influence from factor to measured variables is signified by the arrows in the path diagram. It also assumes that unique factors explain some variance beyond that explained by common factors. Conceptually, unique factors are composed of specific variance (systematic variance specific to a single measured variable) and error variance (unreliable error of measurement).

The purpose of PCA is to take the scores on a large set of observed variables and reduce them to scores on a smaller set of composite variables that retain as much information as possible from the original measured variables. The direction of influence in PCA is from measured variables to factors, which is symbolized by the arrows in the path diagram in Figure 10.2. PCA attempts to explain as much variance as possible and does not differentiate between common (shared) variance and unique (systematic and error) variance. PCA evaluates variance, not covariance. Therefore, principal components are *not* latent variables. Linear functions are properly called components, not factors.

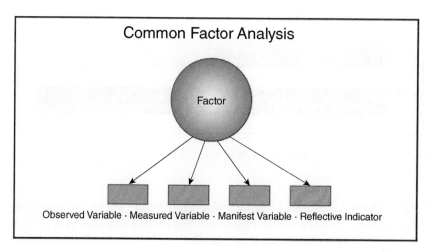

FIGURE 10.1 Common factor analysis model

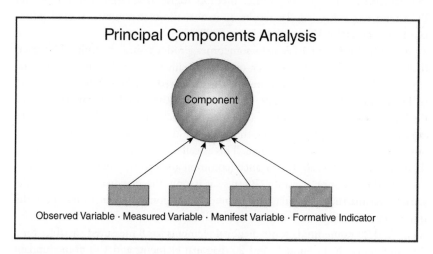

FIGURE 10.2 Principal components analysis model

As summarized in Figure 10.3, the common factor model (called EFA for our purposes) is composed of common variance (general variance shared by all measured variables plus variance shared by subsets of the measured variables) plus unique variance (variance specific to a single measured variable plus error). In contrast, the PCA model does not distinguish common variance from unique variance, analyzing the total variance of the measured variables similar to multiple regression.

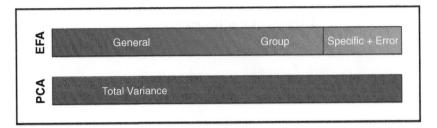

FIGURE 10.3   Variance components of EFA and PCA models

The relative advantages and disadvantages of EFA and PCA models have long been debated. Widaman (1993) found more bias in PCA estimates than in EFA estimates, and Gorsuch (1990) recommended that EFA "should be routinely applied as the standard analysis because it recognizes we have error in our variables, gives unbiased instead of inflated loadings, and is more elegant as a part of the standard model" (p. 39). Other methodologists have argued that EFA and PCA tend to produce similar results, so it does not matter which is used (Hoelzle & Meyer, 2013; Velicer & Jackson, 1990).

In truth, PCA and EFA may sometimes produce similar results. However, that is dependent on the number of variables involved in the analysis and the amount of common variance shared by the measured variables. The computation of PCA and EFA differs in how the diagonal of the correlation matrix is handled. In PCA, the correlations of 1.00 between each variable and itself is used. In contrast, EFA begins by replacing the 1s on the diagonal with an estimate of the communality or common variance. This is called a reduced correlation matrix. Thus, PCA considers all the variance (common and error), whereas EFA considers only the common variance. Because it is only the diagonal elements of the correlation matrix that differ, the number of diagonal elements influences the difference between EFA and PCA results. For example, there are 8 diagonal elements and 28 nonredundant off-diagonal elements for 8 measured variables for a 22% difference in the models, but 20 diagonal elements and 190 nonredundant off-diagonal elements for 20 measured variables is a difference of 10% between EFA and PCA. Thus, EFA and PCA results will tend to be more similar when there are more measured variables in the analysis (10% versus 22% different correlation elements).

As noted, the common factor model recognizes the presence of error in all measurements and therefore substitutes estimates of variable communalities (instead of 1s) in the diagonal of the correlation matrix. Unfortunately, it is not possible to know the communality of variables before conducting an EFA. The solution to this unknown is to estimate the communalities based on some aspect of the data. Potential solutions include the reliability of the variables, partial correlations, multiple correlations, etc. Over time, it has become accepted that a good solution is to initially estimate communalities with the squared multiple correlation of each variable with all other variables (SMC) and then systematically refine that estimate through a series of iterations until a stable estimate is reached (Fabrigar & Wegener, 2012; Pett et al., 2003; Tabachnick & Fidell, 2019).

Widaman (2018) concluded that "PCA should never be used if the goal is to understand and represent the latent structure of a domain; only FA techniques should be used for this purpose" (p. 829). Similar opinions were expressed by Bandalos (2018), Bandalos and Boehm-Kaufman (2009), Carroll (1978, 1985), Fabrigar et al. (1999), Fabrigar and Wegener (2012), Finch (2013), Haig (2018), Hair et al. (2019), Preacher and MacCallum (2003), Russell (2002) and Schmitt (2011).

Report

The purpose of this study was to uncover the latent structure underlying these eight measured variables. Accordingly, a common factor model (EFA) was selected (Widaman, 2018). Squared multiple correlations (SMC) were used for initial communality estimates (Tabachnick & Fidell, 2019).

11

STEP 6

Factor Extraction Method

After selecting the common factor model, the next step in exploratory factor analysis (EFA) is to choose an extraction method. This might also be called the model fitting procedure or the parameter estimation procedure (Fabrigar & Wegener, 2012). In simple terms, this is the mathematical process of deriving the underlying factors from the correlation matrix.

In current practice, the EFA software applies mathematical routines to complete factor extraction. Before computers, extraction was completed by humans who used a geometric approach. That approach retains conceptual clarity, and a simple case of two variables will be used for illustration purposes.

Beginning with a correlation matrix, a scatterplot can be used to display the relationship between X and Y variables in two-dimensional space, as in Figure 11.1. Each data point represents an individual unit's standardized scores on variables X and Y (i.e., z scores). The center is now the mean of both variables. Notice that X–Y score pairs fall into four quadrants. Score pairs that fall into quadrants 1 and 3 tend toward positive correlations, those in quadrants 2 and 4 tend toward negative, and if evenly distributed across all four quadrants, then correlation will be zero. This is a geometric display of what could be called *data* space. More variables would necessitate a view of multidimensional space that is difficult to visualize.

One geometric way to identify the factor(s) underlying a correlation matrix is to convert from data space to *factor* space. The first step in conversion to factor space is to identify the one straight line that lies closer to all the data points than any other line. This is called the "least squares best-fitting line" because the sum of the squared deviations of each of the data points from one and only one straight line is at a minimum. This particular best-fitting line is the first principal component if extracted from the full correlation matrix and the first principal factor

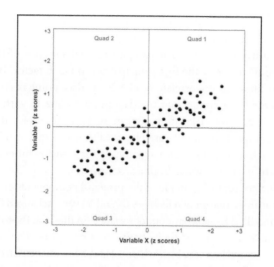

FIGURE 11.1   Scatterplot of two standardized variables in data space

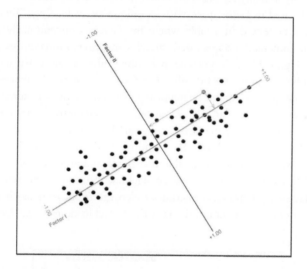

FIGURE 11.2   Conversion from data space to factor space

if extracted from the reduced correlation matrix. This first component or factor "accounts for" more of the variance common to variables X and Y than any other possible component or factor. This best-fitting line is designated by the Roman numeral I. By convention, these lines are scaled from −1.00 to +1.00.

Each individual X–Y data point can be converted from its X–Y location in data space to a location in factor space by connecting the data point to line I with an orthogonal projection. As depicted in Figure 11.2, the new location is approximately 0.77 on Factor I.

The second principal component or factor, labeled II, is defined as a straight line at a right angle to the first principal component/factor. It too is a best-fitting straight line, and it accounts for that part of the total variance of the test score that was *not* accounted for by the first principal component/factor. Being at right angles, the two lines are uncorrelated. The X–Y data point is converted to a location on Factor II by connecting the data point to line II with an orthogonal projection. The factor II location appears to be near −0.43. If this analysis had included additional measured variables, additional factors would have been extracted with each succeeding factor accounting for a smaller proportion of variance analogous to wringing water from a wet towel.

In this simplest conceptual example of the principal components or principal axis variant of factor analysis, one set of references (X and Y) was exchanged for another set of references (I and II). The same amount of variance (in this case, the total or reduced variance of X and Y) is accounted for by both sets of references. The only difference is that X and Y are correlated variables, whereas I and II are uncorrelated components or factors. For now, the factor space references will be called factor loadings.

Theoretically, as many factors as measured variables can be extracted. Each variable can be located in factor space with its unique factor loadings. Typically, this information is presented in a table where the factors, conventionally identified with Roman numerals, and measured variables are entered in columns and rows, respectively (Figure 11.3). In practice, parsimony often suggests that most of the variance can be accounted for by only a few factors, for example, where two factors are sufficient to account for the majority of variance in five measured variables.

The proportion of each variable's variance accounted for by a factor is the square of that variable's loading on the factor (e.g., Variable A loading of $.73^2 = .533$ for Factor I and $.54^2 = .292$ for Factor II). Communality is symbolized by h^2. It is the proportion of variance in each variable that is accounted for by all factors (e.g., $.533 + .292 = .825$). An eigenvalue is an algebraic solution for the percentage of variance a factor contributes. Sometimes called the latent root or characteristic root, the eigenvalue is the sum of the factor's squared loadings (e.g., $.73^2 + .82^2 +$

Variables	Unrotated Factors I	II	h^2
A	.73	.54	.825
B	.82	.49	.913
C	.72	.69	.995
D	.77	−.43	.778
E	.84	−.44	.899
Eigenvalue	3.02	1.39	4.41
% Total variance	60.40	27.80	88.20
Cumm % total var	60.40	88.20	
% Common variance	68.48	31.52	

FIGURE 11.3   Sample EFA table

.72^2 + .77^2 + .84^2 = 3.02). An eigenvalue is one measure of the relative importance of each factor. Mathematically, the total variance of a set of variables is equal
to the total number of variables. Thus, the total variance for this five variable EFA
is 5.00. Based on this sum, the proportion of the total variance contributed by a
factor is its eigenvalue divided by the total variance (e.g., 3.02 ÷ 5.00 = .604, or
60.4%). The proportion of common variance contributed by a factor is its eigenvalue divided by the sum of eigenvalues (e.g., 3.02 ÷ 4.41 = .6848, or 68.48%).

Methodologists have devised a great number of extraction methods since
Spearman (1904) first imagined EFA. These include image analysis, alpha analysis, non-iterated principal axis (PA), iterated principal axis (IPA), maximum
likelihood (ML), unweighted least squares (ULS), weighted least squares (WLS),
generalized least squares (GLS), minimum residual (MINRES), etc. Some extraction methods are identical yet were given different names. For example, ULS,
OLS, and MINRES all refer to essentially the same method (Flora, 2018). Further, an IPA extraction will converge to an OLS/ULS solution (Briggs & Mac-
Callum, 2003; MacCallum, 2009). Mathematically, extraction methods differ in
the way they go about locating the factors that will best reproduce the original
correlation matrix, whether they attempt to reproduce the sample correlation
matrix or the population correlation matrix, and in their definition of the best
way to measure closeness of the reproduced and original correlation matrices.

The seven extraction methods offered by SPSS are arrayed in Figure 11.4. PCA
is the default extraction method, making it easy for inexperienced researchers to

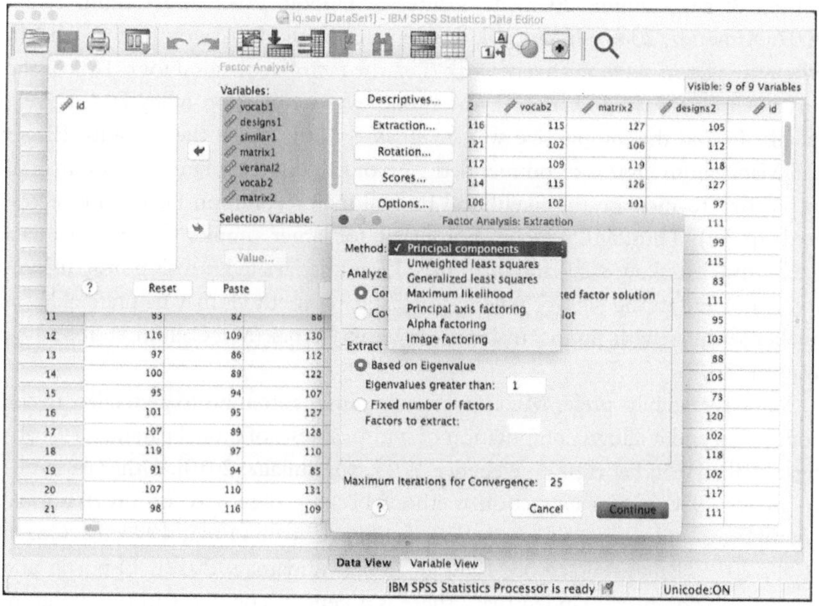

FIGURE 11.4 Factor extraction options in SPSS

apply an inappropriate extraction method. Alpha and image extraction are relatively unusual and perhaps only advantageous in rare, special circumstances that will not be considered here. The most significant distinction between common factor extraction methods is between ML and least squares methods (ULS, GLS, and IPA). ML attempts to reproduce the *population* correlation matrix that most likely generated the sample correlation matrix, whereas the least squares methods attempt to reproduce the *sample* correlation matrix. The population focus of ML extraction leaves it dependent on two critical assumptions: (a) the data are a random sample of some population, and (b) the measured variables have an underlying multivariate normal distribution. In contrast, the least squares methods have no distributional assumptions (Fabrigar & Wegener, 2012). IPA seeks to maximize the variance extracted by forming a weighted combination of all the variables that will produce the highest squared correlations between the variables and the factor, whereas ULS attempts to minimize the differences between the off-diagonal elements of the correlation matrix and the reproduced correlation matrix. IPA and ULS both produce "the best least squares estimate of the entire correlation matrix including diagonal elements" (Gorsuch, 1983, p. 96). Generalized least squares (sometimes called weighted least squares) modifies the ULS method by giving more weight to variables with high correlations. ULS is probably most appropriate when non–positive definite matrices are encountered with another extraction method (Lorenzo-Seva & Ferrando, 2020).

Simulation research has compared ML and least squares extraction methods in terms of factor recovery under varying levels of sample size and factor strength (Briggs & MacCallum, 2003; de Winter & Dodou, 2012; MacCallum et al., 2007; Ximénez, 2009). In general, least squares methods have outperformed ML when the factors were relatively weak (i.e., the factor accounted for ≤ 16% of the variance of a measured variable), the model was wrong (too many factors were specified), and the sample size was small ($N = 100$). Given these results, Briggs and MacCallum (2003) recommended "use of OLS in exploratory factor analysis in practice to increase the likelihood that all major common factors are recovered" (p. 54). Thus, ML may be appropriate for larger samples with normal data (i.e., univariate skew ≤ 2.0 and kurtosis ≤ 7.0; multivariate kurtosis nonsignificant and ≤ 5.0) and strong factors, whereas least squares methods may be preferable for smaller samples with nonnormal data or weak factors (MacCallum et al., 2007; Watson, 2017).

Some researchers prefer ML extraction because it attempts to generalize to the population and it allows computation of statistical tests of model parameters (Fabrigar et al., 1999; Fabrigar & Wegener, 2012; Matsunaga, 2010). Other researchers prefer least squares extraction methods because they have no distributional assumptions and are sensitive to weak factors (Carroll, 1985, 1993; McCoach et al., 2013; Pett et al., 2003; Russell, 2002; Widaman, 2012). Osborne and Banjanovic (2016) concluded that "there is a general consensus in the literature that ML is the preferred choice for when data exhibits multivariate normality and iterated PAF or ULS for when that assumption is violated" (p. 26). Other researchers have endorsed that conclusion (Bandalos & Gerstner, 2016; Costello & Osborne, 2005; Sakaluk & Short, 2017; Schmitt, 2011). However, different extraction methods tend to produce similar results in most cases (Tabachnick & Fidell, 2019).

Regardless of extraction method, researchers must be cautious of improper solutions, that is, solutions that are mathematically impossible, for example, communality values greater than 1.00. Researchers must also be aware that extraction may fail with iterative estimators such as IPA. This happens because EFA software will try to arrive at an optimal estimate before some maximum number of estimation iterations has been completed. If an optimal estimate has not been computed at that point, an error message about nonconvergence will be produced. In that case, the researcher may increase the maximum number of iterations and rerun the analysis. If nonconvergence persists after 1,000 iterations, the results, like those from an improper solution, should not be interpreted (Flora, 2018). "Improper solutions and nonconvergence are more likely to occur when there is a linear dependence among observed variables, when the model includes too many common factors, or when the sample size is too small" (Flora, 2018, p. 257). Alternatively, another extraction method could be employed (e.g., ULS instead of IPA or ML).

Report

The univariate normal distribution of the data and substantial reliability of the measured variables indicated that a maximum likelihood extraction method might be appropriate. Nevertheless, the robustness of ML results will be verified by applying an iterated principal axis method to ensure that weak factors are not overlooked (Briggs & MacCallum, 2003; de Winter & Dodou, 2012).

12

STEP 7

How Many Factors to Retain

As many factors as measured variables can be extracted for exploratory factor analysis (EFA), but it is usually possible to explain the majority of variance with a smaller number of factors. The problem arises in determining the *exact* number of factors to retain for interpretation. Methodologists have observed that this is probably the most important decision in EFA because there are serious consequences for selecting either too few or too many factors (Benson & Nasser, 1998; Fabrigar et al., 1999; Glorfeld, 1995; Hoelzle & Meyer, 2013; Preacher et al., 2013), whereas the options for other EFA decisions tend to be fairly robust (Hayton et al., 2004; Tabachnick & Fidell, 2019). Retaining too few factors can distort factor loadings and result in solutions in which common factors are combined, thereby obscuring the true factor solution. Extracting too many factors can focus on small, unimportant factors that are difficult to interpret and unlikely to replicate (Hayton et al., 2004). "Choosing the number of factors is something like focusing a microscope. Too high or too low an adjustment will obscure a structure that is obvious when the adjustment is just right" (Hair et al., 2019, p. 144).

"In the end, the overriding criteria for choosing a particular number of factors are interpretability and theoretical relevance because a factor solution is useful only if it can be interpreted in a meaningful way" (Bandalos, 2018, p. 324). A delicate balance between *comprehensiveness* and *parsimony* is needed to achieve an interpretable solution. Unfortunately, no infallible method to determine the "true" number of factors to retain has been discovered (Bandalos, 2018; Barrett & Kline, 1982; Cattell, 1966; Comrey & Lee, 1992; Fabrigar & Wegener 2012; Gorsuch, 1983; Nunnally & Bernstein, 1994; Pett et al., 2003; Preacher et al., 2013; Rummel, 1970; Widaman, 2012). It appears that the nature of the data (e.g., the number of indicators per factor, communality level, factor intercorrelations, complex loadings, sample size) differentially affects each method. Given this uncertainty, methodologists have recommended that both empirical evidence and theoretical knowledge be applied to determine the number of factors to retain for interpretation (Bandalos, 2018; Finch, 2020a; Hair et al., 2019; Osborne, 2014; Pituch & Stevens, 2016). Additionally, it has generally been agreed that under-extraction is more dangerous than overextraction, so it may not be a bad strategy to risk the overextraction of one or two factors (Cattell, 1978; Fava & Velicer, 1992, 1996; Gorsuch, 1983; Kline, 2013; MacCallum et al., 2001; Stewart, 1981; Wood et al., 1996).

Empirical Guidelines

A variety of simulation studies have provided empirical guidelines for determining the number of factors to retain. Based on these simulations, some empirical methods have been found to perform better than others. For example, the parallel analysis (PA) criterion of Horn (1965) has generally performed well (Auerswald & Moshagen, 2019; Finch, 2020b; Peres-Neto et al., 2005; Ruscio & Roche, 2012; Velicer et al., 2000; Zwick & Velicer, 1986). Conceptually, PA involves generating a set of random data with the same number of variables and participants as the real data and then comparing the mean eigenvalues from multiple sets of random data with the corresponding eigenvalues from the real data. In this comparison, only factors with eigenvalues that are above the mean of those from the random data should be retained. PA has remained accurate with nonnormal data and non-Pearsonian correlations (Buja & Eyuboglu, 1992; Dinno, 2009; Garrido et al., 2013) and has performed better than modified PA versions (Lim & Jahng, 2019). Some methodologists have noted that PA tends to overextract by one or two factors and recommended that the upper 95th or 99th percentile of each eigenvalue be retained rather than the mean (Glorfeld, 1995; Hoyle & Duvall, 2004). However, Crawford et al. (2010) found that PA tended to underextract if there was a strong general factor, and Caron (2019) reported that PA also tended to underextract if there were correlated factors. Given these competing results, it seems reasonable to compare mean eigen-values rather than risk underextraction. PA is easily computed with modern computers, so it is recommended that at least 100 random datasets be generated (Hoelzle & Meyer, 2013).

A second empirical guideline that has been found to be relatively accurate in simulation studies is the minimum average partial (MAP) method of Velicer (1976). A matrix of partial correlations is calculated after each principal component is extracted. The average of the squared off-diagonal partial correlations is computed from each matrix. This average is expected to reach a minimum when the correct number of components is extracted. The logic of this procedure is that as common variance is partialed out of the matrix, the MAP criterion will decrease. At the point where the common variance has been removed and only unique variance remains, the MAP criterion will begin to rise. Thus, the MAP criterion separates common and unique variance and retains only components consisting of common variance.

A third, more subjective, method relies on graphing the eigenvalues derived from extraction and using visual analysis to detect any abrupt change in their slope. Developed by Cattell (1966), this scree graph plots the eigenvalues on the Y axis against their extraction order on the X axis. The concept is that the eigenvalues for the "true" common factors tend to form a more or less straight line, whereas the error factors form another line with a different, smaller slope (analogous to the scree or rubble at the base of a cliff). This assumes that as succeeding factors are extracted from the factor matrix, error variance will begin to predominate and will represent only minor, random fluctuations. To follow the geology analogy, this will separate important early factors (bedrock) from the rubble (scree) of random error. Some methodologists supplement the scree with a minimum variance guideline, but these guidelines are subjective (e.g., 40% to 75%) and unlikely to be reasonable for social science research (Beavers et al., 2012; Reio & Shuck, 2015).

To analyze a scree plot, draw a straight line through the eigenvalues from right to left. The eigenvalues above and to the left of the straight line are the factors to retain (Pett et al., 2003). An ideal scree plot, as illustrated in Figure 12.1, may be relatively easy to interpret. The three largest eigenvalues are clearly above the trajectory of the straight line. However, most scree plots are more ambiguous, and researchers tend to be unreliable when using scree plots to determine the number of factors to retain (Streiner, 1998).

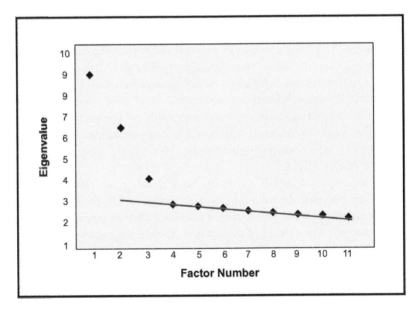

FIGURE 12.1   Simplified scree plot

Attempts have been made to interpret scree plots more objectively via empirical methods. These include the optimal coordinates method (Raîche et al., 2013) that uses eigenvalues as predictors in a multiple regression and identifies the cut point when an observed eigenvalue exceeds its estimated value. Another empirical approach is the acceleration factor (Yakovitz & Szidarovszky, 1986) that identifies where the slope in the curve of the scree plot changes abruptly. Finally, the standard error scree (Zoski & Jurs, 1996) is based on the standard error of the estimate of each eigenvalue. Unfortunately, results from simulation studies have been inconsistent, and it is not clear if any empirical scree method is superior (Nasser et al., 2002; Raîche et al., 2013).

Numerous other empirical guidelines have been suggested by researchers. For example, innovative network graphing methods (Golino & Epskamp, 2017; Golino et al., 2020), a very simple structure (VSS) approach that minimizes factor complexity (Revelle & Rocklin, 1979), the Hull method that attempts to balance goodness-of-fit and parsimony (Lorenzo-Seva et al., 2011), and model fit indices commonly used in confirmatory factor analysis (Clark & Bowles, 2018; Finch, 2020b). Sufficient evidence has not accumulated yet to justify use of these methods. In contrast, there are several methods of determining the number of factors to retain that are *not* supported and should be ignored. These include the so-called Eigenvalue 1 rule as well as the chi-square test with ML extraction (Flora, 2018; Hayashi et al., 2007; Russell, 2002; Velicer et al., 2000).

Velicer et al. (2000) recommended that a combination of PA and MAP should be employed, with scree reserved as a potentially useful adjunct. Other methodologists have also recommended PA and/or MAP (Bandalos, 2018; DeVellis, 2017; Fabrigar & Wegener, 2012; Fabrigar et al., 1999; Ford et al., 1986; Hair et al., 2019; Hayton et al., 2004; Hoelzle & Meyer, 2013; Howard, 2016; Hoyle & Duvall, 2004; Kanyongo, 2005; Lawrence & Hancock, 1999; Osborne, 2014; Sakaluk & Short, 2017), noting that PA tends to slightly overextract, whereas MAP tends to slightly underextract.

Empirical Criteria With SPSS

Scree plot. Unfortunately, the only empirical criterion provided by SPSS is the scree plot. It can be created via the ***Analyze > Dimension Reduction > Factor > Extraction > Scree plot*** menus (Figure 12.2).

Alternatively, command code (also found in Figure 12.2) can produce the same scree plot. The scree plot for the iq data appears to favor the extraction of two factors.

Parallel analysis. Although PA is not natively available in SPSS, O'Connor (2000) provided SPSS syntax that can be downloaded from https://people. ok.ubc.ca/brioconn/nfactors/nfactors.html. First, download O'Connor's parallel .sps syntax file. Second, load that file into SPSS via ***File > Open > Syntax***

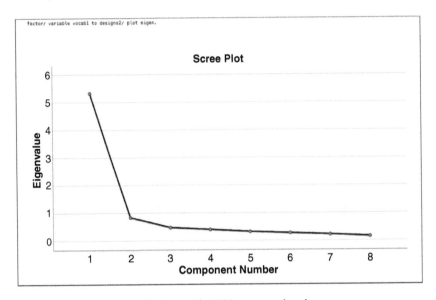

FIGURE 12.2 Scree plot of iq data with SPSS command code

> *parallel .sps*. Third, ensure that the iq data file with only the eight measured variables (delete the id variable for this analysis) is loaded in the **Data Editor** window. Fourth, edit the parallel .sps syntax file to reflect the correct number of cases (152), variables (8), and number of random datasets (500) in lines 8–11, as demonstrated in Figure 12.3. For this example, the 95th percentile criterion will be retained because it produces the same decision as the 50th percentile criterion. Change "95" in line 11 to "50" to obtain only the mean random eigenvalue. Finally, execute the command code via *Run > All*.

SPSS will open an **Output Viewer** window with the mean random eigenvalues and their 95th percentile values (see Figure 12.4).

PA can also be conducted with online calculators available at www.statstodo.com/ParallelAnalysis_Exp.php and https://analytics.gonzaga.edu/parallelengine. The later calculator is displayed in Figure 12.5. Note that the two methods produced almost identical random eigenvalues. Alternatively, a standalone program called *Monte Carlo PCA for Parallel Analysis* can be downloaded from edpsychassociates.com/Watkins3.html.

Finally, the random eigenvalues must be compared to real eigenvalues from the iq data to determine the number of factors to retain. The real eigenvalues can be computed via the *Analyze > Dimension Reduction > Factor > Extraction > Fixed number of factors to extract: 8* menu options (see Figure 12.6).

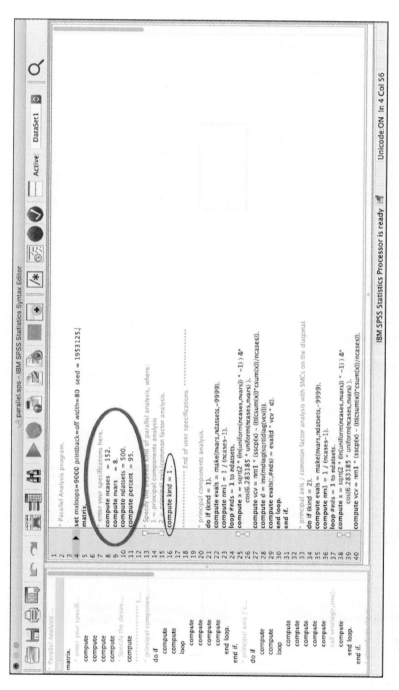

FIGURE 12.3   Syntax file for parallel analysis with SPSS

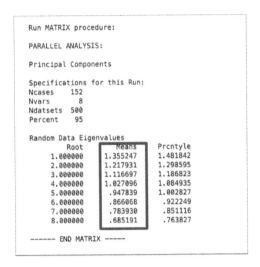

```
Run MATRIX procedure:

PARALLEL ANALYSIS:

Principal Components

Specifications for this Run:
Ncases    152
Nvars       8
Ndatsets  500
Percent    95

Random Data Eigenvalues
        Root        Means       Prcntyle
    1.000000     1.355247      1.481842
    2.000000     1.217931      1.298595
    3.000000     1.116697      1.186823
    4.000000     1.027096      1.084935
    5.000000      .947839      1.002827
    6.000000      .866068       .922249
    7.000000      .783930       .851116
    8.000000      .685191       .763827

------ END MATRIX -----
```

FIGURE 12.4   Parallel analysis output for iq data

Parallel Analysis

Number of Variables in Your Dataset to be Factor Analyzed (Please change)

8

Sample Size of Your Dataset (Please change)

152

Type of Analysis

Principal Components ▼

Number of Random Correlation Matrices to Generate (default of 100 currently set)

500

Percentile of Eigenvalues (default of 95th percentile currently set)

95

Seed

1000

About this Application

Patil et al. (2008) presented a web-based parallel analysis engine (Patil et al. 2007) that used SAS. This engine was published at

Citing this Application:

Patil Vivek H, Surendra N. Singh, Sanjay Mishra, and D. Todd Donavan (2017). Parallel Analysis Engine to Aid in Determining Number of Factors to Retain using R [Computer software], available from https://analytics.gonzaga.edu/parallelengine/.

Using this Application

Based on parameters provided by the researcher, this engine calculates eigenvalues from randomly generated correlation matrices. These can be then compared with eigenvalues extracted from the researcher's dataset. The number of factors to retain will be the number of eigenvalues (generated from the researcher's dataset) that are larger than the corresponding random eigenvalues (Horn 1965).

The default (and recommended) values for number of random correlation matrices and percentile of eigenvalues are 100 and 95 respectively (see Cota et al. 1993; Glorfeld 1995; Turner 1998; Velicer et al. 2000). Based on the nature of their particular dataset, researchers can override these default options. Higher (lower) values of number of correlation matrices generated increase (decrease) computation time but provide more (fewer) data points in the distribution of different eigenvalues. The percentile determines the desired eigenvalue from this distribution, which is then used for comparison purposes. Lower values of the percentile tend to lead to over extraction (extraction of more factors than necessary).

Component or Factor	Mean Eigenvalue	Percentile Eigenvalue
1	1.352472	1.477139
2	1.217003	1.296170
3	1.116722	1.179092
4	1.031649	1.087980
5	0.949538	1.003631
6	0.866667	0.923723
7	0.782495	0.848226
8	0.683454	0.763328

FIGURE 12.5   Online parallel analysis output

```
factor/ variables vocab1 to designs2/ extraction pc.
```

Total Variance Explained

Component	Initial Eigenvalues			Extraction Sums of Squared Loadings		
	Total	% of Variance	Cumulative %	Total	% of Variance	Cumulative %
1	5.328	66.600	66.600	5.328	66.600	66.600
2	.837	10.463	77.063			
3	.474	5.929	82.992			
4	.399	4.986	87.979			
5	.320	4.005	91.984			
6	.268	3.355	95.339			
7	.219	2.742	98.081			
8	.154	1.919	100.000			

Extraction Method: Principal Component Analysis.

FIGURE 12.6 PCA eigenvalues for iq data

Eigenvalue #	Real	Random
1	5.33	1.36
2	0.84	1.22
3	0.47	1.12
4	0.40	1.03
5	0.32	0.95
6	0.27	0.87
7	0.22	0.78
8	0.15	0.69

FIGURE 12.7 Comparison of real and random eigenvalues for iq data

Alternatively, command code (also presented in Figure 12.6) can produce eigenvalues from the iq data.

By comparing the real eigenvalues with the random eigenvalues, respectively, in Figure 12.7 it appears that only one component is sufficient (real eigenvalue of 5.33 vs. random eigenvalue of 1.36). In contrast, the second random eigenvalue of 1.22 exceeds the second real eigenvalue of 0.84.

Parallel analysis can be also conducted with the eigenvalues extracted from a reduced correlation matrix by specifying a common factor extraction method, and some researchers prefer this approach (Crawford et al., 2010). However, the unre-duced correlation matrix was used in the development of parallel analysis (Horn, 1965) and in much of the simulation research (Velicer et al., 2000; Zwick & Velicer, 1986) and has been found more accurate than results from the reduced matrix (Auerswald & Moshagen, 2019; Garrido et al., 2013; Lim & Jahng, 2019). Additionally, the unreduced matrix was the foundation for development of both

MAP and scree, so it seems reasonable to "use it to determine the spread of variance across the factors and as the basis for deciding on the number of factors to be extracted for the next stage" (Child, 2006, p. 153).

Minimum average partial. Although MAP is not natively available in SPSS, O'Connor (2000) provided SPSS syntax that can be downloaded from https://people.ok.ubc.ca/brioconn/nfactors/nfactors.html. First, download O'Connor's map .sps syntax file. Second, load that file into SPSS via *File > Open > Syntax > map .sps*. Third, ensure the iq data file is loaded in the **Data Editor** window. Fourth, edit the map .sps syntax file to select data entry "Method 2" by uncommenting line 61 (delete the asterisk) and providing the variable names, as demonstrated in Figure 12.8. Finally, execute the command code in Figure 12.8 via *Run > All*.

SPSS will open an **Output Viewer** window with the MAP output (see Figure 12.9). The MAP value sequentially drops from .0697 for one factor to 0.0626 for two factors and then increases to 0.0949 for three factors. The lowest MAP value identifies the number of factors to retain. In this case, MAP reached a minimum at two factors.

Theoretical Knowledge

Although empirical guidelines are useful, there is no guarantee that they are correct (Bandalos, 2018; Cattell, 1966; Fabrigar & Wegener, 2012; Gorsuch, 1983; Pett et al., 2003; Preacher et al., 2013; Widaman, 2012). The accuracy of empirical guidelines is more likely to be compromised when factors are highly correlated, factor loadings are low, the number of factors is large, and the sample size is small (Lim & Jahng, 2019). Given this fundamental uncertainty, methodologists have recommended that multiple criteria, including relevant theory and previous research, be used to determine the number of factors to retain (Bandalos, 2018; Bandalos & Boehm-Kaufman, 2009; Bandalos & Finney, 2019; Basto & Pereira, 2012; Brown, 2015; Fabrigar et al., 1999; Finch, 2013, 2020a, 2020b; Flora, 2018; Hoelzle & Meyer, 2013; McCoach et al., 2013; Norman & Streiner, 2014; Nunnally & Bernstein, 1994; Osborne, 2014; Pituch & Stevens, 2016; Preacher & MacCallum, 2003; Preacher et al., 2013; Reio & Shuck, 2015; Velicer & Fava, 1998; Widaman, 2012). There is no prior research with these eight measured variables, but research with similar verbal and nonverbal measures have suggested two factors, and development of these tests was guided by that theoretical expectation.

Model Selection

Given that there is no infallible method to identify the "true" number of factors, Cattell (1978) said, "taking out the right number of factors does not mean in most cases a number correct in some absolute sense, but in the sense of not

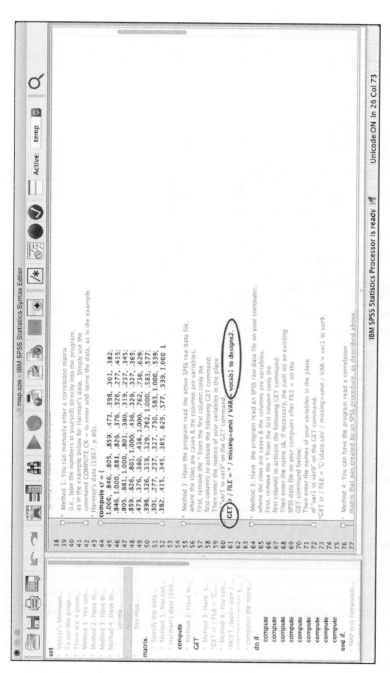

FIGURE 12.8   Syntax file for minimum average partial (MAP) with SPSS

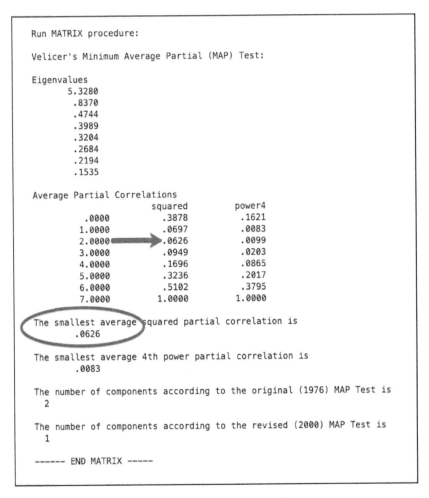

```
Run MATRIX procedure:

Velicer's Minimum Average Partial (MAP) Test:

Eigenvalues
        5.3280
         .8370
         .4744
         .3989
         .3204
         .2684
         .2194
         .1535

Average Partial Correlations
                        squared         power4
        .0000           .3878           .1621
       1.0000           .0697           .0083
       2.0000           .0626           .0099
       3.0000           .0949           .0203
       4.0000           .1696           .0865
       5.0000           .3236           .2017
       6.0000           .5102           .3795
       7.0000          1.0000          1.0000

The smallest average squared partial correlation is
        .0626

The smallest average 4th power partial correlation is
        .0083

The number of components according to the original (1976) MAP Test is
   2

The number of components according to the revised (2000) MAP Test is
   1

------ END MATRIX -----
```

FIGURE 12.9 Minimum average partial (MAP) output for iq data

missing any factor of more than trivial size" (p. 61). This suggests a strategy of "selecting from among a set of competing theoretical explanations the model that best balances the desirable characteristics of parsimony and fit to observed data" (Preacher et al., 2013, p. 29). Each candidate model contains a different number of factors and is judged on its interpretability and conceptual sense in this model selection process (Bandalos, 2018; Carroll, 1993; Cudeck, 2000; Fabrigar & Wegener, 2012; Fabrigar et al., 1999; Finch, 2013; Flora, 2018; Ford et al., 1986; Gorsuch, 1983, 1988, 1997; Hair et al., 2019; Hoelzle & Meyer, 2013; Kahn, 2006; McCoach et al., 2013; Nunnally & Bernstein, 1994; Osborne, 2014; Osborne & Banjanovic, 2016; Pituch & Stevens, 2016; Preacher & MacCallum, 2003; Preacher et al., 2013; Schmitt et al., 2018; Tabachnick & Fidell, 2019;

Velicer et al., 2000; Widaman, 2012). Of course, a model that is generalizable to other samples is scientifically desirable, but multiple samples and multiple EFAs may be required to achieve that goal (Preacher et al., 2013).

Report

Velicer et al. (2000) recommended that a combination of parallel analysis (Horn, 1965) and minimum average partial (Velicer, 1976) methods should be employed for determining the number of factors to retain for rotation, with scree as a potentially useful adjunct. Using these three criteria, it appeared that one or two factors would be sufficient for an optimal balance between comprehensiveness and parsimony. Two factors were also signaled as sufficient by prior research and theory. To ensure that underextraction did not occur, a model with three factors might also be considered (Cattell, 1978). Therefore, models with three, two, and one factor(s) will be sequentially evaluated for their interpretability and theoretical meaningfulness.

13

STEP 8

Rotate Factors

Exploratory factor analysis (EFA) extraction methods have been mathematically optimized to account for the covariance among measured variables, but they do not take interpretability into account (Bandalos, 2018; Comrey & Lee, 1992; DeVellis, 2017; Nunnally & Bernstein, 1994; Pituch & Stevens, 2016). As previously described, the orientation of the factor axes is fixed in factor space during factor extraction. Those axes can be rotated about their origin to make the loadings more interpretable without changing the underlying structure of the data (Tabachnick & Fidell, 2019). The rotated structure accounts for the same proportion of variance as the unrotated structure, but it distributes that variance across factors differently. For example, an orthogonal rotation of two factors from the iq data found that the first and second factors accounted for 62.3% and 7.3% of the variance, respectively, before rotation. However, 35.8% of that variance was allocated to the first factor and 33.8% to the second factor following rotation. Thus, the total variance of 69.6% was distributed differently between unrotated and rotated factors. Rotation is akin to taking a photograph of a person from multiple angles. The person remains the same, but some of the photographs better represent the person than others. DeVellis (2017, pp. 171–176) described several other analogies to help understand the concept of rotation.

For a simple example, the two-factor initial (unrotated) solution for the iq data was obtained and conceptually plotted on a two-dimensional graph in factor space in Figure 13.1. It is apparent that the variables tend to form two clusters in multidimensional space, but they are not particularly well aligned with the factor axes.

Perhaps the factor axes could be rotated about their origin to bring them closer to the center of the variable clusters (Osborne & Banjanovic, 2016). As displayed in gray in Figure 13.2, the rotated Factor II axis is now closer to the

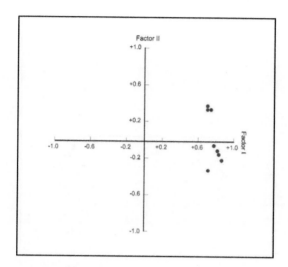

FIGURE 13.1   Unrotated factor plot

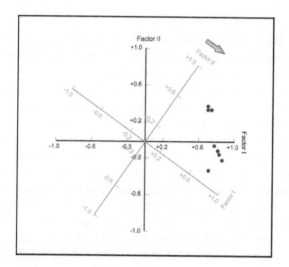

FIGURE 13.2   Orthogonally rotated factor plot

cluster of three variables, but that has moved the axis of Factor I away from the second variable cluster. This is called an orthogonal rotation because the factor axes have been restrained to right angles. Due to this restraint, the two factors also remain uncorrelated.

Alternatively, the factor axes could be rotated independent of each other to bring each of them closer to the centroids of the variable clusters. That is, rotate the axes without constraining them to orthogonality. Independent rotation of the

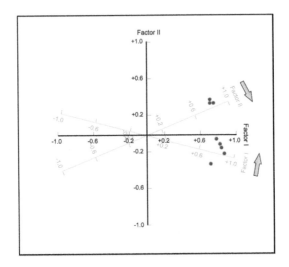

FIGURE 13.3   Obliquely rotated factor plot

axes is called oblique rotation. This allows the factors to become correlated if that results in improved simplicity of loadings. As displayed in gray in Figure 13.3, that has brought both axes closer to the variable clusters.

These geometric representations of factor rotation have been only approximate, sufficient for illustration of the concept of rotation but not precise enough for use in practice. They also intimate that "there is an infinite number of equally fitting ways those factors may be oriented in multidimensional space" (Sakaluk & Short, 2017, p. 3), which is called rotational indeterminacy (Fabrigar & Wegener, 2012). Rotational indeterminacy is an additional reason that methodologists stress that factor models must be judged on their interpretability and theoretical sense (Bandalos, 2018; Cudeck, 2000; Fabrigar & Wegener, 2012; Fabrigar et al., 1999; Ford et al., 1986; Gorsuch, 1983, 1988; Hair et al., 2019; Kahn, 2006; Nunnally & Bernstein, 1994; Osborne, 2014; Preacher & MacCallum, 2003; Preacher et al., 2013; Tabachnick & Fidell, 2019; Velicer et al., 2000; Widaman, 2012).

Orthogonal Versus Oblique Rotation

Researchers differ on their preference for orthogonal or oblique rotations. Those who prefer orthogonal rotations cite simplicity and ease of interpretation (Mertler & Vannatta, 2001). However, orthogonal rotations are inappropriate when there is a higher-order factor (see the later chapter on higher-order and bifactor models) because they disperse the general factor variance across the first-order factors, thereby artificially obscuring the higher-order factor (Gorsuch,

1983). Other researchers prefer oblique rotations due to their accuracy and to honor the reality that most variables are correlated to some extent (Bandalos & Boehm-Kaufman, 2009; Bandalos & Finney, 2019; Brown, 2013, 2015; Costello & Osborne, 2005; Cudeck, 2000; Fabrigar & Wegener, 2012; Fabrigar et al., 1999; Finch, 2013; Flora, 2018; Flora et al., 2012; Ford et al., 1986; Gorsuch, 1983; McCoach et al., 2013; Meehl, 1990; Mulaik, 2010, 2018; Osborne, 2014; Pett et al., 2003; Pituch & Stevens, 2016; Preacher & MacCallum, 2003; Reio & Shuck, 2015; Reise et al., 2000; Rummel, 1967; Russell, 2002; Sakaluk & Short, 2017; Sass, 2010; Widaman, 2012; Worthington & Whittaker, 2006; Zhang & Preacher, 2015).

Some researchers suggest using oblique rotation only if the correlation between factors exceeds .20 (Finch, 2020a) or .32 (Roberson et al., 2014; Tabachnick & Fidell, 2019), whereas others believe there is no compelling reason to select one type of rotation over another, so both should be applied (Child, 2006; Hair et al., 2019). Nonetheless, the arguments in favor of oblique rotations are compelling. As articulated by Schmitt (2011):

> because oblique rotation methods generally produce accurate and comparable factor structures to orthogonal methods even when interfactor correlations are negligible, it is strongly recommend [sic] that researchers only use oblique rotation methods because they generally result in more realistic and more statistically sound factor structures.
>
> *(p. 312)*

In practice, rotation is accomplished with algebraic algorithms (analytic rotations). The most prominent orthogonal rotation is varimax (Kaiser, 1958). Others include quartimax, equamax, and parsimax. As shown in Figure 13.4, SPSS includes varimax, quartimax, and equamax orthogonal rotation options. The most popular oblique rotations are promax (Hendrickson & White, 1964) and oblimin (Jennrich & Sampson, 1966). Other oblique rotations include geomin, maxplane, orthoblique, direct quartimin, bigquartmin, promin, and covarimin. SPSS only offers promax and oblimin oblique rotation options (Figure 13.4). Technical reviews of analytic rotations are available if further details are desired (Browne, 2001; Sass & Schmitt, 2010; Schmitt & Sass, 2011). In many cases, different rotations within the orthogonal and oblique families are likely to produce similar results (Bandalos & Finney, 2019; Nunnally & Bernstein, 1994; Sass & Schmitt, 2010).

Many methodologists have recommended that varimax be selected if an orthogonal rotation is employed (Child, 2006; Gorsuch, 1983, 2003; Kline, 1994; Nunnally & Bernstein, 1994). It is not clear whether there is a superior oblique method (Schmitt & Sass, 2011). Methodologists have variously recommended oblimin (Child, 2006; Flora, 2018; McCoach et al., 2013; Mulaik, 2018), geomin (Hattori et al., 2017), and promax (Finch, 2006; Gorsuch, 1983, 1988,

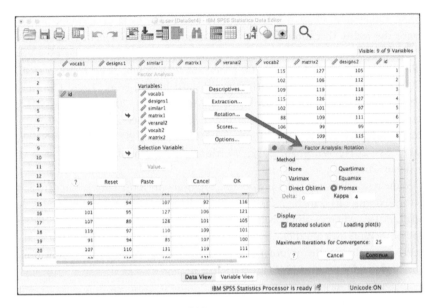

FIGURE 13.4   Rotation options in SPSS

2003; Matsunaga, 2010; Morrison, 2009; Russell, 2002; Sass, 2010; Thompson, 2004). These oblique rotations require that a parameter be set that specifies the extent to which the factors are allowed to be correlated. That parameter is referred to as delta in oblimin, k or kappa in promax, and ε in geomin. Oblimin and geomin solutions seem to be very sensitive to the parameter setting, whereas promax is relatively insensitive to the k setting (Gorsuch, 2003; Tataryn et al., 1999). For oblimin rotations, Howard (2016) noted that delta values of zero were preferred, which is the SPSS default value. For geomin rotations, ε values of .01 and .05 were recommended by Hattori et al. (2017) and Morin et al. (2020), respectively. Unfortunately, geomin may converge on solutions that are not optimal (Hattori et al., 2017). For promax rotations, a kappa value of four will probably be adequate and is the default value in SPSS (Gorsuch, 2003; Tataryn et al., 1999). Given this choice among oblique rotations, many methodologists recommend that results from another rotation method be compared to the initial choice to ensure that results are robust to rotation method (Finch, 2020a; Hattori et al., 2017). Promax and oblimin would be the obvious choice for this comparison.

Factor Loadings

To this point, factor loadings have been specified as quantifications of the relationship between measured variables and factors. By allowing factors to correlate, oblique rotations produce two types of factor loadings: pattern coefficients and structure coefficients. Pattern coefficients quantify the relationship between a measured variable and its underlying factor, after the effects of the other variables have been considered or partialed out. Pattern coefficients are regression-like weights and may occasionally be greater than ± 1.00. In contrast, structure coefficients reflect the simple correlation of a measured variable with its underlying factor and ignore the effects of other factors and must, therefore, range from −1.00 to +1.00. Consequently, it is no longer sufficient to refer to factor loadings after an oblique rotation has been applied. Rather, the appropriate coefficient *must* be identified (pattern or structure).

Pattern and structure coefficients will be identical if the factors are perfectly uncorrelated with each other and will increasingly deviate from each other as the factor intercorrelations increase. Methodologists typically recommend that both pattern and structure coefficients should be interpreted (Gorsuch, 1983; Matsunaga, 2010; McClain, 1996; McCoach et al., 2013; Nunnally & Bernstein, 1994; Pett et al., 2003; Reio & Shuck, 2015; Thompson, 2004) because that "increases the interpretative insights gained from a factor analysis" (Hetzel, 1996, p. 183). However, pattern coefficients and factor intercorrelations should receive primary attention during the model evaluation process (Bandalos, 2018; Brown, 2015; Cattell, 1978; Fabrigar & Wegener, 2012; Flora, 2018; Gibson et al., 2020; Hair et al., 2019; McCoach et al., 2013; Mulaik, 2010; Pituch & Stevens, 2016; Rencher & Christensen, 2012; Roberson et al., 2014; Sakaluk & Short, 2017). Comrey and Lee (1992) suggested that loadings greater than .70 are excellent, .63 are very good, .55 are good, .45 are fair, and .32 are poor. Morin et al. (2020) concluded that loadings ≥ .50 are "fully satisfactory" (p. 1052). Structure coefficients can be consulted after the final model has been tentatively accepted to ensure that the factors have been named appropriately and that anomalous results have not been inadvertently accepted (Kahn, 2006).

Eigenvalues and Variance Extracted

The unrotated and rotated factor solutions will explain the same amount of total variance (computed with eigenvalues), but rotation spreads that variance across the factors to improve interpretation and parsimony. Given this redistribution of variance across factors, it is necessary to identify whether the unrotated or rotated solution is referenced when considering the proportion of total variance that was attributed to each factor. Given that rotation apportions variance away from the first factor to later factors, it would be inappropriate to interpret the proportion of variance following rotation as an indicator of factor importance.

Report

An oblique rotation was selected because it honors the ubiquity of intercorrelations among social science variables (Meehl, 1990). Among the potential oblique analytic rotations, promax was chosen because it is an oblique modification of the widely accepted varimax procedure (Gorsuch, 1983; Thompson, 2004). To ensure stability across extraction methods, oblimin extraction was also employed (Finch, 2020a).

14

STEP 9

Interpret Exploratory Factor Analysis Results

Model Selection Guidelines

Exploratory factor analysis (EFA) models with different numbers of factors should be sequentially evaluated for their interpretability and theoretical meaningfulness (Fabrigar & Wegener, 2012; Finch, 2020a; Flora, 2018). There are a variety of guidelines that can be used to judge models. It is crucial that the researcher explicitly detail the judgment guidelines that will be applied *prior* to implementation. This a priori explanation will reduce the possibility of self-serving judgments (Rubin, 2017; Simmons et al., 2011). Following is an enumerated list of guidelines that are most likely to be helpful:

1. Establish a threshold at which factor loadings (pattern coefficients for oblique rotations) will be considered meaningful (Worthington & Whittaker, 2006). Conventionally, loadings that meet this threshold are characterized as *salient*. It is common to arbitrarily consider factor loadings of .30, .32, or .40 as salient (Child, 2006; Comrey & Lee, 1992; Hair et al., 2019; Pituch & Stevens, 2016), that is, variables with around 9%, 10%, or 16% (factor loading squared) of their variance explained by the factor. Some researchers consider .30 or .32 salient for EFA and .40 salient for PCA. These thresholds honor practical significance but ignore statistical significance. That is, a loading of .32 might account for 10% of a variable's variance, but it might not be statistically significantly different from zero, thereby calling into question its stability (Schmitt & Sass, 2011; Zhang & Preacher, 2015). Norman and Streiner (2014) suggested an approximation based on Pearson correlation coefficients to compute the statistical significance ($p = .01$) of factor loadings: $\dfrac{5.152}{\sqrt{N-2}}$ For the iq data, statistical significance ($p = .01$) would equate to

$5.152 \div 12.25 = .42$. A more relaxed $p = .05$ standard would modify the numerator: $\dfrac{3.92}{\sqrt{N-2}}$ or $3.92 \div 12.25 = .32$. Thus, establish a threshold for salience that is both practically and statistically significant *before* conducting EFA.

2. Respect the concept of simple structure (Thurstone, 1947). Variables with salient loadings on more than one factor are said to cross-load and are called complex variables. Complex loadings might be appropriate for some structures but will complicate interpretation. Simple structure solutions will probably be more interpretable and more likely to replicate. Conceptually, simple structure implies that each variable will exhibit salient loadings on a few factors (the fewer the better) and weak loadings on all other factors (Pituch & Stevens, 2016). At its simplest, several variables will saliently load onto each factor, and each variable will saliently load onto only one factor. In practice, the goal is a reasonable approximation of simple structure (Morin et al., 2020). Simple structure recognizes "the purpose of science [which] is to uncover the relatively simple deep structure principles or causes that underlie the apparent complexity observed at the surface structure level" (Le et al., 2010, p. 112) and embodies the scientific principle of parsimony (Harman, 1976).

3. If the measured variables are items or are otherwise meant to be combined into a scale, the alpha reliability (Cronbach, 1951) of each factor should exceed the threshold established for the use of such scales (Pett et al., 2003). For example, reliability coefficients in the .90s are excellent and likely sufficient for clinical decisions (DeVellis, 2017), coefficients in the .80s are good and sufficient for non-critical decisions, coefficients in the .70s are adequate for group experimental research, and coefficients less than .70 are inadequate for most applications (Hunsley & Mash, 2007; Kline, 2013).

4. Measures of model fit, including:

    a. Residuals. The difference between the actual correlation matrix and a correlation matrix reproduced by the model. The average overall residual misfit is quantified by the root mean squared residual (RMSR). The smaller the RMSR value the better, with values ≤ .08 preferred (Brown, 2015). RMSR values will continue to decrease as more factors are extracted, so several models may exhibit RMSR values ≤ .08. The goal is to select the model where RMSR is substantially smaller than a model with one more factor but does not appreciably decrease when another factor is removed.

    Individual residual correlations should also be considered. Ideally, the proportion of non-redundant residual correlations greater than the absolute value of .05 should be small (Basto & Pereira, 2012; Finch, 2020a; Garson, 2013; Johnson & Morgan, 2016; Maydeu-Olivares, 2017), with absolute residuals > .10 more strongly indicating the presence of another factor (Cudeck, 2000; Flora, 2018; Kline, 2013; McDonald,

2010). If the residuals "are not both small and without apparent pattern, additional factors may be present in the data" (Nunnally & Bernstein, 1994, p. 471). As summarized by Flora (2018), "although there is no concrete guideline or cut-off for how small residual correlations should be, I suggest that any residual correlation > .10 is worthy of further consideration with respect to potential model misfit" (p. 255). Maydeu-Olivares (2017) found that RMSRs from samples tended to be higher than RMSRs from populations and suggested that the standard of close fit should be an RMSR value of .05 with no individual residual larger than .10.

b.   Bayesian information criterion (BIC; Schwarz, 1978). An index that balances model simplicity versus goodness of fit. There is no absolute good or bad BIC value: the model with the lowest BIC value is preferred. The BIC was designed to detect the "true" model if it is among the set of candidate models and emphasizes parsimony by including a penalty for model complexity (Burnham & Anderson, 2004). Unfortunately, the BIC tends to overestimate the number of factors as sample size increases (Schmitt et al., 2018), has received little research attention for use with EFA models, and is not computed by SPSS.

c.   Indices of model fit used in CFA, including the comparative fit index (CFI), Tucker–Lewis index (TLI), root mean square error of approximation (RMSEA), etc. Like the BIC, these indices have received little research attention in the EFA context. However, one study found that they were of "questionable utility" for determining the number of factors in EFA (Clark & Bowles, 2018, p. 544), although CFI/TLI values ≥ .95 might protect against underfactoring. Another study found that RMSEA difference values ≥ .015 might be helpful in determining the number of factors to retain (Finch, 2020b). Garrido et al. (2016) found that all fit indices were influenced by properties of the data and model, making them less accurate than parallel analysis. No indices of model fit are provided by SPSS.

5.   Symptoms of model misfit due to overfactoring:

a.   Factors with only one (singlet) or two (doublet) salient loadings. Such factors are relatively weak and unlikely to replicate (Bandalos, 2018; Bandalos & Finney, 2019; Benson & Nasser, 1998; Brown, 2015; Fabrigar & Wegener, 2012; Nunnally & Bernstein, 1994; Preacher & MacCallum, 2003; Velicer & Fava, 1998). Factors with at least three salient loadings are preferred (Comrey & Lee, 1992; Garson, 2013; Johnson & Morgan, 2016; Mulaik, 2010, 2018; Reio & Shuck, 2015; Velicer & Fava, 1998) because "no meaningful component can be identified unless each factor is overdetermined with three or four or more tests" (Thurstone, 1937, p. 75). Singlet and doublet variables will likely exhibit low communality (Fabrigar & Wegener, 2012) and therefore little explanatory power.

b. Factors that are very highly correlated. Interfactor correlations that exceed .80 or .85 might be a sign of overfactoring and pose a threat to discriminant validity (Brown, 2015; Finch, 2020a; McCoach et al., 2013; Schmitt et al., 2018), whereas interfactor correlations > .90 probably mean that "the two factors are clearly not distinct" (Kline, 2013, p. 185).

c. Factors based on similarities in variable distributions rather than similarity of variable content (Bandalos, 2018).

d. Unreasonable parameter estimates called Heywood cases (e.g., communalities > 1.00) or a failure of iterations to converge on a factor extraction solution may indicate a misspecified factor model (Flora, 2018; Lorenzo-Seva & Ferrando, 2020; Pituch & Stevens, 2016; Wothke, 1993).

e. Factor splitting. Measured variables that are known to load on a single factor in the population are split onto multiple factors after rotation (Wood et al., 1996).

6. Symptoms of model misfit due to underfactoring:

a. Measured variables that saliently load on a factor do not seem to reflect a common unifying theme. This may indicate that two or more factors have collapsed onto the same factor (Fabrigar & Wegener, 2012).

b. Poor model fit indices and modest loadings of measured variables on all factors or many complex loadings (Benson & Nasser, 1998; Zhang, 2014).

7. Robustness of results across extraction and rotation methods. As suggested by Gorsuch (1983), "factor the data by several different analytic procedures and hold sacred only those factors that appear across all the procedures used" (p. 330).

Report

Models with three, two, and one factor(s) will be sequentially evaluated for their interpretability and theoretical meaningfulness using several guidelines. Given oblique rotation, pattern coefficients and factor intercorrelations will receive primary attention during the model evaluation process (Bandalos, 2018; Hair et al., 2019). To ensure both practical (10% variance explained) and statistical significance ($p < .05$) of pattern loadings, the threshold for salience will be set at .32 (Norman & Streiner, 2014) with a goal of approximate simple structure (Morin et al., 2020; Thurstone, 1947). The models will be compared on average model misfit (RMSR) and the proportion of residual coefficients that exceed absolute values of .05 and .10 (Flora, 2018; Nunnally & Bernstein, 1994). Close model fit will be indicated by an RMSR value of .05 or smaller and no individual residual coefficient greater than .10 (Maydeu-Olivares, 2017). Additionally, the alpha reliability of scales created from the salient variables of each factor should approach .90, given the intended clinical use of these scales (DeVellis, 2017). Finally, each model will be examined for symptoms of overextraction, such as statistically inadmissible solutions, fewer than three salient loadings, or technical factors, and symptoms of underextraction, such as no common unifying theme or many complex loadings (Bandalos, 2018; Fabrigar & Wegener, 2012).

Model Evaluation

The first model to be evaluated will be illustrated with both menu and command code for users with and without access to syntax commands. Thereafter, only syntax commands will be demonstrated. Given the many objects created by SPSS during the EFA procedure, objects will be presented individually and sequentially rather than in total.

Model 3

Access to EFA via the SPSS menu system begins with *Analyze > Dimension Reduction > Factor*, which opens a **Factor Analysis** window.

After moving the eight measured variables (vocab1–designs2) into the *Variables:* list, each of the buttons to the right will be systematically invoked (Figure 14.1). The *Determinant, KMO and Bartlett's test of sphericity, Reproduced* (residuals), and *Anti-image* coefficients will be requested, along with *Univariate descriptives* and the *Initial solution* from the **Factor Analysis: Descriptives** window. *Maximum likelihood* extraction, the *Unrotated factor solution, Scree plot*, and three factors are requested from the **Factor Analysis: Extraction** window. *Promax* rotation and the *Rotated solution* are requested from the **Factor Analysis: Rotation** window. Given that there is no missing data, the missing value selection is irrelevant in this case. However, the pattern coefficients will be *Sorted by size* for better readability, as specified in the **Factor Analysis: Options** window.

Alternatively, the command code in Figure 14.2 will accomplish the same results.

When executed, these EFA options produce the determinant, KMO and Bartlett's test, scree plot, descriptive statistics, etc. that have been considered in prior decision steps (i.e., Figures 9.1–9.5), so they will not be repeated. The first new object is the *Communalities* table displayed in Figure 14.3. As previously discussed, a variable's communality is the proportion of its variance explained by all the factors. The SPSS display of communalities can be confusing because its "Communalities" table actually displays the value placed in the diagonal (i.e.,

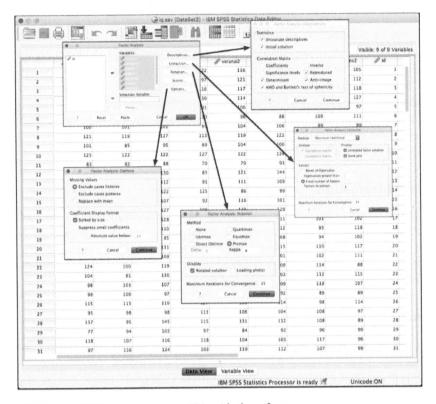

FIGURE 14.1 SPSS menu access to EFA with three factors

```
FACTOR
    /VARIABLES vocab1 designs1 similar1 matrix1 veranal2 vocab2 matrix2 designs2
    /MISSING LISTWISE
    /ANALYSIS vocab1 designs1 similar1 matrix1 veranal2 vocab2 matrix2 designs2
    /PRINT UNIVARIATE INITIAL DET KMO REPR AIC EXTRACTION ROTATION
    /FORMAT SORT
    /PLOT EIGEN
    /CRITERIA FACTORS(3) ITERATE(25)
    /EXTRACTION ML
    /CRITERIA ITERATE(25)
    /ROTATION PROMAX(4).
```

FIGURE 14.2 Syntax command code for EFA with three factors

squared multiple correlation [SMC] of that variable with the other variables) in the "Initial" column. In contrast, the "Extraction" column displays the variance of the measured variables that can be explained by the three retained factors (i.e., their communality). Note that SPSS gave a warning about the communality of the matrix2 variable but restrained its value to .999 and continued. Technically,

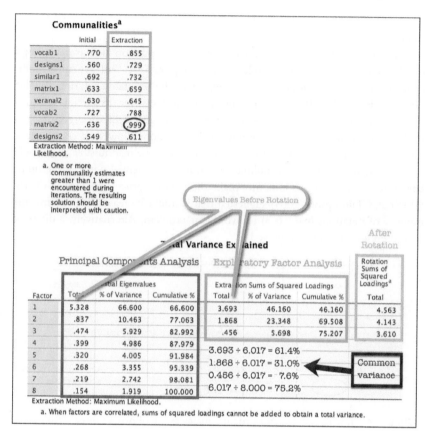

Communalities[a]

	Initial	Extraction
vocab1	.770	.855
designs1	.560	.729
similar1	.692	.732
matrix1	.633	.659
veranal2	.630	.645
vocab2	.727	.788
matrix2	.636	.999
designs2	.549	.611

Extraction Method: Maximum Likelihood.

a. One or more communalitiy estimates greater than 1 were encountered during iterations. The resulting solution should be interpreted with caution.

Eigenvalues Before Rotation

After Rotation

Total Variance Explained

Principal Components Analysis   Exploratory Factor Analysis

							Rotation Sums of Squared Loadings[a]
	Initial Eigenvalues			Extraction Sums of Squared Loadings			
Factor	Total	% of Variance	Cumulative %	Total	% of Variance	Cumulative %	Total
1	5.328	66.600	66.600	3.693	46.160	46.160	4.563
2	.837	10.463	77.063	1.868	23.348	69.508	4.143
3	.474	5.929	82.992	.456	5.698	75.207	3.610
4	.399	4.986	87.979				
5	.320	4.005	91.984				
6	.268	3.355	95.339				
7	.219	2.742	98.081				
8	.154	1.919	100.000				

$3.693 \div 6.017 = 61.4\%$
$1.868 \div 6.017 = 31.0\%$
$0.456 \div 6.017 = 7.6\%$
$6.017 \div 8.000 = 75.2\%$

Common variance

Extraction Method: Maximum Likelihood.

a. When factors are correlated, sums of squared loadings cannot be added to obtain a total variance.

FIGURE 14.3   Communalities and variance explained for EFA with three factors

a communality value > 1.0 is statistically impossible, so this is a fatal problem for this model and these results cannot be trusted (Lorenzo-Seva & Ferrando, 2020; Wothke, 1993).

The *Total Variance Explained* table can also be confusing because it presents both PCA and EFA as well as before and after rotation information in the same table. The first set of values (within the red box in Figure 14.3) are from a PCA that extracted eight unrotated components, whereas the second set of values (within the green box) are the results of the unrotated EFA with three factors. Of course, a PCA that extracted as many factors as there are variables will account for 100% of the variance. However, 75.2% of the total variance was accounted for by three factors before rotation. The proportion of total variance is the sum of the eigenvalues divided by the total number of variables ($6.017 \div 8 = 75.2\%$). The common variance is the proportion of the total variance contributed by each factor. Thus, the first factor accounted for ($3.693 \div 6.017$) 61.4% of the common variance before rotation. Given the oblique solution, the variance after rotation cannot be interpreted.

An oblique solution can produce an unrotated solution (left panel of Figure 14.4) as well as pattern (middle panel of Figure 14.4) and structure coefficients (right panel of Figure 14.4). As expected, the unrotated solution (labeled "Factor Matrix" by SPSS) was not interpretable. However, extraction required only 6 iterations to converge. SPSS defaults to 25 iterations. If convergence is not reached, the analysis can be rerun with more iterations allowed. If convergence cannot be reached in 100 iterations, the solution may be inadmissible and should be reconsidered. However, sampling error is more influential with a large number of iterations and can sometimes make the iterative process go awry. Gorsuch (1988) and Thompson (2004) suggested that it might be reasonable to limit the number of iterations (e.g., 1–3) to avoid that problem. Alternatively, a different rotation method can be employed.

Factor Matrix[a]

	Factor 1	2	3
matrix2	.999	-.009	-.001
matrix1	.718	.296	.237
veranal2	.652	.451	-.127
designs2	.628	.293	.362
designs1	.591	.397	.472
vocab1	.570	.720	-.104
vocab2	.583	.655	-.135
similar1	.588	.621	-.036

Extraction Method: Maximum Likelihood.
a. 3 factors extracted. 6 iterations required.

Pattern Matrix[a]

	Factor 1	2	3
vocab1	.950	.046	-.093
vocab2	.902	-.021	.001
similar1	.768	.130	-.018
veranal2	.652	-.060	.265
designs1	.027	.896	-.089
designs2	.007	.691	.112
matrix1	.128	.492	.270
matrix2	-.012	.035	.982

Extraction Method: Maximum Likelihood.
Rotation Method: Promax with Kaiser Normalization.
a. Rotation converged in 6 iterations.

Structure Matrix

	Factor 1	2	3
vocab1	.922	.668	.562
vocab2	.887	.634	.576
similar1	.851	.675	.579
veranal2	.782	.604	.648
designs1	.619	.851	.574
matrix1	.661	.779	.708
designs2	.582	.777	.615
matrix2	.656	.734	.999

Extraction Method: Maximum Likelihood.
Rotation Method: Promax with Kaiser Normalization.

FIGURE 14.4 Initial, pattern, and structure matrices for EFA with three factors

Reproduced Correlations

		vocab1	designs1	similar1	matrix1	veranal2	vocab2	matrix2	designs2
Reproduced Correlation	vocab1	.855	.573	.786	.598	.710	.819	.564	.531
	designs1	.573	.729	.576	.653	.504	.541	.586	.658
	similar1	.786	.576	.732	.597	.668	.754	.582	.538
	matrix1	.598	.653	.597	.659	.572	.581	.715	.623
	veranal2	.710	.504	.668	.572	.645	.693	.648	.496
	vocab2	.819	.541	.754	.581	.693	.788	.577	.509
	matrix2	.564	.586	.582	.715	.648	.577	.999	.624
	designs2	.531	.658	.538	.623	.496	.509	.624	.611
Residual[b]	vocab1		.003	.003	.020	-.021	.006	.000	-.024
	designs1	.003		-.006	-.003	.004	-.002	.000	.004
	similar1	.003	-.006		.002	.034	-.019	.000	.013
	matrix1	.020	-.003	.002		-.039	-.015	.000	-.004
	veranal2	-.021	.004	.034	-.039		.013	.000	.018
	vocab2	.006	-.002	-.019	-.015	.013		.000	.021
	matrix2	.000	.000	.000	.000	.000	.000		.000
	designs2	-.024	.004	.013	-.004	.018	.021	.000	

Extraction Method: Maximum Likelihood.
a. Reproduced communalities
b. Residuals are computed between observed and reproduced correlations. There are 0 (0.0%) nonredundant residuals with absolute values greater than 0.05.

FIGURE 14.5 Reproduced and residual correlations for EFA with three factors

Pattern Matrix^a

	Factor		
	1	2	3
vocab1	.950	-.017	.111
vocab2	.909	-.033	.008
similar1	.781	.101	.016
veranal2	.695	.056	-.240
designs2	-.036	.817	.018
designs1	.032	.802	.130
matrix1	.050	.773	-.043
matrix2	.084	.659	-.291

Extraction Method: Principal Axis Factoring.
Rotation Method: Oblimin with Kaiser Normalization.

a. Rotation converged in 15 iterations.

FIGURE 14.6   Pattern matrix for principal axis factor extraction for EFA with three factors

The reproduced and residual matrices are presented in Figure 14.5. The diagonal of the reproduced correlation matrix contains the communalities previously observed in Figure 14.3. SPSS automatically reports the number and percent of residuals > .05. In this case, there were none.

Nevertheless, this analysis was rerun with principal axis extraction and the number of iterations restricted to two, as recommended by Gorsuch (1988). In that alternative analysis, all communality estimates were legitimate, and the pattern matrix revealed that the third factor had no salient loadings (Figure 14.6).

It was hypothesized that the three-factor model would exhibit symptoms of overextraction. The output in Figures 14.4–14.6 confirmed that hypothesis. Thus, there is no support for a model with three factors.

Model 2

As with the prior model, access EFA options with the SPSS menu system is via **Analyze > Dimension Reduction > Factor**.

There is no need for scree plot, descriptive statistics, etc. in subsequent analyses, so the output can be simplified and two factors extracted (Figure 14.7).

The same analysis can be obtained from the command code presented in Figure 14.8.

As shown in Figure 14.9, the communalities for this two-factor oblique solution ranged from .598 to .855 with no inadmissible estimates. Communalities ≥ .60 are often considered to be high (Gibson et al., 2020). The first factor accounted for 62.3% of the variance before rotation, and the second factor added

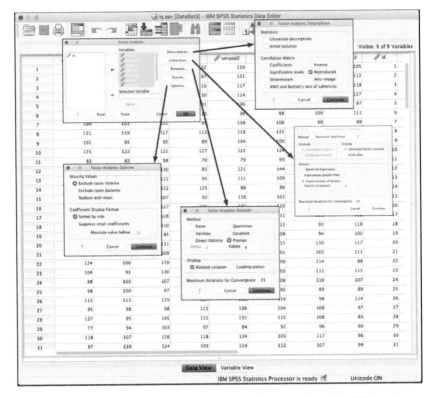

FIGURE 14.7 SPSS menu access to exploratory factor analysis for EFA with two factors

```
FACTOR
  /VARIABLES vocab1 designs1 similar1 matrix1 veranal2 vocab2 matrix2 designs2
  /MISSING LISTWISE
  /ANALYSIS vocab1 designs1 similar1 matrix1 veranal2 vocab2 matrix2 designs2
  /PRINT REPR EXTRACTION ROTATION
  /FORMAT SORT
  /CRITERIA FACTORS(2) ITERATE(25)
  /EXTRACTION ML
  /CRITERIA ITERATE(25)
  /ROTATION PROMAX(4).
```

FIGURE 14.8 Syntax command code to exploratory factor analysis for EFA with two factors

another 7.3%. Thus, two factors accounted for 70% of the variance. Figure 14.3 revealed that the first two components accounted for 77% of the variance, and Figure 14.9 shows that the first two factors accounted for 70% of the variance. Thus, 7% of the variance of these factors could be attributed to uniqueness. Note that PCA extracted 100% of the total variance when eight factors were extracted, whereas the reduced model with two factors accounted for 70% of the total

Communalities

	Extraction
vocab1	.855
designs1	.598
similar1	.731
matrix1	.688
veranal2	.621
vocab2	.787
matrix2	.677
designs2	.611

Extraction Method:
Maximum Likelihood.

Total Variance Explained

Factor	Extraction Sums of Squared Loadings			Rotation Sums of Squared Loadings[a]
	Total	% of Variance	Cumulative %	Total
1	4.985	62.307	62.307	4.530
2	.583	7.285	69.592	4.407

Extraction Method: Maximum Likelihood.

a. When factors are correlated, sums of squared loadings cannot be added to obtain a total variance.

FIGURE 14.9   Communalities and variance explained for EFA with two factors

variance. This is a vivid demonstration of parsimony: two factors explained 70% of the variance of eight measured variables.

The pattern matrix (left panel of Figure 14.10) revealed two clearly defined factors with four variables saliently loading on each factor and no complex loadings. The structure coefficients (middle panel of Figure 14.10) were strong (.58 to .92), and there was no evidence of a suppression effect (Thompson, 2004), namely, a structure coefficient around zero but a high pattern coefficient or vice versa, or pattern and structure coefficients of different signs (Graham et al., 2003). A review of the correlation matrix revealed strong bivariate correlations between the measured variables, making it improbable that this result was simply a mathematical artifact. Finally, the factor correlation matrix (right panel of Figure 14.10) indicated that these two factors were

Pattern Matrix[a]			Structure Matrix			Factor Correlation Matrix		
	Factor			Factor				
	1	2		1	2	Factor	1	2
vocab1	.953	-.038	vocab1	.924	.677	1	1.000	.750
vocab2	.890	-.004	vocab2	.887	.664	2	.750	1.000
similar1	.748	.136	similar1	.850	.697			
veranal2	.614	.215	veranal2	.775	.676			
designs2	-.017	.794	matrix1	.657	.828			
matrix2	.063	.775	matrix2	.644	.822			
matrix1	.083	.766	designs2	.579	.781			
designs1	.093	.701	designs1	.619	.771			

Pattern Matrix: Extraction Method: Maximum Likelihood. Rotation Method: Promax with Kaiser Normalization. a. Rotation converged in 3 iterations.

Structure Matrix: Extraction Method: Maximum Likelihood. Rotation Method: Promax with Kaiser Normalization.

Factor Correlation Matrix: Extraction Method: Maximum Likelihood. Rotation Method: Promax with Kaiser Normalization.

FIGURE 14.10 Pattern, structure, and factor correlation matrices for EFA with two factors

correlated at .75, which does not pose a severe threat to discriminant validity (Brown, 2015).

Although SPSS provides the residual matrix and computes the number of residual coefficients greater than .05 (Figure 14.11), it does not tally the number of residual coefficients greater than .10 nor compute the RMSR. A standalone computer program entitled Residuals can be downloaded from edpsychassociates. com/Watkins3.html, if that information is desired.

The Residuals program requires the residual matrix as input. That can be accomplished by copying the residual matrix from the SPSS output and then pasting it as text into an Excel file. This should create a matrix of size v by v, where v is the number of variables in the factor analysis. That Excel file can then be saved as a text file for input to the Residuals program. As shown in Figure 14.12, the RMSR value was .028, and there were no residuals >.10.

Model 2 converged properly, produced reasonable parameter estimates, and exhibited four salient loadings at good to excellent levels (Comrey & Lee, 1992) on each factor in a simple structure configuration. Communalities were high (.60 to .85; Gibson et al., 2020; Watson, 2017), RMSR was small (.028), and only two off-diagonal residual coefficients exceeded the absolute value of .05 (none exceeded .10). This meets the standard of close fit defined by Maydeu–Olivares (2017). The interfactor correlation of .75 was somewhat elevated, but that might be due to a strong general factor that permeates all the variables (Gorsuch, 1983).

An interesting graph can be produced by SPSS with the addition of one line of command code (/PLOT ROTATION) or by selecting the *Loading plot(s)* option in the **Factor Analysis: Rotation** window (Figure 14.13).

SPSS can compute the alpha reliability of each set of variables identified in the EFA. Menu access is via *Analyze > Scale > Reliability Analysis* and selecting the

Reproduced Correlations

		vocab1	designs1	similar1	matrix1	veranal2	vocab2	matrix2	designs2
Reproduced Correlation	vocab1	.855ᵃ	.560	.783	.595	.713	.820	.582	.522
	designs1	.560	.598ᵃ	.568	.641	.546	.548	.636	.602
	similar1	.783	.568	.731ᵃ	.604	.672	.754	.593	.539
	matrix1	.595	.641	.604	.688ᵃ	.581	.582	.682	.646
	veranal2	.713	.546	.672	.581	.621ᵃ	.687	.572	.523
	vocab2	.820	.548	.754	.582	.687	.787ᵃ	.570	.512
	matrix2	.582	.636	.593	.682	.572	.570	.677ᵃ	.642
	designs2	.522	.602	.539	.646	.523	.512	.642	.611ᵃ
Residualᵇ	vocab1		.016	.005	.023	-.024	.004	-.018	-.014
	designs1	.016		.002	.008	-.037	-.009	-.050	.060
	similar1	.005	.002		-.006	.030	-.019	-.012	.011
	matrix1	.023	.008	-.006		-.049	-.016	.032	-.027
	veranal2	-.024	-.037	.030	-.049		.019	.076	-.010
	vocab2	.004	-.009	-.019	-.016	.019		.007	.018
	matrix2	-.018	-.050	-.012	.032	(.076)	.007		-.017
	designs2	-.014	(.060)	.011	-.027	-.010	.018	-.017	

Extraction Method: Maximum Likelihood.

a. Reproduced communalities

b. Residuals are computed between observed and reproduced correlations. There are 2 (7.0%) nonredundant residuals with absolute values greater than 0.05.

FIGURE 14.11   Reproduced and residual coefficients for EFA with two factors

FIGURE 14.12   Residual matrix analysis with the Residuals program

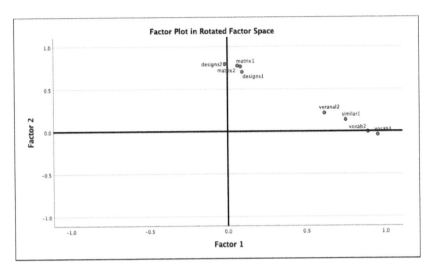

FIGURE 14.13 Factor plot for EFA with two factors

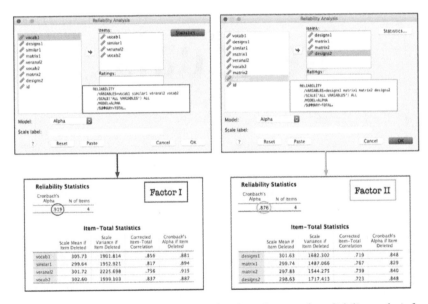

FIGURE 14.14 Menu and syntax command code and output for reliability analysis for two factors

Scale if item deleted option from the *Statistics* button. As revealed in Figure 14.14, coefficient alpha values of .919 and .876 were computed for these two factors.

Although somewhat convoluted, it is possible to compute confidence intervals for coefficient alpha estimates in SPSS (Figure 14.15). Based on these estimates,

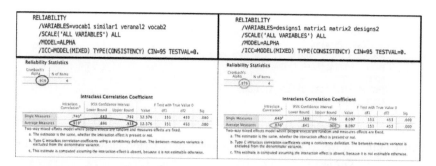

FIGURE 14.15   Menu and syntax command code and output for confidence intervals
of reliability coefficients

internal consistency reliability of the first factor was .92 with 95% CI [.90, .94],
and the reliability of the second factor was .88 with 95% CI [.84, .91]. Reliability
coefficients of this magnitude are generally considered to be strong and useful for
clinical decisions (DeVellis, 2017).

The two-factor model was robust to different extraction and rotation methods, as very similar results were obtained when iterated principal axis extraction
and direct oblimin rotation were employed. Additionally, the measured variables
were distributed across the two factors as predicted by prior theory (verbal versus
nonverbal measures), and the structure was interpretable and theoretically meaningful. In sum, the two-factor model appears to be a good EFA solution and
offers the optimum balance between comprehensiveness (accounting for the most
variance) and parsimony (with the fewest factors).

Model 1

Although the two-factor model appeared to be satisfactory, a one-factor model
was also evaluated to ensure that it did not exhibit superior fit characteristics.

The command code in Figure 14.16 was used to analyze this one-factor model.

Model 1 converged properly, produced reasonable parameter estimates, and
exhibited eight salient loadings on its single factor. However, communalities were
weaker in comparison to Model 2 (means of .61 and .70 for Models 1 and 2,
respectively), as displayed in Figure 14.17.

Further, the RMSR value was .077, 57% of the residual coefficients exceeded
.05, and 18% of the residuals exceeded .10 (Figure 14.18). These residual values
suggest that another factor might be extracted. Most critically, the single factor
does not seem to reflect a common unifying theme because it encompasses both
verbal and nonverbal reasoning variables. This is evidence that two factors have
collapsed onto one (Fabrigar & Wegener, 2012). Thus, measures of model fit and
theoretical convergence remove this model from consideration, leaving Model 2
as the preferred solution.

110   Step 9

```
FACTOR
    /VARIABLES vocab1 designs1 similar1 matrix1 veranal2 vocab2 matrix2 designs2
    /MISSING LISTWISE
    /ANALYSIS vocab1 designs1 similar1 matrix1 veranal2 vocab2 matrix2 designs2
    /PRINT INITIAL REPR EXTRACTION
    /FORMAT SORT
    /CRITERIA FACTORS(1) ITERATE(25)
    /EXTRACTION ML
    /ROTATION NOROTATE.
```

FIGURE 14.16   Syntax command code to exploratory factor analysis for EFA with one factor

Communalities

	Initial	Extraction
vocab1	.770	.765
designs1	.560	.494
similar1	.692	.728
matrix1	.633	.553
veranal2	.630	.636
vocab2	.727	.731
matrix2	.636	.548
designs2	.549	.462

Extraction Method: Maximum Likelihood.

Factor Matrix[a]

	Factor 1
vocab1	.875
vocab2	.855
similar1	.853
veranal2	.797
matrix1	.744
matrix2	.740
designs1	.703
designs2	.680

Extraction Method: Maximum Likelihood.

Total Variance Explained

Factor	Initial Eigenvalues			Extraction Sums of Squared Loadings		
	Total	% of Variance	Cumulative %	Total	% of Variance	Cumulative %
1	5.328	66.600	66.600	4.917	61.467	61.467
2	.837	10.463	77.063			
3	.474	5.929	82.992			
4	.399	4.986	87.979			
5	.320	4.005	91.984			
6	.268	3.355	95.339			
7	.219	2.742	98.081			
8	.154	1.919	100.000			

Extraction Method: Maximum Likelihood.

FIGURE 14.17   Communalities, variance explained, and pattern/structure matrix for EFA with one factor

Although these models were derived from raw data, similar results (depending on the precision of the correlation matrix) can be obtained with correlation input via syntax command code. For this normally distributed data, Pearson correlations were chosen, but Kendall's *tau* and Spearman's *rho* matrices can also be obtained from SPSS. Unfortunately, using a correlation matrix as input for EFA in SPSS can only be accomplished with command code syntax and is not possible

Reproduced Correlations		vocab1	designs1	similar1	matrix1	veranal2	vocab2	matrix2	designs2
Reproduced Correlation	vocab1	.765ᵃ	.615	.747	.651	.697	.748	.648	.595
	designs1	.615	.494ᵃ	.600	.523	.561	.601	.520	.478
	similar1	.747	.600	.728ᵃ	.635	.680	.729	.632	.580
	matrix1	.651	.523	.635	.553ᵃ	.593	.636	.550	.506
	veranal2	.697	.561	.680	.593	.636ᵃ	.681	.590	.542
	vocab2	.748	.601	.729	.636	.681	.731ᵃ	.633	.581
	matrix2	.648	.520	.632	.550	.590	.633	.548ᵃ	.503
	designs2	.595	.478	.580	.506	.542	.581	.503	.462ᵃ
Residualᵇ	vocab1		−.039	.042	−.033	−.008	.076	−.084	−.087
	designs1	−.039		−.030	.127	−.052	−.062	.066	.184
	similar1	.042	−.030		−.036	.021	.006	−.050	−.030
	matrix1	−.033	.127	−.036		−.060	−.070	.164	.113
	veranal2	−.008	−.052	.021	−.060		.024	.058	−.028
	vocab2	.076	−.062	.006	−.070	.024		−.055	−.051
	matrix2	−.084	.066	−.050	.164	.058	−.055		.121
	designs2	−.087	.184	−.030	.113	−.028	−.051	.121	

Extraction Method: Maximum Likelihood.

a. Reproduced communalities

b. Residuals are computed between observed and reproduced correlations. There are 16 (57.0%) nonredundant residuals with absolute values greater than 0.05.

FIGURE 14.18 Reproduced and residual correlations for EFA with one factor

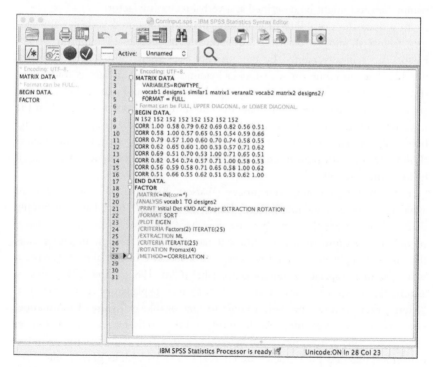

FIGURE 14.19 Syntax command code for EFA with two factors using correlation matrix as input

via the menu system. Figure 14.19 displays the **Syntax** window with a command code for reproducing the two-factor model using a correlation matrix as input.

Factor Names

For convenience, researchers typically name the factors identified through EFA. Names can be given to factors to facilitate the communication of results and advance cumulative knowledge. Rummel (1967) suggested that factors can be named symbolically, descriptively, or causally. Symbolic names are without any substantive meaning, for example, F1 and F2 or A, B, and C. These names merely denote the factors without adding any meaning. Descriptive names are clues to factor content that can categorize the factor in terms of its apparent contents. For example, measures of word meaning, synonyms, and paragraph comprehension might be described as verbal. Causal names involve reasoning from the salient loadings to the underlying influences that caused them. Given that a factor is a construct operationalized by its factor loadings, the researcher tries to understand the underlying dimension that unifies the variables that define the factor. "Thus, the naming of a factor is based on its conceptual underpinnings" (Reio & Shuck, 2015, p. 20). For example, measures of word meaning, synonyms, and paragraph comprehension might be described as a verbal reasoning factor.

To reduce the possibility of confusion between measured variables and factors, factors should *not* be named after measured variables (Thompson, 2004). Factors are typically named by considering what their most salient measured variables have in common with higher loadings receiving greater consideration (Kahn, 2006; Thompson, 2004). Although both pattern and structure coefficients are considered, structure coefficients may be more useful for naming when the interfactor correlations are modest because they reflect the simple relationship between a variable and a factor without the confounding effect of other factors (Kahn, 2006). With high interfactor correlations, the pattern coefficients might become more useful.

Factor naming is a subjective process (Watson, 2017), and the researcher must avoid the construct identity fallacy (Larsen & Bong, 2016). That is, assuming that two factors are the same because they have the same name (jingle fallacy) or different because they have different names (jangle fallacy). In either case, the unwary might be tempted to accept an inaccurate factor label. Likewise, it would be inappropriate to reify a factor label (Cliff, 1983; Kline, 2013), that is, assume that it is a real, physical thing rather than an explanatory latent construct. "Merely because it is convenient to refer to a factor (like g), by use of a noun does not make it a physical thing. At the most, factors should be regarded as sources of variance, dimensions, intervening variables, or latent traits that are useful in explaining manifest phenomena, much as abstractions such as gravity, mass, distance, and force are useful in describing physical events" (Carroll, 1995b, p. 126). There is ample evidence that jingle-jangle fallacies are widespread in practice and have resulted in construct proliferation and empirically redundant measures (Le et al., 2010; Shaffer et al., 2016).

Report

Three plausible models were evaluated. It was hypothesized that the three-factor model would exhibit symptoms of overextraction. This hypothesis was confirmed by a factor with no salient loadings and an inadmissible communality estimate. In contrast, the one-factor model exhibited symptoms of underextraction: failure to reflect a common unifying theme (Fabrigar & Wegener, 2012) and many large residuals, strongly indicating the presence of another factor (Cudeck, 2000). Model 2 converged properly, produced reasonable parameter estimates, and exhibited four salient loadings on each factor in a simple structure configuration. Communalities were robust (.60 to .86), and only two off-diagonal residual coefficients exceeded the absolute value of .05. When the variables that saliently loaded each factor were combined to create a scale, their internal consistency reliability was .92 and .88.

The four measured variables that saliently loaded on the first factor contained verbal content and seemed to require reasoning with that content: defining words, describing how words are similar, and explaining verbal analogies. The four measured variables that saliently loaded on the second factor contained nonverbal content that involved analysis for patterns, inductive discovery of relationships, and deductive identification of missing components. Thus, the first factor might be called verbal reasoning and the second nonverbal reasoning. Performance on the verbal measures is obviously affected by experience, learning, and acculturation, whereas performance on the nonverbal measures is less affected by prior learning and experience. These attributes can be found in the taxonomy of cognitive abilities elucidated by Carroll (1993) and are probably better labeled crystalized and fluid ability, respectively, to reduce construct redundancy (Le et al., 2010; Shaffer et al., 2016). The high interfactor correlation of .75 is also consistent with Carroll's (1993) model of a general ability that accounts for the correlation between cognitive factors (Carretta & Ree, 2001; Gorsuch, 1983).

15

STEP 10

Report Exploratory Factor Analysis Results

As previously documented, many published exploratory factor analysis (EFA) studies employ inappropriate methods and are deficient in detail (Conway & Huffcutt, 2003; Fabrigar et al., 1999; Ford et al., 1986; Gaskin & Happell, 2014; Henson & Roberts, 2006; Howard, 2016; Izquierdo et al., 2014; Lloret et al., 2017; McCroskey & Young, 1979; Norris & Lecavalier, 2010; Park et al., 2002; Roberson et al., 2014; Russell, 2002; Sakaluk & Short, 2017). EFA reports should provide a clear presentation of the decisions made and a comprehensive presentation of the results. In other words, the EFA process must be made transparent (Flake & Fried, 2020). Enough detail must be provided to allow "informed review, replication, and cumulation of knowledge" (Ford et al., 1986, p. 307) yet remain succinct enough for journal presentation. Ideally, "the description of the methods used in the analysis should be sufficiently clear that a reader could replicate the study exactly" (Finch, 2020a, p. 94). To that end, report the name and version of the software used to conduct the EFA. There may be differences in results due to software or version, and this will allow readers to understand how your results were achieved (Grieder & Steiner, 2020). The Report paragraphs in prior sections are preliminary models of how each decision step could be reported.

The EFA report should echo the previously enumerated decision steps. Following is an outline for the EFA report:

1. Describe the measured variables and justify their inclusion.
2. Describe the participants and justify their adequacy in terms of number and representativeness.
3. Present descriptive statistics. Ensure that linearity, outliers, and normality are addressed. Report the extent of missing data and how it was addressed.

Report the correlation matrix if journal space allows. If not, present it in a supplemental table.

4. Verify that data are appropriate for EFA with Bartlett's test of sphericity, KMO sampling adequacy, and magnitude of coefficients in the correlation matrix.
5. Justify the model: principal components or common factor analysis.
6. Detail the method of factor extraction and justify its use with the data. Report the method of estimating communalities if applicable. Report and justify the type of correlation matrix employed (Pearson, Spearman, polychoric, etc.).
7. Describe a priori criteria for determination of how many factors to retain for interpretation. Ensure that multiple criteria are applied within a model testing approach. Report the results of each criterion.
8. Identify the rotation method (orthogonal or oblique) and type (varimax, promax, oblimin, etc.). Justify those selections.
9. Interpret each model using a priori guidelines for acceptability (including salience of loadings, scale reliability, model fit standards, symptoms of over- and underextraction). For the final model, present all pattern coefficients (do not omit non-salient values), communalities, and factor intercorrelations. Also, present structure coefficients if journal space allows. If not, present them in a supplemental table.

Factor Scores

It is possible to weight variable scores according to their relationship to each factor and thereby create factor score estimates for each participant that can subsequently be included in other investigations. Conceptually, a factor score is an estimate of the latent variable that underlies the measured variables. Unfortunately, "an infinite number of ways for scoring the individuals on the factors could be derived that would be consistent with the same factor loadings" (Grice, 2001, p. 431). Consequently, numerous ways to compute factor scores have been developed over the years, but none have been found to be superior in all circumstances (Finch, 2013; Gorsuch, 1983; Revelle, 2016). Some methodologists prefer complex computations involving multiple regression and maximum likelihood estimation (Comrey & Lee, 1992; Hair et al., 2019). Others believe that simple unit weights (e.g., adding the scores from variables that saliently load) may be superior (Carretta & Ree, 2001; Gorsuch, 2003; Kline, 1994; Russell, 2002; Wainer, 1976). Given the current state of knowledge about factor score indeterminacy (Rigdon et al., 2019), it is best to be cautious about the use of factor scores (Osborne & Banjanovic, 2016).

SPSS offers only three ways to compute factor scores via *Analyze > Dimension Reduction > Factor* menu choices followed by selection of the *Scores* button from the **Factor Analysis** window (Figure 15.1).

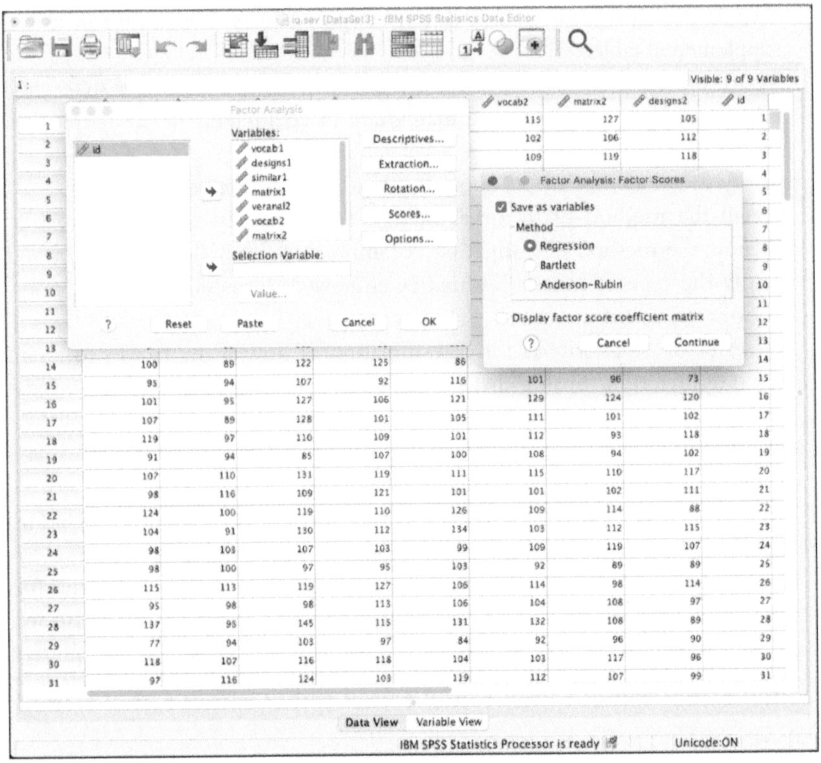

FIGURE 15.1 SPSS menu options to compute factor scores

If factor scores are estimated, Nunnally and Bernstein (1994) suggested that they should exhibit strong multiple correlations with the variables that comprise each factor and should not correlate with other factor scores beyond the underlying factor intercorrelations. Mulaik (2018) recommended that factor scores be avoided unless the R^2 for predicting the common factors exceeds .95. Gorsuch (1983) recommended that the factor score correlations with factors should, at a minimum, exceed .80. An extended discussion of the benefits and liabilities of factor scores was provided by DiStefano et al. (2009).

Cautions

Factor analysis only provides models of the world. By definition, models cannot capture the complexities of the real world. "At best, they can provide an approximation of the real world that has some substantive meaning and some utility" (MacCallum, 2003, p. 115). Therefore, the researcher should not fall prey to the nominalistic fallacy or the construct identity fallacy, nor should they reify factors (Cliff, 1983; Kline, 2013; Larsen & Bong, 2016), that is, believe that naming a factor means that the factor is a real physical entity, well understood, or even correctly named. As cogently argued by Feynman (1974), the first duty of a scientist is "that you must not fool yourself—and you are the easiest person to fool" (p. 12).

A basic premise of the philosophy of science is that data do not confirm a model, they can only fail to disconfirm it (Popper, 2002). Thus, "factor analysis is not an end in itself but a prelude to programmatic research on a particular psychological construct" (Briggs & Cheek, 1986, p. 137). Factor analysis addresses only one type of construct validity evidence: the internal structural aspect that "appraises the fidelity of the scoring structure to the structure of the construct domain (Messick, 1995, p. 745). "Strong factorial evidence is necessary, but not sufficient, for establishing evidence of validity" (McCoach et al., 2013, p. 111).

The value of factors must be judged by their replicability across samples and methods and by the meaningfulness of their relationships with external criteria (Comrey & Lee, 1992; Goldberg & Velicer, 2006; Gorsuch, 1983; Mulaik, 2018; Nunnally & Bernstein, 1994; Preacher et al., 2013). Replication is critical because results that cannot be reproduced cannot contribute to the cumulative growth of knowledge necessary for scientific progress (Open Science Collaboration, 2015). Of course, replication with independent samples would be ideal but is not always possible. If the sample is sufficiently large, it can be randomly split into two samples, and EFA results can be compared across those replication samples (Osborne & Fitzpatrick, 2012). A variety of cross-validation techniques that might be implemented with a single sample were presented by Koul et al. (2018). Absent replication, the researcher should employ alternative extraction and rotation methods to ensure the EFA results are at least robust across those methods (Gorsuch, 1983).

It is essential that a construct validation program be implemented to delineate the external ramifications of replicated structural validity studies (Comrey & Lee, 1992; Goodwin, 1999; Gorsuch, 1983; Lubinski & Dawis, 1992; Rencher & Christensen, 2012). See Benson (1998) and Simms and Watson (2007) for tutorials on construct validation programs and Messick (1995) for a discussion of construct validity.

16

EXPLORATORY FACTOR ANALYSIS WITH CATEGORICAL VARIABLES

The measured variables in the original application of exploratory factor analysis (EFA) by Spearman (1904) were scores on school tests of math, spelling, etc. Thus, each variable was the sum of multiple math or spelling items called a scale, and EFA was developed for the analysis of such scales (Gorsuch, 1997). Scales are more reliable than items because they rely on the aggregation principle whereby common variance accumulates, whereas measurement error, being random, does not (Lubinski & Dawis, 1992). Additionally, response options for items often take the form of a set of ordered categories rather than a continuous range of values. For ability and achievement items, responses may allow only two categories: correct or incorrect. For attitude items, 3- to 7-category Likert-type responses (*strongly agree* to *strongly disagree*) are often used, with five alternatives being the most common (Likert, 1932). These ordered categorical responses constitute ordinal variables (Stevens, 1946). The psychometric characteristics of items (compared to scales) require careful consideration when conducting an EFA (Gorsuch, 1997; Nunnally & Bernstein, 1994; Reise et al., 2000; Widaman, 2012).

Data

The sdq.xlsx file can be imported via the *File > Import Data > Excel* menu options.

The *Variable View* of the imported sdq dataset reveals that SPSS categorized these 30 variables as nominal when, in fact, they were measured at the ordinal level (Figure 16.1). Clicking on that column header will allow the measurement level to be changed for each variable. For efficiency, copy and paste can be used to change this characteristic for multiple variables. Notice that there are no missing data indicators, which implies but does not guarantee that there is no missing data

	Name	Type	Width	Decimals	Label	Values	Missing	Columns	Align	Measure	Role
1	sdq1	Numeric	1	0		None	None	11	Right	Nominal	Input
2	sdq2	Numeric	1	0		None	None	11	Right	Nominal	Input
3	sdq3	Numeric	1	0		None	None	11	Right	Nominal	Input
4	sdq4r	Numeric	1	0		None	None	11	Right	Nominal	Input
5	sdq5r	Numeric	1	0		None	None	11	Right	Nominal	Input
6	sdq6	Numeric	1	0		None	None	11	Right	Nominal	Input
7	sdq7	Numeric	1	0		None	None	11	Right	Nominal	Input
8	sdq8	Numeric	1	0		None	None	11	Right	Nominal	Input
9	sdq9r	Numeric	1	0		None	None	11	Right	Nominal	Input
10	sdq10r	Numeric	1	0		None	None	11	Right	Nominal	Input
11	sdq11r	Numeric	1	0		None	None	11	Right	Nominal	Input
12	sdq12	Numeric	1	0		None	None	11	Right	Nominal	Input
13	sdq13	Numeric	1	0		None	None	11	Right	Nominal	Input
14	sdq14	Numeric	1	0		None	None	11	Right	Nominal	Input
15	sdq15r	Numeric	1	0		None	None	11	Right	Nominal	Input
16	sdq16r	Numeric	1	0		None	None	11	Right	Nominal	Input
17	sdq17r	Numeric	1	0		None	None	11	Right	Nominal	Input
18	sdq18	Numeric	1	0		None	None	11	Right	Nominal	Input
19	sdq19	Numeric	1	0		None	None	11	Right	Nominal	Input
20	sdq20	Numeric	1	0		None	None	11	Right	Nominal	Input
21	sdq21r	Numeric	1	0		None	None	11	Right	Nominal	Input
22	sdq22r	Numeric	1	0		None	None	11	Right	Nominal	Input
23	sdq23r	Numeric	1	0		None	None	11	Right	Nominal	Input
24	sdq24	Numeric	1	0		None	None	11	Right	Nominal	Input
25	sdq25	Numeric	1	0		None	None	11	Right	Nominal	Input
26	sdq26	Numeric	1	0		None	None	11	Right	Nominal	Input
27	sdq27r	Numeric	1	0		None	None	11	Right	Nominal	Input
28	sdq28r	Numeric	1	0		None	None	11	Right	Nominal	Input
29	sdq29r	Numeric	1	0		None	None	11	Right	Nominal	Input
30	sdq30	Numeric	1	0		None	None	11	Right	Nominal	Input

Data View   Variable View

IBM SPSS Statistics Processor is ready   Unicode:ON

FIGURE 16.1   Variable View of sdq data

in this dataset. The **Data View** option will display the scores of 425 participants on 30 measured variables. For future convenience, this data might be saved in SPSS format via **File > Save As > sdq**. SPSS automatically recognizes that is a data file and applies the .sav suffix.

Participants

Participants were 425 elementary school children. The communality of the variables under study is unknown, but prior international research and the ordinal nature of the response scale indicate that it would be reasonable to estimate communality to be in the low range (Mucherah & Finch, 2010). With 30 items and three anticipated factors, the number of items per factor is 10. Rouquette and Falissard (2011) simulated typical attitudinal scale data and reported that scales with that item to factor ratio required a sample of 350 to 400 participants. The ratio of participants to measured variables is 14 to 1, exceeding the recommendations of several measurement specialists (Child, 2006; Gorsuch, 1983). Given these considerations, the current sample size of 425 participants was judged to be adequate.

Data Screening

Pearson correlations assume normality, which requires continuous scores. Thus, categorical scores are not, by definition, normally distributed (Bandalos, 2018; Hancock & Liu, 2012; Puth et al., 2015; Walsh, 1996). In addition, categorization of continuous scores causes imprecise estimation of Pearson correlations. For example, Bollen and Barb (1981) used simulated data and demonstrated the effect of categorizing two continuous scores with a correlation of .90. As illustrated in Figure 16.2, the reduction in precision is relatively modest for seven categories, falling from .90 to .85. However, the fewer the categories, the more imprecise the correlation estimates. With only two categories, the estimated correlation dropped to .72, a reduction of 20%. Additionally, the Pearsonian correlation for dichotomous items (phi) is strongly influenced by differences in item endorsement frequencies. Rummel (1970) suggested deleting dichotomous variables with > 90 to 10 splits between categories because the correlation coefficients between these variables and others are truncated and because the scores for the cases in the small category are more influential than those in the category with numerous cases. Of course, imprecise correlation estimates impact EFA results.

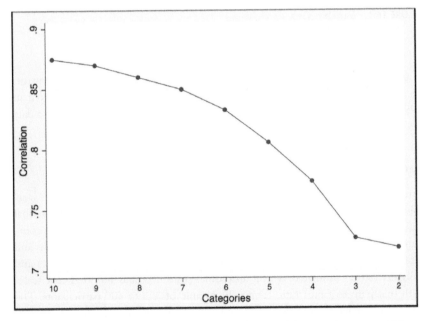

FIGURE 16.2   Effect on correlation coefficient of categorizing continuous variables

Given that EFA is conducted on a correlation matrix, it is important to utilize the optimal type of correlation for ordinal data. Bollen and Barb (1981) suggested "that under certain conditions it may be justifiable to use Pearson correlations and analyze categorical data as if it were continuous" (p. 232). Lozano et al. (2008) conducted a statistical simulation study and found that four response categories were minimal and seven were optimal to ensure adequate factorial validity. Other methodologists have suggested the use of Pearson correlations when there are at least five ordered categories (DiStefano, 2002; Mueller & Hancock, 2019).

However, nonnormality, especially kurtosis, can bias Pearson correlation estimates and thereby bias EFA results (Cain et al., 2017; DeCarlo, 1997; Greer et al., 2006). The extent to which variables can be nonnormal and not substantially affect EFA results has been addressed by several researchers. Curran et al. (1996) opined that univariate skew should not exceed 2.0, and univariate kurtosis should not exceed 7.0. Other measurement specialists have agreed with those guidelines (Bandalos, 2018; Fabrigar et al., 1999; Wegener & Fabrigar, 2000). In terms of multinormality, statistically significant multivariate kurtosis values > 3.0 to 5.0 might bias factor analysis results (Bentler, 2005; Finney & DiStefano, 2013; Mueller & Hancock, 2019). Thus, Pearson correlations might not be appropriate for ordinal data with five to seven categories if the variables are severely nonnormal.

In fact, some methodologists recommend that "it is often not appropriate to pretend that categorical variables are continuous" (Flora et al., 2012, p. 12) and have studied the characteristics of alternative types of correlation coefficients for factor analysis of ordinal data. These alternatives include the nonparametric correlations of Kendall and Spearman (Revelle, 2016) as well as polychoric and tetrachoric correlations (Basto & Pereira, 2012; Choi et al., 2010; McCoach et al., 2013).

Polychoric correlations assume that a normally distributed continuous, but unobservable, latent variable underlies the observed ordinal variable and are a maximum likelihood estimate of the Pearson correlations for those underlying normally distributed continuous variables (Basto & Pereira, 2012). A tetrachoric correlation is a special case of the polychoric correlation applicable when the observed variables are dichotomous (Panter et al., 1997). Although some researchers prefer Spearman correlations for kurtotic distributions or when outliers are present (de Winter et al., 2016), factor analysis results based on polychoric correlations have better reproduced the measurement model than Pearsonian correlations (Barendse et al., 2015; Carroll, 1961; Choi et al., 2010; Flora et al., 2012; Flora & Flake, 2017; Holgado-Tello et al., 2010; Lloret et al., 2017; van der Eijk & Rose, 2015; Zhang & Browne, 2006). In fact, Flora and Curran (2004) found that polychoric correlations tended to be robust to violations of univariate nonnormality until nonnormality became extremely severe (skew = 5.0, kurtosis = 50.0). However, polychoric correlations are estimates of the latent correlation between assumed continuous variables, and that estimation process can sometimes go amiss, producing imprecise estimates or a statistically inadmissible matrix (Lorenzo-Seva & Ferrando, 2020). If there are few or no responses to more than 20% of the items on a factor, it may be beneficial to recode the data into fewer categories for estimation of the polychoric matrix (DiStefano et al., 2020). Further, polychoric correlations would not be appropriate if the assumption of an underlying normally distributed latent variable is not tenable.

Given the ordinal nature of the sdq data, it was anticipated that nonnormality would be readily apparent. Screening of the sdq data begins with a review of the univariate descriptive statistics via the menu options *Analyze > Descriptive Statistics > Descriptives* and then selecting the *Mean, Std. deviation, Minimum, Maximum, Kurtosis,* and *Skewness* options from the **Descriptives: Options** window.

Figure 16.3 displays the resulting descriptive statistics as well as the command code for producing those statistics. The minimum and maximum values of all

```
DESCRIPTIVES VARIABLES=sdq1 sdq2 sdq3 sdq4r sdq5r sdq6 sdq7 sdq8 sdq9r sdq10r sdq11r sdq12 sdq13
    sdq14 sdq15r sdq16r sdq17r sdq18 sdq19 sdq20 sdq21r sdq22r sdq23r sdq24 sdq25 sdq26 sdq27r sdq28r
    sdq29r sdq30
/STATISTICS=MEAN STDDEV MIN MAX KURTOSIS SKEWNESS.
```

Descriptive Statistics

	N	Minimum	Maximum	Mean	Std. Deviation	Skewness		Kurtosis	
	Statistic	Statistic	Statistic	Statistic	Statistic	Statistic	Std. Error	Statistic	Std. Error
sdq1	425	1	6	4.17	1.796	-.570	.118	-1.046	.236
sdq2	425	1	6	4.83	1.371	-1.213	.118	.745	.236
sdq3	425	1	6	4.82	1.422	-.968	.118	-.171	.236
sdq4r	425	1	6	3.82	1.920	-.247	.118	-1.489	.236
sdq5r	425	1	6	5.32	1.270	-1.959	.118	2.923	.236
sdq6	425	1	6	4.00	1.815	-.450	.118	-1.167	.236
sdq7	425	1	6	4.05	1.799	-.484	.118	-1.132	.236
sdq8	425	1	6	4.77	1.383	-1.219	.118	.837	.236
sdq9r	425	1	6	4.86	1.578	-1.277	.118	.408	.236
sdq10r	425	1	6	4.79	1.581	-1.167	.118	.152	.236
sdq11r	425	1	6	5.02	1.294	-1.396	.118	1.312	.236
sdq12	425	1	6	4.44	1.485	-.840	.118	-.202	.236
sdq13	425	1	6	3.85	1.866	-.312	.118	-1.347	.236
sdq14	425	1	6	4.77	1.382	-1.284	.118	1.032	.236
sdq15r	425	1	6	5.14	1.457	-1.667	.118	1.529	.236
sdq16r	425	1	6	4.30	1.795	-.674	.118	-.954	.236
sdq17r	425	1	6	4.96	1.594	-1.451	.118	.797	.236
sdq18	425	1	6	4.19	1.788	-.577	.118	-1.033	.236
sdq19	425	1	6	4.24	1.694	-.627	.118	-.868	.236
sdq20	425	1	6	4.81	1.452	-1.272	.118	.764	.236
sdq21r	425	1	6	5.04	1.532	-1.530	.118	1.104	.236
sdq22r	425	1	6	4.87	1.663	-1.344	.118	.433	.236
sdq23r	425	1	6	5.13	1.467	-1.675	.118	1.637	.236
sdq24	425	1	6	4.46	1.549	-.880	.118	-.217	.236
sdq25	425	1	6	3.97	1.777	-.469	.118	-1.147	.236
sdq26	425	1	6	5.52	1.012	⟨-2.779⟩	.118	⟨8.305⟩	.236
sdq27r	425	1	6	3.82	1.882	-.176	.118	-1.492	.236
sdq28r	425	1	6	4.68	1.758	-1.036	.118	-.393	.236
sdq29r	425	1	6	5.58	.961	⟨-2.604⟩	.118	6.391	.236
sdq30	425	1	6	4.71	1.455	-1.117	.118	.393	.236
Valid N (listwise)	425								

FIGURE 16.3 Descriptive statistics command code and output for sdq data

items range from one to six, indicating no illegal or out-of-bounds values. There is no missing data (as the *n* for each item is 425), and there was no item with zero variance. The mean and median values are high (many in the five to six range for a scale with a maximum score of six). Univariate skew reflects that distributional tilt. Two variables exhibited high skew (-2.78 and -2.60) and one variable high kurtosis (8.31). Although these values suggest univariate nonnormality, only one variable exceeded the guidelines established by Curran et al. (1996).

SPSS does not include a test of multivariate normality. However, an online calculator at https://webpower.psychstat.org/models/kurtosis/ can accept an SPSS data file or an Excel file as input. This calculator does not provide a reference, but it seems to be using an implementation of Mardia's multivariate tests (1970). As expected from the univariate distributions, the data are not multivariate normal, as indicated by multivariate kurtosis of $1,208.1$ ($p < .001$).

Given the violation of multivariate normality, a polychoric correlation matrix might be more appropriate input for this data than a Pearson correlation matrix. Unfortunately, SPSS does not provide that option. A polychoric correlation matrix might be computed by another statistical program (e.g., SAS, **R**, Stata) and then used as input to an EFA in SPSS, as illustrated in Figure 14.19. Alternatively, SPSS command code has been authored by Lorenzo-Seva and Ferrando (2015) that will compute polychoric correlations. In both cases, typing a 30 x 30 matrix into the Syntax window will be a laborious and error-prone process. Accordingly, a Pearson correlation matrix will be employed because the data have six ordered categories, which should make them continuous-enough (DiStefano, 2002; Lozano et al., 2008; Mueller & Hancock, 2019).

Figure 16.3 demonstrated that none of the data values were illegal or out of bounds, so they will be retained. Given that these are ordinal data, it might be useful to view frequency distributions or cross-tabulations of responses (McCoach et al., 2013). Although each item has six response options, it is possible that the participants never selected one or more options, effectively reducing the actual number of response options (empirical underidentification).

Frequency tables for all 30 variables can be produced via *Analyze > Descriptive Statistics > Frequencies* and moving all 30 variables into the *Variable(s)* box in the resulting **Frequencies** window.

The Frequencies output is quite lengthy, so only the first three frequency tables are displayed in Figure 16.4. A review of all 30 tables reveals that items 26 and 29 had few responses for some categories, but both had at least one participant for all six options. If there are few or no responses to more than 20% of the items on a factor, it may be beneficial to recode the data into fewer categories (DiStefano et al., 2020). If desired, more intelligible tables can be obtained from the Crosstabs procedure via *Analyze > Descriptive Statistics > Crosstabs* menu options.

```
FREQUENCIES VARIABLES=sdq1 sdq2 sdq3 sdq4r sdq5r sdq6 sdq7 sdq8 sdq9r sdq10r sdq11r sdq12 sdq13
    sdq14 sdq15r sdq16r sdq17r sdq18 sdq19 sdq20 sdq21r sdq22r sdq23r sdq24 sdq25 sdq26 sdq27r sdq28r
    sdq29r sdq30
  /ORDER=ANALYSIS.
```

Frequency Table

sdq1

		Frequency	Percent	Valid Percent	Cumulative Percent
Valid	1	62	14.6	14.6	14.6
	2	25	5.9	5.9	20.5
	3	62	14.6	14.6	35.1
	4	51	12.0	12.0	47.1
	5	80	18.8	18.8	65.9
	6	145	34.1	34.1	100.0
	Total	425	100.0	100.0	

sdq2

		Frequency	Percent	Valid Percent	Cumulative Percent
Valid	1	17	4.0	4.0	4.0
	2	18	4.2	4.2	8.2
	3	33	7.8	7.8	16.0
	4	63	14.8	14.8	30.8
	5	114	26.8	26.8	57.6
	6	180	42.4	42.4	100.0
	Total	425	100.0	100.0	

sdq3

		Frequency	Percent	Valid Percent	Cumulative Percent
Valid	1	11	2.6	2.6	2.6
	2	24	5.6	5.6	8.2
	3	56	13.2	13.2	21.4
	4	53	12.5	12.5	33.9
	5	78	18.4	18.4	52.2
	6	203	47.8	47.8	100.0
	Total	425	100.0	100.0	

FIGURE 16.4 Frequencies command code and tables for sdq data

Ordinal scale data is often obtained from surveys that rely on respondents to provide honest and thoughtful answers. Thus, it is assumed that respondents were motivated to respond accurately and thoughtfully about their self-concept on the sdq. Unfortunately, that assumption may not be correct, and participants may provide invalid responses due to linguistic incompetence, deliberate misrepresentation, or careless inattentiveness (Curran, 2016). Linguistic incompetence is related to how the scale was constructed and its proper application to a specific sample. For example, asking preschool children to respond to a written self-concept scale would likely produce invalid responses because most of them cannot read. Misrepresentation typically involves respondents cheating or faking (either good or bad), usually on high-stakes tests or surveys (Curran, 2016), whereas carelessness is the result of responding without consideration of the content of the items (Dunn et al., 2018).

A variety of screening techniques have been developed to detect invalid responses (Curran, 2016; DeSimone et al., 2015; Dunn et al., 2018), but only the Mahalanobis distance (D^2) as a general method of outlier detection is available through SPSS. As demonstrated with the iq data, an indirect method must be used. First, create a new variable in the **Data Editor** via *Transform > Compute Variable* that will open a **Compute Variable** window. Name the *Target Variable:* "id" and identify the **Numeric Expression:** as "$casenum." This creates a new variable named id that contains consecutive numbers 1 through 425 for the 425 participants.

SPSS computes D^2 values through its *Analyze > Regression > Linear* menus, which will open a **Linear Regression** window. After selecting the id variable as the *Dependent* variable and the 30 sdq variables (sdq1–sdq30) as *Independent* variables, click the *Save* option, which will open a **Linear Regression: Save** window. This window offers many options, but Mahalanobis distance is the only one needed. Check that box and then the *Continue* button. Click on the *Continue* button to return to the **Linear Regression** window and then click the **OK** button to generate D^2 values. The **Data Editor** window will now display a new variable labeled MAH_1 at the end of the variable list. To more easily identify the most extreme D^2 values, sort the MAH_1 values via the *Data > Sort Cases* menu options. Move the MAH_1 variable into the *Sort by* window, enable the *Descending* radio button, and click **OK**.

D^2 values can be tested for statistical significance, but "it is suggested that conservative levels of significance (e.g., .005 or .001) be used as the threshold value for designation as an outlier" (Hair et al., 2019, p. 89). SPSS can compute the chi-square probability level of each D^2 value, or they can be obtained from printed tables or online calculators.

To use SPSS to compute probability values for these D^2 statistics, a new variable must be created. As with the id variable, the *Transform > Compute Variable* menu options will generate a **Compute Variable** window where the new variable is named and filled with values (Figure 16.5). Name the new variable "probM." Complete the Numeric Expression field by typing "1 -" and then clicking on the chi-square distribution functions. That will generate "CDF.CHISQ(X1,X2)." Replace X1 with the MAH_1 variable and X2 with the number of sdq variables, thus: 1 - CDF.CHISQ(MAH_1,30). Given the small probability values, go to

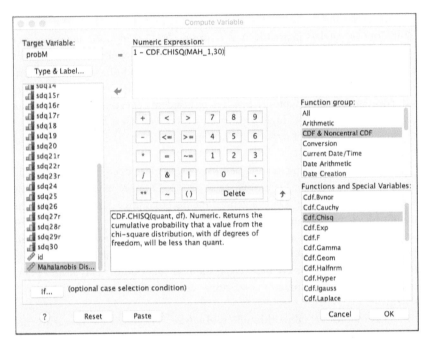

FIGURE 16.5 Compute Variable window for computing chi-square probability of D^2 values

the **Variable View** option of the Data Editor and allow the probM variable to be displayed with four decimal places.

Figure 16.6 reveals that case 187 has the largest D^2 value (96.89), case 416 the next largest (84.68), etc. Several D^2 values are displayed as $p = .0000$, but that figure is deceptive because SPSS reported these results to four decimal places so the D^2 value is less than .0001 but not zero. Using the conservative level of significance ($p < .001$) recommended by Hair et al. (2019), there are 29 cases that might be outliers. There is no obvious explanation for why these values are discrepant. As recommended by Hair et al. (2019), data "should be retained unless demonstrable proof indicates that they are truly aberrant and not representative of any observations in the population" (p. 91). However, as with continuous data (Bandalos & Finney, 2019; Leys et al., 2018; Tabachnick & Fidell, 2019; Thompson, 2004), results with and without the outlier data should be reported (Curran, 2016; DeSimone et al., 2015; Dunn et al., 2018). Inconsistent results may raise questions about the scale or the sample, whereas consistent results will allow greater confidence in the results. In this case, results did not differ when the 30 discrepant cases were deleted, so the full dataset is retained for subsequent analyses.

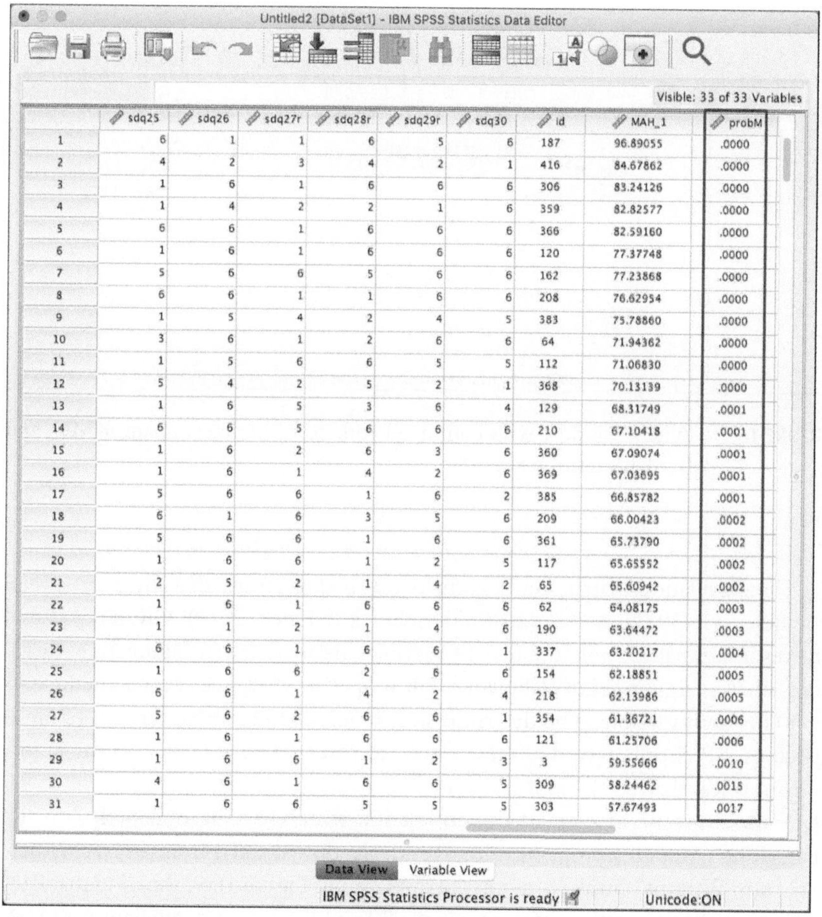

	sdq25	sdq26	sdq27r	sdq28r	sdq29r	sdq30	id	MAH_1	probM
1	6	1	1	6	5	6	187	96.89055	.0000
2	4	2	3	4	2	1	416	84.67862	.0000
3	1	6	1	6	6	6	306	83.24126	.0000
4	1	4	2	2	1	6	359	82.82577	.0000
5	6	6	1	6	6	6	366	82.59160	.0000
6	1	6	1	6	6	6	120	77.37748	.0000
7	5	6	6	5	6	6	162	77.23868	.0000
8	6	6	1	1	6	6	208	76.62954	.0000
9	1	5	4	2	4	5	383	75.78860	.0000
10	3	6	1	2	6	6	64	71.94362	.0000
11	1	5	6	6	5	5	112	71.06830	.0000
12	5	4	2	5	2	1	368	70.13139	.0000
13	1	6	5	3	6	4	129	68.31749	.0001
14	6	6	5	6	6	6	210	67.10418	.0001
15	1	6	2	6	3	6	360	67.09074	.0001
16	1	6	1	4	2	6	369	67.03695	.0001
17	5	6	6	1	6	2	385	66.85782	.0001
18	6	1	6	3	5	6	209	66.00423	.0002
19	5	6	6	1	6	6	361	65.73790	.0002
20	1	6	6	1	2	5	117	65.65552	.0002
21	2	5	2	1	4	2	65	65.60942	.0002
22	1	6	1	6	6	6	62	64.08175	.0003
23	1	1	2	1	4	6	190	63.64472	.0003
24	6	6	1	6	6	1	337	63.20217	.0004
25	1	6	6	2	6	6	154	62.18851	.0005
26	6	6	1	4	2	4	218	62.13986	.0005
27	5	6	2	6	6	1	354	61.36721	.0006
28	1	6	1	6	6	6	121	61.25706	.0006
29	1	6	6	1	2	3	3	59.55666	.0010
30	4	6	1	6	6	5	309	58.24462	.0015
31	1	6	6	5	5	5	303	57.67493	.0017

FIGURE 16.6 Data Editor window with D^2 (MAH_1) and probability (probM) variables displayed

Is EFA Appropriate?

As with the continuous iq data, correlation coefficients, the determinant, Bartlett's test of sphericity (1950), and the Kaiser–Meyer–Olkin measure of sampling adequacy (KMO; Kaiser, 1974) will be considered.

Syntax command code for Bartlett's test and the KMO measure of sampling adequacy is presented in Figure 16.7. This information can also be generated via the ***Analyze > Dimension Reduction > Factor > Descriptives*** menu options, moving all 30 sdq variables into the ***Variables:*** box, and then selecting the ***Coefficients***, ***Determinant***, and ***KMO and Bartlett's test of sphericity*** options.

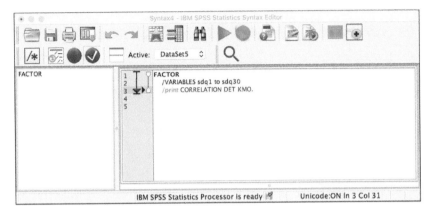

FIGURE 16.7 Syntax window with command code to print determinant, KMO, and Bartlett's test for sdq data

The correlation matrix can be visually scanned to ensure that there are several coefficients ≥ .30 (Hair et al., 2019; Tabachnick & Fidell, 2019). Given the size of the resulting matrix, only the first 14 variables are included in Figure 16.8. Scanning such a large matrix is laborious, but it appears there are several coefficients ≥ .30 for each variable. The determinant is reported to be .000, but this figure is specious. SPSS only reported these results to three decimal places, so the determinant is less than .001 but is not zero.

A more precise analysis of the correlation matrix can be obtained with the standalone computer program titled Residuals, downloaded from edpsychassociates.com/Watkins3.html. Its results are displayed in Figure 16.9, showing that 21% of the correlation coefficients were above .30 and the largest coefficient was .694.

As displayed in Figure 16.10, the KMO measure of sampling adequacy (Kaiser, 1974) was acceptable at .88, and Bartlett's test of sphericity (1950) statistically rejected the hypothesis that the correlation matrix was an identity matrix (chi-square of 5346.3 with 435 degrees of freedom) at $p < .001$ (again, if a probable value is smaller than the specified decimal precision, then SPSS displays a misleading probability value of .000, but it is NOT zero). Altogether, these measures indicated that the Pearson correlation matrix is appropriate for EFA (Hair et al., 2019; Tabachnick & Fidell, 2019).

Factor Analysis Model

The purpose of this study was to uncover the latent structure underlying the 30 sdq items. Accordingly, a common factor model (EFA) was selected (Widaman, 2018).

Correlation Matrix[a]

	sdq1	sdq2	sdq3	sdq4r	sdq5r	sdq6	sdq7	sdq8	sdq9r	sdq10r	sdq11r	sdq12	sdq13	sdq14
Correlation sdq1	1.000	.134	-.035	.575	.163	-.011	.578	.053	-.015	.476	.134	-.091	.694	.117
sdq2	.134	1.000	.186	.073	.335	.105	.109	.379	.192	.123	.381	.147	.162	.413
sdq3	-.035	.186	1.000	.034	.152	.325	-.007	.245	.342	.127	.314	.343	.014	.282
sdq4r	.575	.073	.034	1.000	.162	-.088	.357	.064	.100	.518	.162	-.094	.469	.100
sdq5r	.163	.335	.152	.162	1.000	.064	.137	.290	.175	.186	.407	.072	.182	.256
sdq6	-.011	.105	.325	-.088	.064	1.000	.209	.200	.123	-.078	.188	.295	.102	.112
sdq7	.578	.109	-.007	.357	.137	.209	1.000	.065	.009	.269	.125	-.042	.633	.105
sdq8	.053	.379	.245	.064	.290	.200	.065	1.000	.109	.115	.296	.207	.140	.528
sdq9r	-.015	.192	.342	.100	.175	.123	.009	.109	1.000	.131	.198	.223	.080	.101
sdq10r	.476	.123	.127	.518	.186	-.078	.269	.115	.131	1.000	.296	-.108	.413	.148
sdq11r	.134	.381	.314	.162	.407	.188	.125	.296	.198	.296	1.000	.140	.198	.439
sdq12	-.091	.147	.343	-.094	.072	.295	-.042	.207	.223	-.108	.140	1.000	-.007	.198
sdq13	.694	.162	.014	.469	.182	.102	.633	.140	.080	.413	.198	-.007	1.000	.211
sdq14	.117	.413	.282	.100	.256	.112	.105	.528	.101	.148	.439	.198	.211	1.000
sdq15r	.002	.162	.282	.062	.165	.040	-.040	.143	.365	.125	.133	.127	-.006	.091
sdq16r	.556	.162	.296	.588	.120	-.070	.375	.048	.086	.517	.144	-.099	.503	.127
sdq17r	.099	.542	.010	.046	.344	.052	.076	.285	.225	.180	.386	.005	.127	.290
sdq18	-.095	.084	.439	-.158	.031	.499	-.009	.212	.209	-.155	.088	.552	.018	.115
sdq19	.637	.075	.010	.552	.187	-.068	-.436	.026	.032	.467	.184	-.107	.551	.099
sdq20	.135	.250	.208	.066	.211	.039	.122	.315	.110	.161	.213	.200	.169	.307
sdq21r	.020	.081	.294	-.033	.089	.252	.072	.186	.337	.043	.178	.263	.058	.047
sdq22r	.457	.087	.113	.367	.096	.112	.484	.132	.089	.334	.286	.004	.511	.210
sdq23r	.177	.401	.121	.103	.363	.158	.122	.312	.067	.169	.389	.100	.168	.217
sdq24	-.076	.119	.487	-.075	.116	.321	-.053	.191	.275	.026	.182	.547	-.010	.118
sdq25	.613	.093	-.061	.482	.170	-.016	.420	.050	.028	.433	.172	-.046	.531	.273
sdq26	.098	.187	.164	.059	.121	-.009	.080	.298	.092	.145	.160	.075	.111	.123
sdq27r	.038	.231	.264	.025	.167	.155	-.072	.218	.254	.121	.185	.223	.050	.192
sdq28r	.630	.132	.035	.469	.179	.027	.517	.086	.021	.470	.279	-.056	.587	.462
sdq29r	.177	.408	.172	.107	.483	.116	.137	.324	.157	.253	.533	.087	.194	.230
sdq30	-.122	.174	.443	-.091	.066	.341	-.041	.243	.280	-.028	.199	.594	-.044	

a. Determinant = .000

FIGURE 16.8 Correlation matrix for sdq data

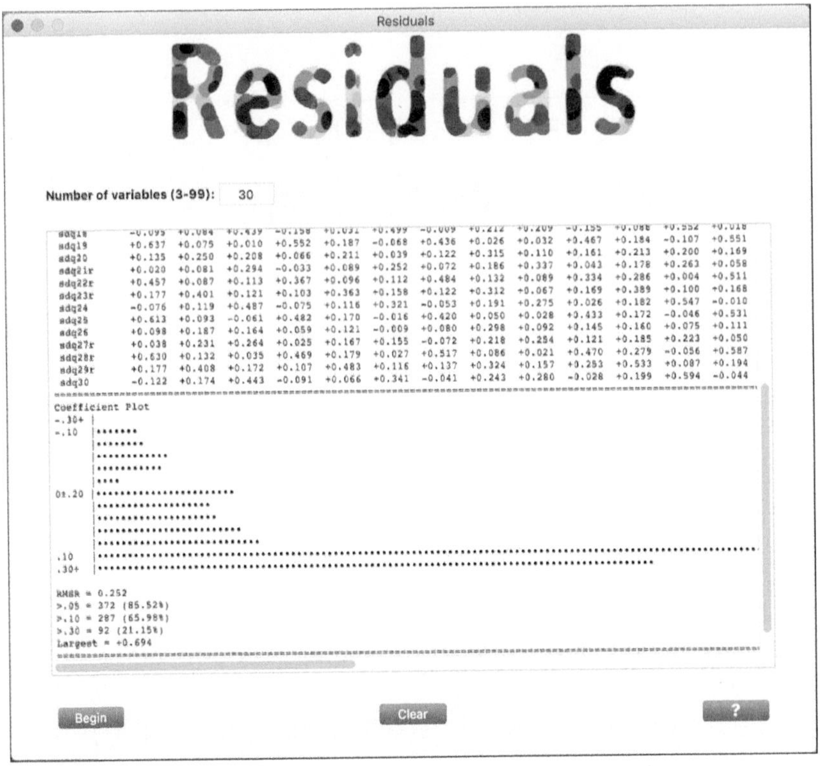

FIGURE 16.9   Analysis of sdq correlation matrix with the Residuals program

KMO and Bartlett's Test		
Kaiser–Meyer–Olkin Measure of Sampling Adequacy.		.884
Bartlett's Test of Sphericity	Approx. Chi–Square	5346.271
	df	435
	Sig.	.000

FIGURE 16.10   KMO and Bartlett's test output for sdq data

Factor Extraction Method

Maximum likelihood estimation can be biased in the presence of multivariate nonnormality. Therefore, an estimation method with greater computational robustness and reduced sensitivity to nonnormality would be preferred (Barendse et al., 2015; Cudeck, 2000; Lee et al., 2012; Rhemtulla et al., 2012; Zhang & Browne, 2006). Accordingly, principal axis extraction was conducted with initial communalities estimated by squared multiple correlations (Tabachnick & Fidell, 2019), which are the default in SPSS.

How Many Factors to Retain

Empirical guidelines include parallel analysis, minimal average partials (MAP), and scree (Velicer et al., 2000). Parallel analysis with Pearson correlations has been shown to perform well with ordinal data (Cho et al., 2009; Garrido et al., 2013). Although PA is not natively available in SPSS, PA can be conducted with online calculators available at www.statstodo.com/ParallelAnalysis_Exp.php and https://analytics.gonzaga.edu/parallelengine. Alternatively, a standalone computer program called *Monte Carlo PCA for Parallel Analysis* can be downloaded from http://edpsychassociates.com/Watkins3.html.

Staying with SPSS, O'Connor (2000) provided a syntax command code that can be downloaded from https://people.ok.ubc.ca/brioconn/nfactors/nfactors.html. First, download O'Connor's parallel .sps syntax file. Second, load that file into SPSS via *File > Open > Syntax > parallel .sps*. Third, ensure that the sdq data file with only the 30 measured variables (delete the id variable for this analysis) is loaded in the **Data Editor** window. Fourth, edit the parallel .sps syntax file to reflect the correct number of cases, variables, etc. in lines 8–16, as demonstrated in Figure 16.11. Finally, execute the command code via *Run > All*.

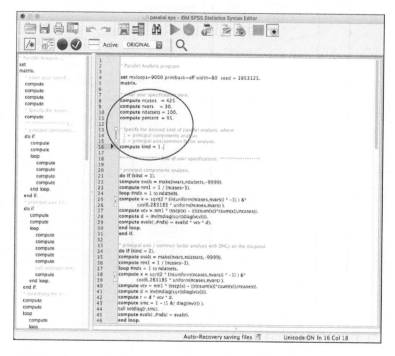

FIGURE 16.11 Syntax window command code for parallel analysis

When the eigenvalues from random data were compared to the eigenvalues from the sdq data (Figure 16.12), the fifth random eigenvalue was larger than the fifth real eigenvalue. Thus, parallel analysis indicates that four factors should be sufficient.

Although MAP is not natively available in SPSS, O'Connor (2000) provided SPSS syntax that can be downloaded from https://people.ok.ubc.ca/brioconn/nfactors/nfactors.html. First, download O'Connor's map .sps syntax file. Second, load that file into SPSS via ***File > Open > Syntax > map .sps***. Third, ensure that the sdq data file with only the 30 measured variables (delete the id variable for this analysis) is loaded in the **Data Editor** window. Fourth, edit the map .sps syntax file to select data entry method 2 by commenting out lines 44–52, uncommenting line 61, and providing the variable names in line 61, as displayed in Figure 16.13. Finally, execute the command code via ***Run > All***.

The MAP values decreased from .0438 at one factor, to .0191 at two factors, to .0119 at three factors, to .0116 at four factors but increased to .0125 at five

Real Data

Total Variance Explained

Component	Initial Eigenvalues Total	% of Variance	Cumulative %
1	6.595	21.983	21.983
2	4.854	16.179	38.162
3	2.467	8.223	46.385
4	1.539	5.131	51.516
5	1.250	4.166	55.682
6	1.052	3.507	59.189
7	.941	3.136	62.325
8	.845	2.818	65.144
9	.810	2.701	67.844
10	.761	2.537	70.381
11	.721	2.402	72.783
12	.700	2.335	75.118
13	.617	2.058	77.176
14	.584	1.947	79.122
15	.575	1.916	81.038
16	.540	1.801	82.839
17	.527	1.756	84.595
18	.496	1.655	86.250
19	.456	1.520	87.770
20	.445	1.482	89.252
21	.421	1.403	90.655
22	.384	1.280	91.935
23	.372	1.238	93.173
24	.359	1.198	94.371
25	.328	1.093	95.463
26	.309	1.029	96.493
27	.294	.980	97.472
28	.280	.932	98.404
29	.257	.857	99.261
30	.222	.739	100.000

Extraction Method: Principal Component Analysis.

Random Data

```
PARALLEL ANALYSIS:

Principal Components

Specifications for this Run:
Ncases     425
Nvars       30
Ndatsets   100
Percent     95

Random Data Eigenvalues
```

Root	Means	Prcntyle
1.000000	1.541351	1.627573
2.000000	1.459331	1.509033
3.000000	1.395133	1.426679
4.000000	1.351669	1.387508
5.000000	1.310063	1.351046
6.000000	1.269792	1.304656
7.000000	1.233607	1.258375
8.000000	1.199180	1.225404
9.000000	1.167237	1.192745
10.000000	1.136227	1.165226
11.000000	1.105289	1.130772
12.000000	1.076261	1.100750
13.000000	1.048549	1.067043
14.000000	1.020927	1.045170
15.000000	.992624	1.019168
16.000000	.963295	.986509
17.000000	.937850	.963892
18.000000	.913698	.935631
19.000000	.888226	.912709
20.000000	.861449	.884016
21.000000	.835681	.859147
22.000000	.809459	.833006
23.000000	.781979	.801854
24.000000	.758791	.780709
25.000000	.731083	.756270
26.000000	.702403	.728225
27.000000	.675008	.700254
28.000000	.645922	.671394
29.000000	.614771	.643787
30.000000	.573143	.616460

------ END MATRIX -----

FIGURE 16.12 Eigenvalues of sdq data compared to eigenvalues of random data

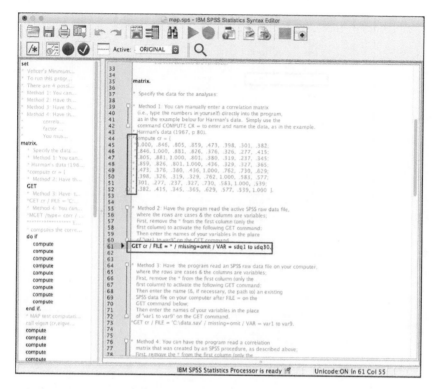

FIGURE 16.13 Syntax window command code for MAP

factors (Figure 16.14). Thus, MAP agrees with PA that four factors should be sufficient (Figure 16.14).

The only empirical criterion provided by SPSS is the scree plot. It can be created via the ***Analyze > Dimension Reduction > Factor > Extraction > Scree plot*** menus. As often happens, the scree plot is ambiguous (Mulaik, 2018; Streiner, 1998). Figure 16.15 shows why the scree plot is considered subjective: analysts might reasonably posit different numbers of factors to extract. In this case, the scree plot indicates as many as six factors or as few as four.

The instrument was designed to measure three dimensions of self-concept. Therefore, models with six (the largest estimate, obtained from the visual scree), five, four, three, and two factors will be sequentially evaluated for their interpretability and theoretical meaningfulness (Preacher et al., 2013).

Rotate Factors

An oblique rotation was selected because it honors the ubiquity of intercorrelations among social science variables (Meehl, 1990). Among the potential oblique

```
Average Partial Correlations
                    squared      power4
        .0000       .0636        .0131
       1.0000       .0438        .0045
       2.0000       .0191        .0009
       3.0000       .0119        .0004
       4.0000       .0116        .0004
       5.0000       .0125        .0005
       6.0000       .0137        .0007
       7.0000       .0148        .0009
       8.0000       .0168        .0012
       9.0000       .0200        .0021
      10.0000       .0229        .0029
      11.0000       .0266        .0037
      12.0000       .0306        .0046
      13.0000       .0355        .0058
      14.0000       .0397        .0067
      15.0000       .0454        .0094
      16.0000       .0515        .0103
      17.0000       .0567        .0126
      18.0000       .0647        .0162
      19.0000       .0751        .0203
      20.0000       .0868        .0246
      21.0000       .0974        .0279
      22.0000       .1153        .0382
      23.0000       .1349        .0486
      24.0000       .1654        .0685
      25.0000       .2001        .0889
      26.0000       .2617        .1419
      27.0000       .3507        .2164
      28.0000       .4897        .3614
      29.0000      1.0000       1.0000

The smallest average squared partial correlation is
   .0116

The smallest average 4rth power partial correlation is
   .0004

The number of components according to the original (1976) MAP Test is
4

The number of components according to the revised (2000) MAP Test is
4
```

FIGURE 16.14   MAP output for sdq data

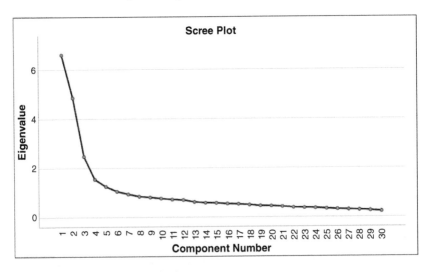

FIGURE 16.15   Scree plot for sdq data

analytic rotations, "promax rotation is almost always a good choice" (Thompson, 2004, p. 43).

Interpret Results

Given the oblique rotation, pattern coefficients and factor intercorrelations will receive primary attention during the model evaluation process (Bandalos, 2018; Hair et al., 2019). To ensure both practical (10% variance) and statistical ($p < .01$) significance of pattern loadings, the threshold for salience will be set at .32 (Norman & Streiner, 2014) with a goal of approximate simple structure (Morin et al., 2020; Thurstone, 1947). This threshold seems reasonable, given that a meta-analysis of EFA outcomes found that the average factor loading of ordinal data was around .32 (Peterson, 2000).

Each model will be examined for symptoms of overextraction, such as inadmissible solutions, fewer than three salient loadings, and technical factors, as well as for symptoms of underextraction, such as no common unifying theme or many complex loadings (Bandalos, 2018; Fabrigar & Wegener, 2012). Finally, the alpha reliability of scales created from the salient variables of each factor should reach .80, given that the intended use of these variables is for group research (DeVellis, 2017).

The use of a syntax command code can make this series of model comparisons relatively easy. The command code in Figure 16.16 can be edited for each model. Thus, line 7 can be changed to "FACTORS(5)" for the five-factor model, to "FACTORS(4)" for the four-factor model, etc.

The six-factor model converged properly and produced reasonable parameter estimates. However, it exhibited symptoms of overextraction (Figure 16.17). For

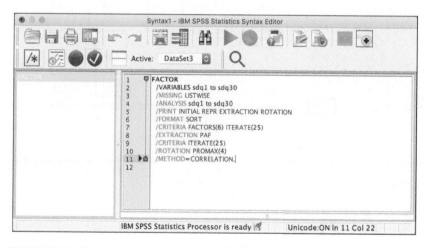

FIGURE 16.16   Syntax window command code for EFA with six factors

Pattern Matrix[a]

Factor

	1	2	3	4	5	6
sdq1	.832	.063	.067	-.136	-.084	.059
sdq19	.822	-.021	.002	.037	-.032	-.038
sdq25	.763	.038	.089	-.079	-.071	-.050
sdq16r	.756	-.099	-.076	.115	.081	.007
sdq4r	.710	-.066	-.059	.077	.047	-.044
sdq13	.690	.076	.124	-.138	-.040	.223
sdq28r	.566	.009	-.121	.033	.067	.396
sdq10r	.561	.038	-.126	.191	.131	-.027
sdq7	.507	.056	.085	-.145	-.125	.383
sdq23r	.014	.698	-.014	-.071	.002	-.040
sdq17r	-.055	.695	-.161	.183	-.075	-.080
sdq2	-.017	.654	.024	.028	.042	-.093
sdq29r	-.014	.627	-.075	.043	.160	.059
sdq5r	.092	.586	-.021	.112	-.074	-.090
sdq11r	.003	.480	-.038	.173	.125	.164
sdq18	.009	-.049	.881	-.032	-.095	.016
sdq12	.001	-.056	.692	-.017	.105	-.041
sdq24	.038	-.051	.690	.137	.088	-.084
sdq30	-.035	-.128	.659	.099	.214	.030
sdq6	-.060	.141	.502	.004	-.225	.287
sdq3	-.037	.016	.377	.330	.127	.102
sdq27r	.108	.160	.316	.224	-.045	-.167
sdq15r	-.012	.107	.010	.608	-.119	.016
sdq9r	.025	.099	.131	.584	-.148	.037
sdq21r	-.067	-.054	.179	.528	-.116	.333
sdq14	-.049	.319	.052	-.201	.574	.097
sdq26	.005	.037	.012	-.104	.484	.013
sdq8	-.076	.307	.133	-.098	.402	.052
sdq20	.125	.208	.199	-.112	.342	-.126
sdq22r	.350	-.147	-.098	.147	.162	.613

Extraction Method: Principal Axis Factoring.
Rotation Method: Promax with Kaiser Normalization.

a. Rotation converged in 9 iterations.

FIGURE 16.17   Pattern matrix for EFA with six factors

example, the final factor in the six-factor model was saliently loaded by four items, but all four were complex with salient loadings on other factors. The five-factor model exhibited similar symptoms of overextraction with its fifth factor saliently loaded by three complex items. Finally, the alpha reliability of the final factors in these models was less than .70. Given these weak factors, these two models were not considered plausible.

Similarly, the final factor in the four-factor model was saliently loaded by only three items, but two were complex (Figure 16.18) and the alpha reliability of this three-item scale was only .60. One item failed to saliently load on any factor (sdq27r). The items containing math and general self-concept content consistently cohered across these three models, whereas the items designed to tap verbal self-concept tended to split into reading versus English content groupings. This is a potential indicator of overextraction and suggested that the three-factor model might be more appropriate.

The three-factor model converged properly and produced reasonable parameter estimates (Figure 16.19). In total, more than 80% of the loadings were good to excellent in magnitude (Comrey & Lee, 1992) in a simple structure configuration. Two items failed to saliently load on any factor, although their highest loadings were in alignment with their anticipated factors. The three factors accounted for 41% of the variance before rotation, and the interfactor correlations of .05 to .32 were low enough to pose no threat to discriminant validity (Brown, 2015). The three-factor model was consistent with the theoretical underpinning of the scale as color coded in Figures 16.19 and 16.20.

Using the highest loadings on each factor, the alpha reliability coefficient was .91 for the math self-concept factor (left panel of Figure 16.21), .82 for the verbal self-concept factor (middle panel of Figure 16.21), and .83 for the general self-concept factor (right panel of Figure 16.21). This three-factor structure was robust to rotation method (promax and oblimin) as well as extraction method (iterated principal axis and generalized least squares). Further, results did not differ when a polychoric correlation matrix was submitted to EFA.

Information about the residuals was obtained from the standalone computer program titled Residuals, downloaded from edpsychassociates.com/Watkins3.html. The RMSR was .04 for four factors and increased to .05 for three factors. Thus, models with three and four factors were close fits on average. More than 24% of the residuals were above the absolute value of .05, and 4% were above the absolute value of .10 in the three-factor model. Examination of this pattern suggested several plausible explanations. First, the verbal scale contained three items that addressed reading and seven items that dealt with English and written expression. The average pattern coefficient for the three reading items was .35, whereas the average pattern coefficient for the English items was .63. Given the content of these items, children in elementary school may see reading and English as different subjects. Thus, a reading self-concept factor might emerge if more

Pattern Matrix[a]

	Factor			
	1	2	3	4
sdq1	.836	−.002	−.011	−.092
sdq13	.788	.063	.132	−.175
sdq19	.775	−.072	−.086	.131
sdq28r	.755	.087	.005	−.078
sdq16r	.738	−.078	−.114	.209
sdq25	.708	−.033	−.021	.011
sdq7	.686	.024	.161	−.282
sdq4r	.667	−.070	−.124	.182
sdq22r	.636	.029	.150	−.046
sdq10r	.532	.089	−.151	.277
sdq29r	.018	.735	−.054	.004
sdq23r	−.006	.691	−.067	−.090
sdq2	−.067	.664	−.032	.037
sdq14	.018	.642	.109	−.105
sdq17r	−.093	.635	−.192	.134
sdq11r	.086	.574	.043	.090
sdq8	−.042	.545	.170	−.041
sdq5r	.040	.524	−.080	.099
sdq20	.057	.378	.140	.038
sdq26	.022	.310	.048	.008
sdq18	−.015	−.099	.846	−.010
sdq30	−.040	.001	.692	.167
sdq12	−.042	−.001	.667	.062
sdq24	−.032	−.015	.659	.230
sdq6	.066	.054	.565	−.148
sdq3	−.001	.099	.464	.318
sdq21r	.085	−.060	.367	.305
sdq15r	−.018	.039	.079	.529
sdq9r	.025	.015	.195	.501
sdq27r	.000	.106	.245	.294

Extraction Method: Principal Axis Factoring.
Rotation Method: Promax with Kaiser Normalization.

a. Rotation converged in 5 iterations.

FIGURE 16.18 Pattern matrix for EFA with four factors

Pattern Matrix[a]

	Factor		
	1	2	3
sdq1	.834	-.037	-.033
sdq19	.787	-.033	-.037
sdq13	.770	.074	.003
sdq28r	.753	-.014	.058
sdq16r	.751	-.035	-.019
sdq25	.714	-.011	-.035
sdq4r	.680	-.054	-.017
sdq7	.653	.060	-.059
sdq22r	.633	.139	.000
sdq10r	.549	-.043	.165
sdq18	-.033	.819	-.156
sdq30	-.040	.751	-.009
sdq24	-.028	.740	-.005
sdq12	-.049	.685	-.036
sdq3	.011	.573	.147
sdq6	.043	.497	-.022
sdq21r	.097	.465	-.004
sdq9r	.051	.357	.133
sdq27r	.015	.348	.163
sdq15r	.014	.254	.168
sdq29r	.016	-.033	.731
sdq17r	-.085	-.128	.678
sdq2	-.068	-.003	.671
sdq23r	-.012	-.080	.660
sdq14	.009	.091	.590
sdq11r	.089	.091	.588
sdq5r	.045	-.031	.551
sdq8	-.049	.169	.512
sdq20	.055	.164	.372
sdq26	.021	.060	.303

Extraction Method: Principal Axis Factoring.
Rotation Method: Promax with Kaiser Normalization.

a. Rotation converged in 5 iterations.

FIGURE 16.19 Pattern matrix for EFA with three factors

No	Description	No	Description
1.	Math is my best subject	16.	Do badly on math tests
2.	Overall, I'm proud	17.	Not much to be proud of
3.	Hopeless in English class	18.	English is one of my best subjects
4.	Need help in math	19.	Good grades in math
5.	Overall, I'm no good	20.	Do things as well as most
6.	Look forward to English class	21.	I hate reading
7.	Look forward to math class	22.	Never want another math course
8.	Most things I do well	23.	My life is not very useful
9.	Do badly on reading tests	24.	Good grades in English
10.	Trouble understanding math	25.	Always done well in math
11.	Nothing ever turns out right	26.	Can do almost anything if I try
12.	English class is easy	27.	Trouble with writing
13.	I enjoy studying math	28.	Hate math
14.	Most things turn out well	29.	Overall, I'm a failure
15.	Not good at reading	30.	Learn quickly in English class

FIGURE 16.20 SDQ items color-coded for two factors

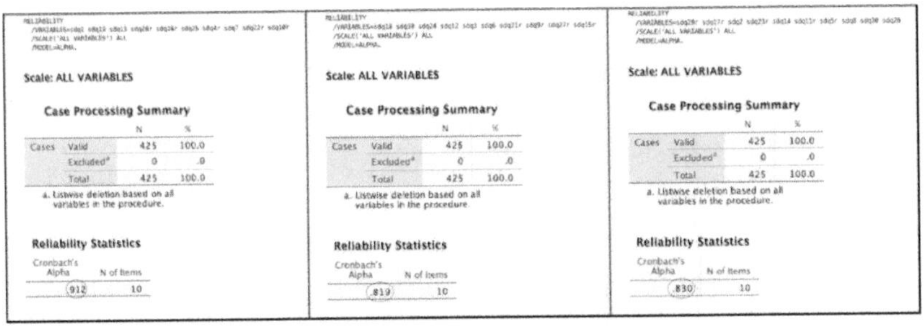

FIGURE 16.21 Alpha reliability command code and output for three sdq factors

reading items were included. Additionally, the mixture of positively and negatively worded items may be responsible because they are known to disrupt the pattern of correlations and thereby create artifactual factors (Spector et al., 1997). That might be especially true for children in elementary school.

Additional support for the three-factor model was provided by analysis of a two-factor model. The two-factor model was marked by large residual values: an RMSR of .08, 51% of the residuals >.05, and 18% of the residuals >.10. In this model, the math self-concept items continued to cohere, but the verbal and general self-concept items collapsed into a single scale. This is a common symptom of underextraction and signals that the three-factor model appears to be the most acceptable solution.

A potential criticism of the scale in its entirety is the possibility of what Cattell (1978) called a "bloated specific," that is, items that are virtual paraphrases of each other. For example: "Do badly on math tests" and "Bad grades in math" might be perceived by young children as essentially the same question. Factors created by boated specifics are narrow and unlikely to replicate (de Winter et al., 2009). Likewise, factors created by combining items with similar vocabulary (e.g., math, reading, English) might be too narrow and unlikely to replicate (Gorsuch, 1997; Podsakoff et al., 2012). These sources of "hidden invalidity" should be considered (Hussey & Hughes, 2020, p. 166).

17

HIGHER-ORDER AND BIFACTOR MODELS

Higher-Order Models

There are situations where constructs of different conceptual breadth exist and should, therefore, be reflected in the exploratory factor analysis (EFA) model. For example, the concept of general intelligence is currently thought to subsume narrower group factors, which, in turn, subsume even narrower abilities (Carroll, 1993). This model reflects the theoretical belief that intelligence is comprised of subdimensions.

Broad, group, and specific abilities are often conceptualized in a higher-order factor model. In the simple higher-order model depicted in Figure 17.1, factors one through three are first-order factors (group factors) responsible for the intercorrelations of their indicator variables, whereas g is a broad general factor responsible for the intercorrelations of the first-order factors.

Gorsuch (1988) maintained that "correlated factors imply the existence of higher-order factors" (p. 250), and higher-order models have been advanced as a solution for the misinterpretation of rotated factors (Carretta & Ree, 2001). When factors are rotated, variance from the first factor is distributed across the remaining factors and seems to strengthen those factors. In actuality, variance from the first factor has simply become a major source of variance in the new rotated factors. This can lead to a mistaken interpretation about the relative importance of the factors (Carroll, 1983; Gignac, 2007). Some researchers object to the use of EFA for higher-order analyses (Osborne & Banjanovic, 2016). However, EFA higher-order models are often encountered in the research literature (e.g., Canivez & Watkins, 2010; Watkins, 2006) and should be utilized if congruous with theory (Gorsuch, 1983; Thompson, 2004).

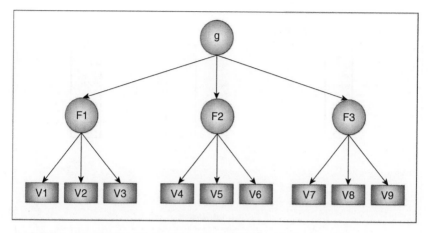

FIGURE 17.1 Simplified path diagram of a higher-order factor model

A second-order factor analysis can be conducted with the first-order factor correlation matrix as input and should be based on at least three first-order factors for identification. This requirement rules out the iq data used in the previous example. Likewise, the sdq data is not appropriate because there is no theoretical expectation of a broader general factor (Marsh, 1990). However, the classic Holzinger and Swineford (1939) data is often used to illustrate higher-order and bifactor models.

The HolzingerSwineford.xlsx file can be imported via an SPSS syntax command code, as in Figure 17.2, or via SPSS menu options (*File > Import Data > Excel*).

```
GET DATA
  /TYPE=XLSX
  /FILE='/Documents/HolzingerSwineford.xlsx'
  /SHEET=name 'HolzingerSwineford1939'
  /CELLRANGE=FULL
  /READNAMES=ON
  /DATATYPEMIN PERCENTAGE=95.0
  /HIDDEN IGNORE=YES.
EXECUTE.
```

FIGURE 17.2 Command code for importing Holzinger–Swineford Excel data

Once imported, the SPSS **Data Editor** window will display the data. Scroll through the data to ensure that there are 9 variables and 301 participants. Click the *Variable View* button and review the characteristics of the data (Figure 17.3). Be sure that SPSS categorized the variables as "Numeric" and at a "Scale" measurement level. There is no missing data indicator, so it is assumed that there are no

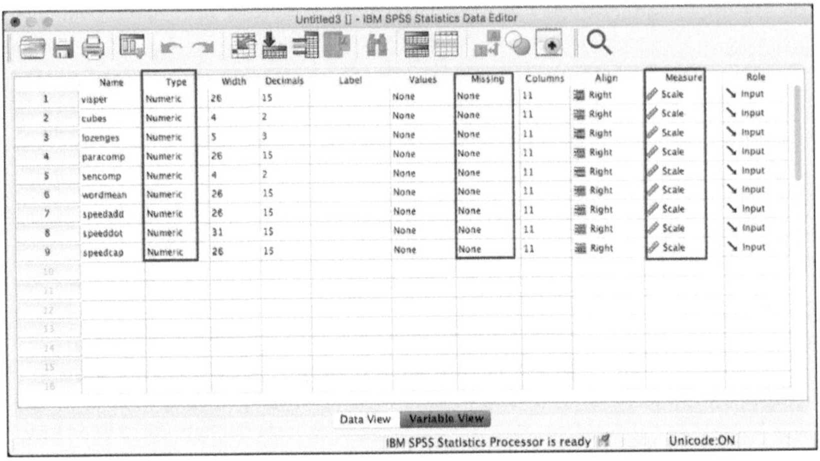

	Name	Type	Width	Decimals	Label	Values	Missing	Columns	Align	Measure	Role
1	visper	Numeric	26	15		None	None	11	Right	Scale	Input
2	cubes	Numeric	4	2		None	None	11	Right	Scale	Input
3	lozenges	Numeric	5	3		None	None	11	Right	Scale	Input
4	paracomp	Numeric	26	15		None	None	11	Right	Scale	Input
5	sencomp	Numeric	4	2		None	None	11	Right	Scale	Input
6	wordmean	Numeric	26	15		None	None	11	Right	Scale	Input
7	speedadd	Numeric	26	15		None	None	11	Right	Scale	Input
8	speeddot	Numeric	31	15		None	None	11	Right	Scale	Input
9	speedcap	Numeric	26	15		None	None	11	Right	Scale	Input

FIGURE 17.3 Data Editor window with Variable View of Holzinger–Swineford data

missing data. Once the data have been verified, they can be saved in SPSS format for future convenience (***File > Save As > HolzingerSwineford***). SPSS will recognize that this is a data file and automatically add the .sav suffix to the file name.

The descriptive statistics (***Analyze > Descriptive Statistics > Descriptives***) do not reveal any obviously incorrect or out-of-bounds values, and there are 301 cases for all 9 variables, so there are no missing data (Figure 17.4). The skewness values were all less than 2.0, and the kurtosis values were all less than 7.0, indicating univariate normality.

```
DESCRIPTIVES VARIABLES=visper cubes lozenges paracomp sencomp wordmean speedadd speeddot speedcap
  /STATISTICS=MEAN STDDEV MIN MAX KURTOSIS SKEWNESS.
```

Descriptive Statistics

	N	Minimum	Maximum	Mean	Std. Deviation	Skewness		Kurtosis	
	Statistic	Statistic	Statistic	Statistic	Statistic	Statistic	Std. Error	Statistic	Std. Error
visper	301	.666666670	8.50000000	4.93576966	1.16743212	-.257	.140	.355	.280
cubes	301	2.25	9.25	6.0880	1.17745	.475	.140	.381	.280
lozenges	301	.250	4.500	2.25042	1.130979	.387	.140	-.888	.280
paracomp	301	.000000000	6.33333330	3.06090809	1.16411628	.270	.140	.123	.280
sencomp	301	1.00	7.00	4.3405	1.29047	-.353	.140	-.525	.280
wordmean	301	.142857140	6.14285710	2.18557190	1.09560314	.867	.140	.876	.280
speedadd	301	1.30434780	7.43478260	4.18590207	1.08953351	.252	.140	-.274	.280
speeddot	301	3.05000000	10.0000000	5.52707641	1.01261514	.531	.140	1.240	.280
speedcap	301	2.77777780	9.25000000	5.37412329	1.00915173	.206	.140	.337	.280
Valid N (listwise)	301								

FIGURE 17.4 Descriptive statistics command code and output for Holzinger–Swineford data

The correlation matrix revealed that there are several coefficients ≥ .30 (Hair et al., 2019; Tabachnick & Fidell, 2019). Bartlett's test of sphericity (1950) rejected the hypothesis that the correlation matrix was an identity matrix (chi-square of

904.1 with 36 degrees of freedom at $p < .001$). The Kaiser–Meyer–Olkin (KMO) measure of sampling adequacy was acceptable with values of .75 (Hoelzle & Meyer, 2013; Kaiser, 1974). Altogether, as illustrated in Figure 17.5, these measures indicate that the correlation matrix is appropriate for EFA (Hair et al., 2019; Tabachnick & Fidell, 2019).

Correlation Matrix[a]

		visper	cubes	lozenges	paracomp	sencomp	wordmean	speedadd	speeddot	speedcap
Correlation	visper	1.000	.297	.441	.373	.293	.357	.067	.224	.390
	cubes	.297	1.000	.340	.153	.139	.193	-.076	.092	.206
	lozenges	.441	.340	1.000	.159	.077	.198	.072	.186	.329
	paracomp	.373	.153	.159	1.000	.733	.704	.174	.107	.208
	sencomp	.293	.139	.077	.733	1.000	.720	.102	.139	.227
	wordmean	.357	.193	.198	.704	.720	1.000	.121	.150	.214
	speedadd	.067	-.076	.072	.174	.102	.121	1.000	.487	.341
	speeddot	.224	.092	.186	.107	.139	.150	.487	1.000	.449
	speedcap	.390	.206	.329	.208	.227	.214	.341	.449	1.000

a. Determinant = .047

KMO and Bartlett's Test

Kaiser-Meyer-Olkin Measure of Sampling Adequacy.		.752
Bartlett's Test of Sphericity	Approx. Chi-Square	904.097
	df	36
	Sig.	.000

FIGURE 17.5   Correlation matrix, KMO, and Bartlett's test output for Holzinger–Swineford data

The scree plot indicated that three factors would be sufficient (Figure 17.6), as did parallel analysis with real eigenvalues displayed in blue and random eigenvalues in red.

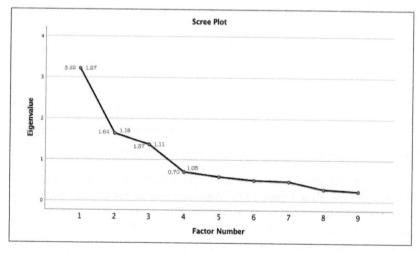

FIGURE 17.6   Scree plot with real (blue) and random (red) eigenvalues for Holzinger–Swineford data

The command code for an EFA with three factors, principal axis extraction, and promax rotation is displayed in Figure 17.7.

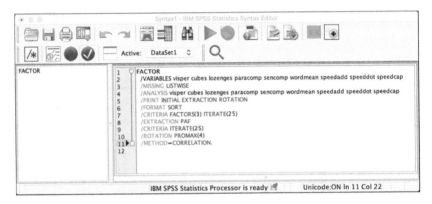

FIGURE 17.7 Syntax window command code for first-order EFA of Holzinger–Swineford data

Before rotation, the first factor accounted for 31.4% of the variance, the second factor for 13.5% of the variance, and the third factor for 9.1% of the variance. Altogether, the three factors accounted for 54% of the variance (Figure 17.8).

Total Variance Explained

	PCA			EFA			Rotation Sums of Squared Loadings[a]
	Initial Eigenvalues			Extraction Sums of Squared Loadings			
Factor	Total	% of Variance	Cumulative %	Total	% of Variance	Cumulative %	Total
1	3.216	35.737	35.737	2.828	31.417	31.417	2.501
2	1.639	18.208	53.945	1.215	13.497	44.914	1.852
3	1.365	15.168	69.114	.814	9.047	53.961	1.645
4	.699	7.766	76.879				
5	.584	6.493	83.372				
6	.500	5.552	88.924				
7	.473	5.257	94.181				
8	.286	3.178	97.359				
9	.238	2.641	100.000				

Extraction Method: Principal Axis Factoring.
a. When factors are correlated, sums of squared loadings cannot be added to obtain a total variance.

FIGURE 17.8 Output of first-order EFA of Holzinger–Swineford data

As anticipated, three factors emerged: verbal ability, spatial ability, and mental speed (left panel of Figure 17.9). Although one of the mental speed items also saliently loaded on the spatial factor, the three-factor solution appears to be adequate. The structure coefficients (middle panel of Figure 17.9) were strong (.49 to .87), and there was no evidence of a suppression effect (Thompson, 2004). However, theory (Carroll, 1993) suggests that there is an overarching general factor that is responsible for the intercorrelations between these three first-order factors (right panel of Figure 17.9), as demonstrated by moderate interfactor correlations (.26 to .39).

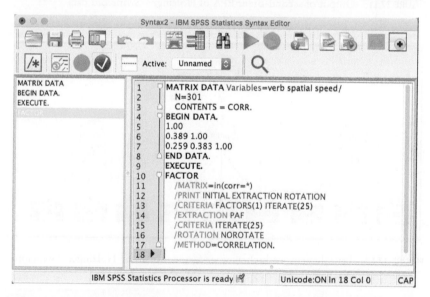

Pattern Matrix[a]			
	Factor		
	1	2	3
sencomp	.893	-.076	.008
paracomp	.849	.008	.006
wordmean	.804	.075	-.016
lozenges	-.106	.706	.003
visper	.160	.605	.018
cubes	.012	.538	-.139
speedadd	.045	-.233	.764
speeddot	-.050	.057	.712
speedcap	.003	.346	.465

Extraction Method: Principal Axis Factoring.
Rotation Method: Promax with Kaiser Normalization.
a. Rotation converged in 5 iterations.

Structure Matrix			
	Factor		
	1	2	3
sencomp	.865	.274	.209
paracomp	.853	.340	.229
wordmean	.829	.382	.220
visper	.399	.674	.291
lozenges	.169	.666	.246
cubes	.185	.489	.070
speeddot	.156	.310	.721
speedadd	.153	.078	.687
speedcap	.258	.525	.598

Extraction Method: Principal Axis Factoring.
Rotation Method: Promax with Kaiser Normalization.

Factor Correlation Matrix			
Factor	1	2	3
1	1.000	.389	.259
2	.389	1.000	.383
3	.259	.383	1.000

Extraction Method: Principal Axis Factoring.
Rotation Method: Promax with Kaiser Normalization.

FIGURE 17.9   Pattern, structure, and factor correlation matrices for Holzinger–Swineford data

A higher-order EFA can be accomplished by entering the interfactor correlation matrix into a syntax command file and then conducting an EFA on that factor intercorrelation matrix. Figure 17.10 uses syntax command code in a slightly different format than was illustrated in Figure 4.5 to import the correlation matrix. Note that the interfactor correlations have been entered on lines 5–7 of this code.

```
MATRIX DATA Variables=verb spatial speed/
   N=301
   CONTENTS = CORR.
BEGIN DATA.
1.00
0.389 1.00
0.259 0.383 1.00
END DATA.
EXECUTE.
FACTOR
   /MATRIX=in(corr=*)
   /PRINT INITIAL EXTRACTION ROTATION
   /CRITERIA FACTORS(1) ITERATE(25)
   /EXTRACTION PAF
   /CRITERIA ITERATE(25)
   /ROTATION NOROTATE
   /METHOD=CORRELATION.
```

FIGURE 17.10   Syntax window command code for second-order factor of Holzinger–Swineford data

Figure 17.11 reveals that the higher-order factor accounts for 36.4% of the variance, with each first-order factor loading on the general factor at high levels (.51 to .76).

Total Variance Explained

Factor	Initial Eigenvalues			Extraction Sums of Squared Loadings		
	Total	% of Variance	Cumulative %	Total	% of Variance	Cumulative %
1	1.691	56.351	56.351	1.091	36.372	36.372
2	.741	24.702	81.053			
3	.568	18.947	100.000			

Extraction Method: Principal Axis Factoring.

Factor Matrix

	Factor 1
verb	.514
spatial	.755
speed	.506

Extraction Method: Principal Axis Factoring.

a. 1 factors extracted. 20 iterations required.

FIGURE 17.11   Output of second-order EFA of Holzinger–Swineford data

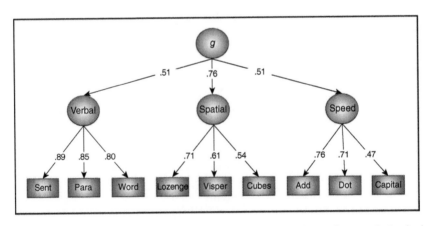

FIGURE 17.12   Path diagram of higher-order factor model for Holzinger–Swineford data

These two analyses can be summarized in a path diagram that displays both first- and second-order loadings (Figure 17.12). This model is conceptually more complicated than a first-order model because each measured variable is influenced by two factors, one of them far removed from the measured variables and thus more abstract and difficult to understand (Hair et al., 2019). Thompson

(2004) suggested the analogy of a mountain range: first-order factors provide a close-up view that focuses on the details of the valleys and the peaks, whereas the second-order factors are like looking at the mountains at a great distance, seeing them as constituents of a mountain range. Alternatively, first- and second-order factors might be compared to viewing a mountain range through a camera's telephoto and wide-angle lenses, respectively (McClain, 1996). These "perspectives complement each other, and each is needed to see patterns at a given level of specificity versus generality" (Thompson, 2004, p. 73).

The primary problem with higher-order models is interpretation because the first-order factor loadings represent two sources of variance (from both the general factor and the group factor). Thus, the relationship between a second-order factor and a measured variable is fully mediated by the first-order factor. The researcher must, therefore, provide a theoretical justification for the full mediation implied by the higher-order model (Gignac, 2008) and must consider the multiple sources of variance when interpreting the factors and measured variables.

Schmid–Leiman Transformation of Higher-Order Models

"Factors are abstractions of measured variables. Second-order factors, then, are abstractions of abstractions even more removed from the measured variables. Somehow, we would like to interpret the second-order factors in terms of the measured variables, rather than as a manifestation of the factors of the measured variables" (Thompson, 2004, p. 74). It is possible to disentangle the variance due to general and group factors and identify the effect of a second-order factor on a measured variable by multiplying the path coefficients (e.g., .51 x .89 = .45; .51 x .85 = .43, etc.). A more elegant solution was provided by Schmid and Leiman (1957), who demonstrated that a higher-order model could be transformed into "orthogonal sources of variance: (1) variance shared between the higher-order general factor and the observed variables; and (2) variance shared between the first-order factors and the respective observed variables specified to load upon them" (Gignac, 2007, p. 40). Orthogonal (uncorrelated) factors are conceptually simpler to interpret because they are independent sources of variance (Carroll, 1983).

Two advantages of the Schmid–Leiman transformation (S–L) are "the calculation of direct relations between higher-order factors and primary variables, and the provision of information about the independent contribution of factors of different levels to variables" (Wolff & Preising, 2005, p. 48). The S–L transformation was extensively employed by Carroll (1993) and has been recommended by other methodologists (Cattell, 1978; Gignac, 2007; Gorsuch, 1983; Humphreys, 1982; Lubinski & Dawis, 1992; McClain, 1996; Thompson, 2004).

The S–L transformation is not included in SPSS. However, Wolff and Preising (2005) published syntax command code to accomplish that transformation that can be downloaded from https://link.springer.com/article/10.3758/

BF03206397. Among the supplementary material on that site is a file labeled "2_ level_SLS .sps" that contains the appropriate command code. Open that syntax file in SPSS and enter the complete first-order pattern matrix, second-order loadings, variable names, and factor names, as demonstrated in Figure 17.13. When completed, select ***Run > All*** to execute that S–L command code.

SPSS automatically places the S–L output into an **Output Viewer** window (Figure 17.14). It is important that the output be checked to ensure that no errors occurred during the entry of pattern coefficients. In Figure 17.14, "h" and "H" indicate communality. For example, the communality of the sentence comprehension variable was .754. Of that amount, .165 was contributed by the general factor and .589 by the verbal ability group factor. On average, the general factor accounted for 34% of the common variance in the measured variables. Gorsuch (1983) suggested that a general factor that accounted for ≥ 40% of the variance would be of interest, but "if the highest-order factors only count for 2% or 3% of the variance, then their impact is negligible and they will be of only limited interest" (p. 253). In this case, the extraction of a general factor appears to be justified.

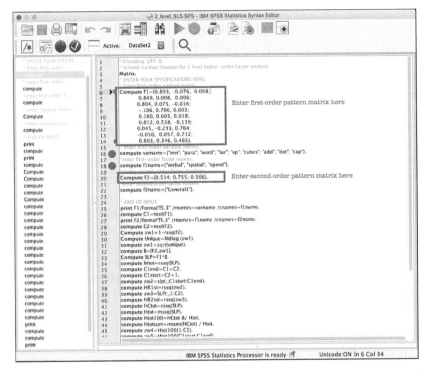

FIGURE 17.13 Syntax window command code for Schmid–Leiman transformation of higher-order model

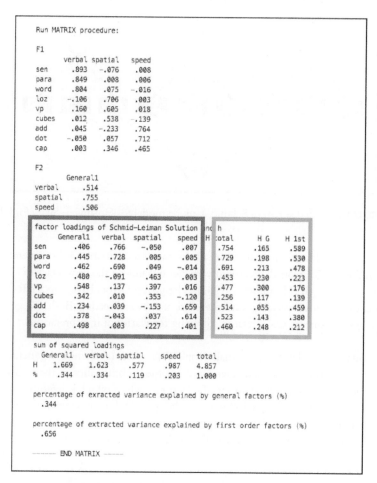

```
Run MATRIX procedure:

F1
         verbal spatial   speed
sen       .893   -.076    .008
para      .849    .008    .006
word      .804    .075   -.016
loz      -.106    .706    .003
vp        .160    .605    .018
cubes     .012    .538   -.139
add       .045   -.233    .764
dot      -.050    .057    .712
cap       .003    .346    .465

F2
         General1
verbal     .514
spatial    .755
speed      .506

factor loadings of Schmid-Leiman Solution  nc h
         General1 verbal spatial speed  H total    H G    H 1st
sen       .406    .766   -.050   .007    .754    .165    .589
para      .445    .728    .005   .005    .729    .198    .530
word      .462    .690    .049  -.014    .691    .213    .478
loz       .480   -.091    .463   .003    .453    .230    .223
vp        .548    .137    .397   .016    .477    .300    .176
cubes     .342    .010    .353  -.120    .256    .117    .139
add       .234    .039   -.153   .659    .514    .055    .459
dot       .378   -.043    .037   .614    .523    .143    .380
cap       .498    .003    .227   .401    .460    .248    .212

sum of squared loadings
      General1 verbal spatial  speed   total
H     1.669   1.623   .577    .987   4.857
%      .344    .334   .119    .203   1.000

percentage of exracted variance explained by general factors (%)
   .344

percentage of extracted variance explained by first order factors (%)
   .656

------ END MATRIX ------
```

FIGURE 17.14 Schmid–Leiman output for higher-order model of Holzinger–Swineford data

Alternatively, a standalone computer program named MacOrtho that computes the S–L transformation can be downloaded from http://edpsychassociates.com/Watkins3.html. That program also requires that the first-order pattern matrix, second-order loadings, variable names, and factor names be entered.

Placing these factor loadings into a path diagram, as in Figure 17.15, visually portrays the orthogonal relationships of group and general factors to the measured variables.

Bifactor Models

Holzinger and Swineford (1937) proposed the bifactor model where each observed variable depends on two factors: a general factor and a smaller group

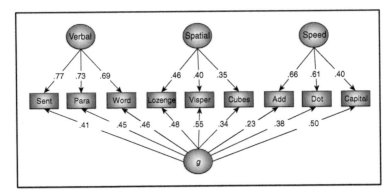

FIGURE 17.15 Path diagram of Schmid–Leiman model for Holzinger–Swineford data

factor characterizing a specific subset of the measured variables. The general factor has direct effects on all measured variables but not on the group factors. Thus, it has wide breadth (Humphreys, 1982). The group factors have direct effects on subsets of measured variables and therefore narrower breadth. Both the general and group factors are uncorrelated, allowing for clarity of interpretation.

> Bifactor models are potentially applicable when (a) there is a general factor that is hypothesized to account for the commonality of the items; (b) there are multiple domain specific factors, each of which is hypothesized to account for the unique influence of the specific domain over and above the general factor; and (c) researchers may be interested in the domain specific factors as well as the common factor that is of focal interest.
>
> *(Chen et al., 2006, p. 190)*

Reise (2012) argued that a bifactor model, "which views the variance in trait indicators as being influenced by both general and group sources of variance, provides a strong foundation for understanding psychological constructs and their measurement" (p. 692).

Bifactor models appear identical to Schmid–Leiman transformed models when illustrated in a path diagram. However, bifactor models are not mathematically equivalent to the S–L transformation of higher-order models (Chen et al., 2006). Rather, the S–L transformed higher-order model includes mediating variables and proportionality constraints that may bias the estimation of population values (Mansolf & Reise, 2016; Reise et al., 2010). Accordingly, Mansolf and Reise (2016) said to "treat this method as a descriptive technique only, and not as an estimator of a bifactor structure in the population" (p. 714).

Nevertheless, exploratory bifactor models have typically been estimated by S–L transformations because software to compute an exploratory bifactor analysis was not readily available (Reise, 2012). That deficiency was remedied by Jennrich and Bentler (2011), who explicated the mathematics of an exploratory bifactor rotation that was subsequently included in the *psych* package within the **R** (R Core Team, 2020) statistical system. It is not included in SPSS.

There has been little research on the properties of Jennrich and Bentler's (2011) exploratory bifactor rotation method, but Mansolf and Reise (2015, 2016) reported that it produced biased parameter estimates in some conditions and was vulnerable to local minima (i.e., erroneous parameter estimates). More recently, it was found to be sensitive to variables with small factor loadings and relatively large cross-loadings (Dombrowski et al., 2019) and less accurate than Schmid–Leiman transformations in recovering population structures (Giordano & Waller, 2020). Given these results, exploratory bifactor analysis should be employed with care. More research is needed to clarify the strengths and weaknesses of exploratory bifactor analysis rotations (Lorenzo-Seva & Ferrando, 2019). Before employing higher-order or bifactor models, the user should consult Brunner et al. (2012), Chen et al. (2006), Mansolf and Reise (2016), and Reise (2012).

Alternative Measures of Reliability

To this point, reliability estimation has consisted of coefficient alpha (Cronbach, 1951). Although popular, most applications of coefficient alpha have ignored its statistical assumptions, resulting in biased estimates of reliability (Watkins, 2017). Model-based reliability estimates have been proposed as alternatives to alpha that make fewer and more realistic assumptions (Reise, 2012). Especially useful are the omega (ω) family of coefficients described by McDonald (1999). Based on an orthogonal factor model, these indices allow a judgment of the relative strength of the general factor and its influence on derived scale scores as well as the viability of global and subscale domains (Rodriguez et al., 2016; Zinbarg et al., 2005). A tutorial on model-based estimates of reliability was provided by Watkins (2017).

SPSS does not contains routines for computing omega reliability estimates but command code was provided by Hayes and Coutts (2020) that can be downloaded from www.afhayes.com. Ensure that a data file is in the **Data Editor** window and then open their omega .sps syntax file (*File > Open > Syntax > omega .sps*). When that **Syntax** window opens, select the *Run > All* menu option without making any changes to the syntax command code.

Next, open a new **Syntax Editor** window and enter the omega code for each factor, as in Figure 17.16. Coefficient alpha coefficients (*Analyze > Scale > Reliability Analysis*) for these three factors were also computed and displayed in Figure 17.16. In agreement with Hayes and Coutts (2020), alpha and omega "typically produce similar estimates of reliability when applied to real data" (p. 20).

Several omega variants can be computed to describe how precisely "total and subscale scores reflect their intended constructs" and determine "whether subscale scores provide unique information above and beyond the total score" (Rodriguez et al., 2016, p. 223). The most general omega coefficient is omega total (ω), "an

FIGURE 17.16 Omega reliability command code and output for Holzinger–Swineford data

estimate of the proportion of variance in the unit-weighted total score attributable to all sources of common variance" (Rodriguez et al., 2016, p. 224). Omega total is essentially a model-based substitute for alpha, as displayed in Figure 17.16. In this case, the omega total estimates for the group factor scores were .886, .633, and .696, respectively. Reliability of the verbal scale is acceptable, given the group nature of this research but might be too unstable for making important decisions about individuals (DeVellis, 2017). Neither the spatial nor the speed scales were sufficiently reliable for even group research. However, the amalgam of general and group factor variance reflected by ω total does not allow the contributions of general and group factor variance to be disentangled.

A second omega variant, called omega hierarchical (ω^h), reflects the proportion of systematic variance in a unit-weighted score that can be attributed to the

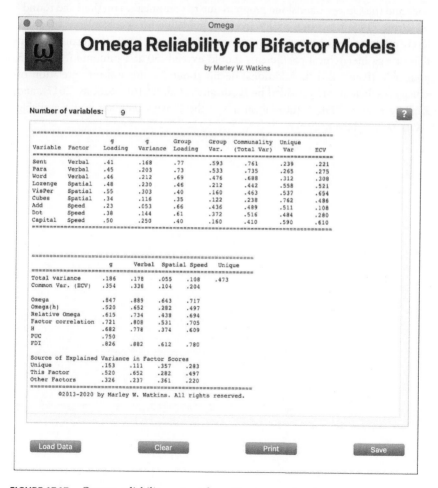

FIGURE 17.17 Omega reliability output from *Omega* program

general factor alone. A third omega variant is called omega hierarchical subscale (ω^{hs}), which indicates the proportion of variance in the subscale score that is accounted for by its intended group factor to the total variance of that subscale score and indexes the reliable variance associated with that subscale after controlling for the effects of the general factor.

SPSS does not include an option to calculate ω^h nor ω^{hs}, but ω^h is promised for version 27.0.1. When available, that reliability estimate can be implemented via the *Analyze > Scale > Reliability Analysis > Model: Omega* menu options. Alternatively, a standalone program called Omega can be downloaded from http://edpsychassociates.com/Watkins3.html to compute those metrics (Figure 17.17). The first- and second-order loadings in Figure 17.15 serve as input to the Omega program.

There are some differences in the values produced by the Omega command code and the Omega standalone program due to computation method and round-off error. There is no universally accepted guideline for acceptable or adequate levels of omega reliability for clinical decisions, but it has been recommended that omega hierarchical coefficients should exceed .50 at a minimum, with .75 preferable (Reise, 2012). Additional details about the use and interpretation of omega coefficients are provided by Rodriguez et al. (2016), Watkins (2017), and Zinbarg et al. (2005). A tutorial on use of the Omega program is also available (Watkins & Canivez, 2021).

18

EXPLORATORY VERSUS CONFIRMATORY FACTOR ANALYSIS

Exploratory (EFA) and confirmatory factor analysis (CFA) are both based on the common factor model, and both attempt to reproduce the correlations among a set of measured variables with a smaller set of latent variables (Brown, 2015). However, the two methods differ in the measurement model: EFA allows all factors to relate to all measured variables, whereas CFA restricts relationships between factors and measured variables to those specified beforehand by the analyst. Consequently, EFA is sometimes called unrestricted factor analysis and CFA is called restricted factor analysis (Widaman, 2012).

EFA and CFA models are symbolized by the path diagrams in Figure 18.1. In the EFA model, every variable loads onto every factor. The researcher must apply the principle of simple structure and specify the magnitude of factor loadings required for salience to remove the presumably trivial variable–factor relationships from consideration. In CFA, the researcher must specify beforehand the number of factors, how the factors relate to each other, and which variables load onto which factor. In a typical CFA (as depicted in Figure 18.1), the loadings of variables V1–V3 onto factor 2 and those of variables V4–V6 onto factor 1 are prespecified to be zero and are therefore omitted from the path diagram. Although other patterns are possible, this independent clusters model (ICM) is most common (each variable is allowed to load onto one factor, and its loadings on all other factors are constrained to zero). This a priori specification of simple structure removes the need for factor rotation in CFA.

Many methodologists believe that "the purpose of EFA is typically to identify the latent constructs or to generate hypotheses about their possible structures, whereas the purpose of CFA is to evaluate hypothesized structures of the latent constructs and/or to develop a better understanding of such structures" (Bandalos & Finney, 2019, p. 98). That is, EFA generates models, whereas CFA

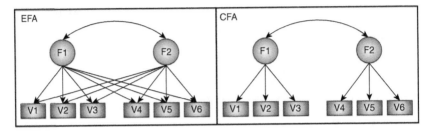

FIGURE 18.1 Simplified path diagrams of EFA and CFA models

tests models (Matsunaga, 2010; Norman & Streiner, 2014). Obviously, any CFA model's veracity depends on the accuracy and thoroughness of its prespecified parameters. As judged by Carroll (1993):

> it is highly desirable, or perhaps mandatory, that the hypotheses to be tested have excellent logical or psychological support in some theory of individual differences and their measurements, or in prior analyses of datasets other than the one on which the hypotheses are to be tested.
>
> *(p. 82)*

Some methodologists consider EFA to be inferior to CFA because EFA "tends to be guided by ad hoc rules and intuition, whereas confirmatory factor analysis is imbued with robust dual tests for both parameters (factor loadings) and the quality of the factor" (Ramlall, 2017, p. 5). Likewise, Little et al. (2017) disparaged EFA, asserting that "EFA is a data-driven enterprise that presents too many misguiding temptations for misunderstanding the nature of the construct of interest. Using CFA with careful and skillful scrutiny of all indicated modifications will reveal the structure of a scale that will retain optimal validity" (p. 127).

CFA Model Fit

Thus, it is often claimed that CFA provides an objective test of factor models (Hoyle, 2000; Ramlall, 2017). Maximum likelihood estimation is typically employed in CFA (Russell, 2002), and CFA models are commonly assessed with a statistical test of overall model fit, the chi-square goodness of fit, that assesses the discrepancy between the observed relationship among the measured variables versus the relationship implied by the prespecified model. The chi-square value will be statistically non-significant if the two are identical but statistically significant if the model and actual data relationships differ (Barrett, 2007). Unfortunately, the chi-square test is sensitive to sample size: large samples may produce statistically significant chi-square values, even when the difference between actual and model implied relationships is trivial and small sample sizes may fail to distinguish between quite discrepant models (Kline, 1994).

In reality, most CFA models produce statistically significant chi-square values, so common practice is to ignore that result and rely on approximate fit indices that measure some aspect of closeness of fit of the actual and implied models (Brown, 2015; Browne, 2001; Hancock & Schoonen, 2015; Hoyle, 2000; Hurley et al., 1997; Maydeu-Olivares, 2017; Ropovik, 2015; Saris et al., 2009). Essentially, this practice acknowledges that the model is not an exact representation of reality but that it might be useful if it sufficiently corresponds to the real world and is not entirely incorrect (MacCallum, 2003). Thus, the idea that CFA provides an objective test of models is both true and false: true that the chi-square test of exact fit is conducted but false that the model is disconfirmed by that test in typical practice (Hurley et al., 1997; Ropovik, 2015). Rather, approximate fit indices are used to subjectively judge that a model is close enough to reality to be useful.

Unfortunately, there is no clear empirical demarcation to the quantification of "close enough" (Berk, 2011). Dozens of approximate-fit indices have been developed to measure a model's "closeness to reality," but many "are subjective in nature or do not follow known statistical distributions" (DiStefano, 2016, p. 167). In practice, fit indices may conflict (i.e., one signaling close fit and another poor fit); thus, "researchers are likely to be confused and potentially make incorrect research conclusions" (Lai & Green, 2016, p. 220). Statistical simulations have been conducted to develop "rules of thumb" for optimal cut-points of approximate fit indices (e.g., Hu & Bentler, 1999), but each fit index is differentially sensitive to estimation method, sample size, distributional characteristics, model size, and model misspecification (Clark & Bowles, 2018; Preacher & Merkle, 2012; Saris et al., 2009; Savalei, 2012; Shi & Maydeu-Olivares, 2020; Tomarken & Waller, 2003) with the result that "cutoff values for fit indices, confidence intervals for model fit/misfit, and power analysis based on fit indices are open to question" (Yuan, 2005, p. 142). As summarized by Greiff and Heene (2017), "there are no golden rules for cutoff values, there are only misleading ones" (p. 315).

Approximate-fit indices are not sensitive in detecting the correct number of factors (Heene et al., 2011), especially with ordinal data (Garrido et al., 2016; Themessl-Huber, 2014), nor do they uniquely identify correctly specified models. This was vividly illustrated by Orcan (2018), who simulated a simple model with two correlated factors, each with four measured variables. CFA fit indices indicated good fit for the correct model as well as for two purposively misspecified models. In common practice, "if a goodness-of-fit index meets the recommended cutoff values, the model is retained and used as if it were correctly specified . . . [and] inferences on the model parameters are made as if the model were correct, when in fact, it is mis-specified" (Maydeu-Olivares, 2017, pp. 538–539). By relying on goodness of fit, "essentially unidimensional measures might require multidimensional specifications for the degree of fit to be acceptable. And the resulting solution generally consists of minor, ill-defined factors that yield poor factor score estimates" (Ferrando et al., 2019, p. 124).

Browne and Cudeck (1993) reminded researchers that "fit indices should not be regarded as measures of usefulness of a model. They contain some information about the lack of fit of a model, but none about plausibility" (p. 157). Even worse, subjectivity in model selection is enhanced by the availability of numerous fit indices, each with different cut-points (Hayduk, 2014; Heene et al., 2011; McCoach et al., 2013; McDonald, 2010). The probability that "close enough" models are scientifically useful is usually neglected, but it is also unlikely, according to basic principles of logic and science (Meehl, 2006; Platt, 1964; Popper, 2002; Roberts & Pashler, 2000; Ropovik, 2015; Wasserstein & Lazar, 2016).

CFA Model Respecification

If a model with acceptable fit cannot be found among the candidate models, model modifications or respecifications are often guided by "modification indices" produced by the CFA software (MacCallum, 2003; Marsh et al., 2009; Maydeu-Olivares, 2017; McCoach et al., 2013; Tarka, 2018). Modification indices statistically approximate how much the chi-square goodness of fit test and accompanying approximate fit indices might improve if a particular prespecified fixed parameter (e.g., factor loading, interfactor correlation) were allowed to be estimated rather than fixed (Brown, 2015). According to Brown (2015), model modifications "should only be pursued if they can be justified on empirical or conceptual grounds" (Brown, 2013, p. 265). However, "if a model modification is highly interpretable, then why was it not represented in the initial model?" (MacCallum et al., 1992, p. 492). In fact, it does not seem difficult for researchers to find theoretical justifications for most respecifications (Armstrong & Soelberg, 1968; Steiger, 1990). Additionally, respecifications tend not to generalize to new samples nor to the population (Bandalos & Finney, 2019; Kline, 2012, 2013; MacCallum et al., 1992), especially when there are fewer than 1,200 participants in the sample (Hutchinson, 1998). This respecification procedure has been called "a dangerous practice because it capitalizes on chance. . . . [N]one of the significance tests nor the goodness-of-fit measures take this capitalization into account" (Gorsuch, 2003, p. 151). Almost identical warnings have been sounded by other methodologists (Cliff, 1983; Cribbie, 2000; Jebb et al., 2017; McArdle, 2011; Sass & Schmitt, 2010; Tomarken & Waller, 2003). If not disclosed, respecification based on examination of the data is unethical and can impede scientific progress (Breckler, 1990; Murphy & Aguinis, 2019; Rubin, 2017; Simmons et al., 2011).

Box (1976) provided cogent scientific guidance more than 40 years ago: "Since all models are wrong the scientist cannot obtain a 'correct' one by excessive elaboration. On the contrary following William of Occam he should seek an economical description of natural phenomena. . . . [O]verelaboration and overparameterization is often the mark of mediocrity" (p. 792). Therefore, even if justified by theory, respecification means that the analysis has become exploratory rather than confirmatory (Brown, 2015; Browne, 2001; Gorsuch, 1997;

Hancock & Schoonen, 2015; Ropovik, 2015; Schmitt, 2011; Tarka, 2018) and "has the worst of both exploratory and confirmatory factor analysis and cannot be recommended" (Gorsuch, 1988, p. 235). Accordingly, "it is better to identify potential problems [via EFA] prior to fitting a confirmatory model than it is to fit a confirmatory model, find problems in fit, and try to diagnose (and 'fix') them" (Reise et al., 2018, p. 699).

CFA Model Assumptions

Researchers often overlook these complexities (Hayduk, 2014; Hoyle, 2000; Ramlall, 2017; Schmitt et al., 2018). Additionally, they tend to ignore the statistical assumptions necessary for unbiased CFA results (Kline, 2012), and "the sheer technical complexity of the [CFA] method tends to overwhelm critical judgement" (Freedman, 1987, p. 102). Kline (2012) reported that several assumptions must be considered in CFA. These include attentiveness to the direction of causal influence from factor to measured variables and the absence of other plausible explanations.

At the most basic level, it is assumed that the model is correctly specified (DiStefano, 2016; Kline, 2012). Three primary model specifications are assumed: (a) the correct number of factors, (b) the correct pattern of factor loadings, and (c) the absence of unmodeled subfactors (Hoyle, 2000). Assumptions about the data in CFA include those assumptions that underlie use of maximum likelihood estimation applied to the covariance, rather than the correlation, matrix (Brown, 2013; Kline, 2012), specifically, "linearity, independent observations, sufficiently large sample size, multivariate normality of indicators, and a correctly specified model" (DiStefano, 2016, p. 167). Thus, CFA results will be unbiased if the measured variables are multivariate normally distributed, the number of participants is sufficiently large, and the model is correctly specified (DiStefano, 2016). However, correct model specification is unlikely in many practical situations (Bandalos, 2018; DiStefano, 2016; Hurley et al., 1997; Kline, 2012; Orcan, 2018; Tomarken & Waller, 2003, 2005). In fact, CFA has been found to be especially prone to overfactoring with ordinal data (Garrido et al., 2011, 2016; van der Eijk & Rose, 2015; Xia & Yang, 2019). Additionally, data in the social sciences are rarely multivariate normally distributed (Cain et al., 2017), and "all inferences based on [misspecified models] are suspect" (Maydeu-Olivares, 2017, p. 533); consequently, "the interpretation of results in the typical [CFA] may be unwarranted" (Kline, 2012, p. 111).

The limitations of CFA have become especially apparent to researchers who investigate the structure of psychological instruments (Hoelzle & Meyer, 2013; Hopwood & Donnellan, 2010; Marsh et al., 2009). The typical independent clusters model (ICM) approach appears to be too restrictive because test items are often ordinal and exhibit small cross-loadings on several factors (Hurley et al., 1997; Schmitt, 2011). Thus, some items may manifest localized weak discriminant validity (i.e., equivalent loadings on multiple factors) that is hidden within the overall CFA model fit. In an EFA, these small cross-loadings are assumed to be indicators of ill-defined factors of no substantive interest and are therefore ignored. However, constraining these minor loadings to zero in CFA causes a degradation of model fit and systematic inflation of the interfactor correlations. For example, Marsh et al. (2009) found a median correlation of .34 among factors in an exploratory analysis that increased to .72 in a CFA. These artificially inflated factor correlations may negatively impact subsequent efforts to identify unique external correlates of the factors (Molina et al., 2020). As summarized by Schmitt et al. (2018), violation of the ICM assumption can lead to "rather arbitrary modifications, unrealistic factor loadings, and elevated interfactor correlations" (p. 349). However, an EFA model will be unaffected by these conditions. See Morin et al. (2020) for an in-depth discussion of this issue.

Exploratory Use of CFA

Reliance on approximate fit indices, post-hoc modification of models based on data characteristics, and violation of statistical assumptions have created a situation where CFA is often used in an exploratory manner (Bandalos & Finney, 2019; Browne, 2001; Cliff, 1983; DiStefano, 2016; Gerbing & Hamilton, 1996; Gorsuch, 1988; Hancock & Schoonen, 2015; Heene et al., 2011; Kline, 2012; MacCallum et al., 1992; Maydeu-Olivares, 2017; Tomarken & Waller, 2003, 2005). Some methodologists have suggested that CFA is superior to EFA because it provides a statistical test of models and its decisions are more objective (Little et al., 2017; Ramlall, 2017). However, exploratory use of CFA leaves researchers vulnerable to confirmatory bias (MacCallum & Austin, 2000; Roberts & Pashler, 2000). That is, they may "persevere by revising procedures until obtaining a theory-predicted result" (Greenwald et al., 1986). As previously described, statistical tests in CFA are conducted but often ignored (Hayduk, 2014). Likewise, the decision steps in CFA are not nearly as objective as claimed: "with all its breadth and versatility come many opportunities for misuse" (Hancock & Schoonen, 2015, p. 175). For example, DiStefano and Hess (2005) reviewed published CFA studies and found that more than 50% provided inadequate theoretical support for the tested models, failed to consider statistical assumptions of CFA, and appeared to select approximate fix indices and their thresholds opportunistically. Literature reviews have also found that published CFA studies often fail to report critical information such as method of estimation, type of matrix analyzed, justification of sample size, and distributional characteristics of the data (MacCallum & Austin, 2000; Ropovik, 2015; Russell, 2002).

EFA Versus CFA

Given the increased popularity of CFA methods and the widespread belief that EFA is not acceptable, researchers may be criticized by journal editors for choosing EFA over CFA (Haig, 2018; Hayduk, 2014; Hurley et al., 1997; Marsh et al., 2009). However, the differences between EFA and CFA are not as distinct as sometimes claimed (Child, 2006; Fabrigar & Wegener, 2012; Hoelzle & Meyer, 2013; Hoyle, 2000). EFA and CFA are both valuable statistical tools for scientific inquiry (Gorsuch, 1988). Haig (2018) discussed the role of factor analysis in scientific method and argued that "science is as much concerned with theory generation as it is with theory testing" (p. 84) and that "EFA has a legitimate, and important, role as a method of theory generation, and that EFA and CFA should be viewed as complementary, not competing, methods of common factor analysis" (p. 83). Clark and Bowles (2018) noted that to the extent that EFA and CFA "methods converge on a conceptually coherent solution, it is possible to have greater confidence in that solution, even if there are documented flaws with any one method" (p. 555). Other methodologists have also suggested that EFA can be productively used in conjunction with CFA (Bandalos & Finney, 2019; Carroll, 1995a; DeVellis, 2017; Fabrigar et al., 1999; Gerbing & Hamilton, 1996; Goldberg & Velicer, 2006; Gorsuch, 2003; Hurley et al., 1997; Jebb et al., 2017; Morin et al., 2016; Nesselroade, 1994; Schmitt, 2011; Schmitt et al., 2018; Selbom & Tellegen, 2019; Wegener & Fabrigar, 2000).

In summary, both EFA and CFA require thoughtful and evidence-based methodological decisions that offer many opportunities for error (Bandalos & Boehm-Kaufman, 2009; Fabrigar et al., 1999; Hancock & Schoonen, 2015; Hurley et al., 1997; McCoach et al., 2013; Steiger, 2001; Stewart, 2001; Tarka, 2018; Widaman, 2012). The users of CFA, in particular, are often unaware of the limitations of that methodology (Brannick, 1995; DiStefano & Hess, 2005; Hayduk, 2014; Kline, 2000, 2012; Ropovik, 2015; Schmitt et al., 2018), possess misconceptions about its application (MacCallum & Austin, 2000), and "tend to overstate both the strength and certainty of [its] conclusions" (Tomarken & Waller, 2005, p. 48). It appears that many users of CFA are unaware that the many possible choices for each decision lead to a "garden of forking paths" (Gelman & Loken, 2014, p. 460), resulting in findings that do not replicate. Hussey and Hughes (2020) referred to this practice as v-hacking: "selectively choosing and reporting a combination of metrics, including their implementations and cutoffs, and taking advantage of other degrees of experimenter freedom so as to improve the apparent validity of measures" (p. 180).

Accordingly, the use of EFA may be preferable when: (a) "a strong empirical or conceptual foundation to guide the specification and evaluation of factor model" (Brown, 2013, p. 258) is missing; (b) the measured variables are not multivariate normally distributed (Lei & Wu, 2012); or (c) the model is incorrectly specified (Browne, 2001). Additionally, categorical measured variables, especially test items, may be more productively analyzed with EFA (Ferrando & Lorenzo-Seva, 2000; Schumacker & Lomax, 2004), especially when the number of factors is in doubt because Garrido et al. (2016) demonstrated that parallel analysis was more accurate than fit indices in determining the number of factors. Likewise, EFA may be more appropriate when items fail to meet the assumption of the independent clusters model (Marsh et al., 2009; Molina et al., 2020). EFA may also be superior to the post-hoc model respecification of poor-fitting CFA models (Bandalos & Finney, 2019; Browne, 2001; Flora & Flake, 2017; Gorsuch, 1997; Schmitt, 2011; Schmitt et al., 2018; Warne & Burningham, 2019; Wegener & Fabrigar, 2000). In contrast, CFA may be a more appropriate choice when: (a) strong conceptual and empirical foundations are available for specification of a model (Orcan, 2018; Thompson, 2004); (b) the purpose is to test the invariance of a factor model across multiple groups (Osborne et al., 2007); or (c) direct estimation of a bifactor model is desired (Mansolf & Reise, 2015, 2016). Therefore, researchers should "not abandon EFA for the more recently developed confirmatory methods, but develop a heuristic strategy that builds on the comparative strengths of the two techniques" (Gerbing & Hamilton, 1996, p. 63).

Interestingly, similar issues have been explored in the past but within different contexts. Tukey (1980) asserted that "neither exploratory nor confirmatory is sufficient alone" (p. 23), and Box (1976) noted that science can only progress via "a motivated *iteration* between theory and practice" (p. 791). Thus, some facts lead to a tentative theory and then deductions from that tentative theory are found to be discrepant with other facts, which, in turn, generates a modified theory. This abductive, deductive, and inductive cycle continues almost indefinitely as science progresses (Haig, 2018; Mulaik, 2018; Rummel, 1967). However, there are two impediments to this progress described by Box (1976) as *cookbookery* and *mathematistry*. "The symptoms of the former are a tendency to force all problems into the molds of one or two routine techniques," whereas mathematistry "is characterized by development of theory for theory's sake" (p. 797). Cookbookery can be recognized by the routine use of a statistical method without consideration of its assumptions, whereas mathematistry can be seen when researchers adopt inappropriate statistical procedures they do not understand. Consequently, the choice of factor analysis method must not degenerate into cookbookery and should not be determined solely by statistical complexity.

19

PRACTICE EXERCISES

Exercise 1

To this point, readers have had the opportunity to conduct best-practice, evidence-based exploratory factor analysis (EFA) with both continuous and categorical datasets. Each EFA has followed a step-by-step process, and each EFA has included SPSS code and output along with a discussion of the relevant principles. This practice dataset is provided as an independent exercise. Readers are encouraged to analyze this dataset and check their results with the sample report provided at the end of this exercise.

Data

The Rmotivate.xlsx dataset can be downloaded as per the Data chapter and imported into the SPSS environment as per the Importing and Saving Data and Results chapter. Remember to check the imported data to ensure that its type and level of measurement are accurate. Alternatively, both Pearson and polychoric correlation matrices are provided in the RmotivateCorr.xlsx file.

Variables Included

The 20 reading motivation items (Figure 19.1) in this dataset were hypothesized to reflect two aspects of reading motivation: reading self-concept (odd items) and value of reading (even items). Each item offered four ordered response options.

No.	Description	No.	Description
1.	My friends think I am	11.	I have trouble with reading
2.	Read a book	12.	Reading well is
3.	Reading skill	13.	I can answer teacher questions
4.	My friends think reading is	14.	I think reading is boring/interesting
5.	Can figure out unknown words	15.	For me, reading is easy/hard
6.	Tell friends about books	16.	Will spend time reading when adult
7.	Understand what I read	17.	I understand reading assignments
8.	People who read are	18.	Would like more reading time
9.	As a reader, I am	19.	When reading aloud
10.	I think libraries are	20.	Would like books as presents

FIGURE 19.1   Description of the variables in the Rmotivate dataset

Participants

The 20 reading motivation items were answered by 500 elementary school students equally distributed across Grades 2–6.

Are the Data Appropriate?

Are data values accurate and plausible? Is there missing data, and if so, how much and how was it handled? Are there outliers that bias the results? Are these data normally distributed? If not, how nonnormal are they? Consequently, what correlation matrix should be employed for the EFA and why?

Is EFA Appropriate?

Why or why not? Be sure to report quantitative evidence to support that decision.

What Model of Factor Analysis Was Employed?

Choose between principal components analysis and common factor analysis. Provide rationale for that choice.

What Factor Extraction Method Was Used?

Specify and provide a rationale for that choice.

How Many Factors Were Retained?

What methods were selected to guide this decision? Provide rationale for the choice of methods.

What Factor Rotation Was Applied?

Provide rationale for the choice of orthogonal or oblique rotation and the specific type of orthogonal or oblique rotation.

Interpretation of Results

Employ a model-selection approach with a priori guidelines for interpretation.

Report Results

Provide sufficient detail to demonstrate that evidence-based decisions were made and the results are professionally competent and reasonable. Follow the step-by-step checklist. Compare your report to the sample report that follows.

Exercise 1 Report

Method

Participants were 500 elementary school students equally distributed across Grades 2–6. Rouquette and Falissard (2011) simulated ordinal scale data and reported that scales with 10 items and 2 factors required at least 350 participants to obtain stable and accurate factor analysis results. Consequently, the current sample size of 500 participants was judged to be adequate.

Given the uncertainty surrounding the structure of this reading motivation scale, exploratory rather than confirmatory factor analysis was employed (Flora, 2018). Common factor analysis was selected over principal components analysis because the goal of this study was to identify the scale's latent structure (Widaman, 2018). Additionally, common factor analysis may produce more accurate estimates of population parameters than does principal components analysis (Widaman, 1993). Principal axis extraction was applied due to its relative tolerance of multivariate nonnormality and its superior recovery of weak factors (Briggs & MacCallum, 2003). Communalities were initially estimated by squared multiple correlations (Flora, 2018). Lozano et al. (2008) conducted a statistical simulation study and found that four response categories, as offered by this reading motivation scale, were minimal to ensure adequate factorial validity with Pearson correlations.

Following the advice of Velicer et al. (2000), minimum average partials (MAP; Velicer, 1976) and parallel analysis (Horn, 1965), supplemented by a visual scree test (Cattell, 1966), were used to determine the number of factors to retain for rotation. For both theoretical and empirical reasons, it was assumed that factors would be correlated (Gorsuch, 1997; Meehl, 1990). Thus, a Promax rotation with a k value of 4 was selected (Tataryn et al., 1999). To ensure both practical (10% variance explained) and statistical significance ($p < .01$), the threshold for salience was set at .32 (Norman & Streiner, 2014).

Some evidence favors overestimating rather than underestimating the number of factors (Wood et al., 1996); therefore, experts suggest that the highest to lowest number of factors be examined until the most interpretable solution is found (Fabrigar et al., 1999; Flora, 2018). Guidelines for model acceptability included: (a) three salient item loadings (pattern coefficients) are necessary to form a factor with the exclusion of complex loadings (Gorsuch, 1997); (b) an internal consistency reliability coefficient (alpha) of at least .80 for each factor because the intended use of this scale is for non-critical decisions about individual students (DeVellis, 2017); (c) no obvious symptoms of model misfit due to overfactoring or underfactoring; and (d) robustness of results across alternative extraction and rotation methods.

Results

There were no obvious illegal or out-of-bounds values, and there was no missing data. Univariate skew and kurtosis values were not extreme (maximum of 2.07 and 3.80, respectively), but Mardia's multivariate kurtosis was large and statistically significant (535.9, $p < .001$).

The Kaiser–Meyer–Olkin (KMO) measure of sampling adequacy (Kaiser, 1974) was acceptable (.93 for the total group of variables and .91 to .94 for each of the measured variables). Bartlett's test of sphericity (1950) statistically rejected the hypothesis that the correlation matrix was an identity matrix (chi-square of 3687.5 with 190 degrees of freedom at $p < .001$). A visual scan of the correlation matrix revealed numerous coefficients $\geq .30$ (Tabachnick & Fidell, 2019). Altogether, these measures indicate that factor analysis is appropriate.

Parallel analysis, MAP, and scree criteria were in agreement that two factors should be extracted for rotation and subsequent interpretation. However, models with three, two, and one factor(s) were sequentially evaluated for acceptability with the aforementioned guidelines. The three-factor model explained 43% of the total variance before rotation, with the first, second, and third factors accounting for 31.4%, 9.3%, and 2.2% of the variance, respectively. The root mean squared residual (RMSR) was .028, and there were no residual coefficients greater than .10. Thus, there was no indication that another factor should be extracted. The third factor was saliently loaded by only two items, and both were complex. This is an indicator of overextraction and suggests that one fewer factor might be more appropriate.

The two-factor model explained 41% of the total variance before rotation. Prior to rotation, the first factor (reading self-concept) accounted for 31% of the total variance, while the second factor (value of reading) accounted for 9% of the total variance. This two-factor model was consistent with the theoretical underpinning of the scale with 10 items loading saliently on a value of reading factor (.42 to .82) and 10 items on a reading self-concept factor (.45 to .80) in a simple structure configuration. The interfactor correlation of .54 was low enough to pose no threat to discriminant validity (Brown, 2015), and the factors exhibited alpha reliability coefficients of .86, 95% CI [.85, .88] for the reading self-concept factor and .87, 95% CI [.85, .88] for the value of reading factor.

The RMSR for the two-factor model was .035, and there was only one residual coefficient greater than .10, suggesting that little residual variance remained after extracting two factors. Essentially, this model appeared to be a close fit to the data (Maydeu-Olivares, 2017).

The one-factor model accounted for 31% of the total variance. All 20 items loaded saliently in the one-factor model, but the RMSR reached an unacceptable level (.098) and 37% of the nonredundant residuals were > .10 (Brown, 2015). This is evidence that two factors collapsed onto one (Fabrigar & Wegener, 2012). Thus, measures of model fit as well as theoretical convergence remove this model from consideration, leaving the two-factor model as the preferred solution.

Similar results were obtained when the extraction method was changed to generalized least squares and the rotation method to oblimin. Given nonnormal categorical data with only four response options, a polychoric correlation matrix was also submitted for analysis and also identified two factors (Flora & Flake, 2017; Mueller & Hancock, 2019). Thus, these results were robust in demonstrating that this reading motivation scale is best described by two factors, reading self-concept and value of reading.

Command code to complete this EFA is provided in Figure 19.2.

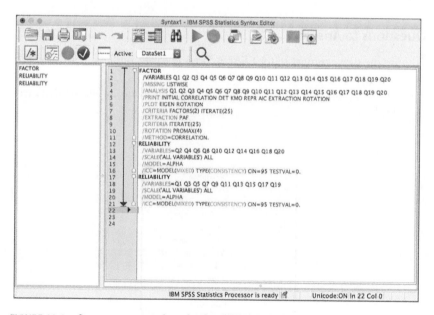

FIGURE 19.2 Syntax command code for EFA with two factors and their alpha reliability

Exercise 2

This fourth dataset (second practice exercise) is also provided for independent practice. Readers are encouraged to analyze this dataset while answering the questions found at the end of this chapter. No report, SPSS command code, nor SPSS output are provided with this practice exercise.

Data

This dataset is also in spreadsheet format and contains 10 variables (Figure 19.3). Each variable is one item from a rating scale designed to tap the symptoms of attention-deficit hyperactivity disorder (ADHD) that was completed by 500 respondents. This data file, labeled "adhd.xlsx," can be imported, as was previously described in the Importing Raw Data section, using the menu commands *File > Import Data > Excel*. Respondents reported the frequency of each item on a four-point Likert scale: 0 (*Never or Rarely*), 1 (*Sometimes*), 2 (*Often*), and 3 (*Very Often*). Thus, the data are ordered and not continuous.

These 10 items are hypothesized to reflect two behavioral aspects of ADHD: attention problems and over-activity/impulsivity problems. It was assumed that the first five items tap the attention problems dimension of ADHD, while the final five items tap over-activity/impulsivity. Scales with more items have typically found internal consistency reliability coefficients of around .85 to .90 for these factors (Nichols et al., 2017).

Questions to Answer

1. Are the data appropriate for EFA? Address linearity, outliers, normality, and missing data.
2. Is EFA appropriate? Verify with KMO sampling adequacy and Bartlett's test of sphericity.

Item	Description
instruct	Follow instructions
effort	Sustain mental effort
organize	Organization problems
forget	Forgetful
attention	Sustain attention
go	Constantly on the go
talks	Talk excessively
fidgets	Fidget
turns	Difficulty waiting turn
runs	Runs about

FIGURE 19.3 Description of the variables in the ADHD dataset

3. What correlation matrix should be used? See Figure 2.7 for both Pearson and polychoric matrices.
4. What factor analysis model is appropriate? Justify the choice of principal components or common factor models.
5. What factor extraction method is appropriate? Detail the method of factor extraction and the correlation matrix employed.
6. How many factors to retain? Describe and justify the selection criteria.
7. What factor rotation method is appropriate? Justify the rotation method (orthogonal or oblique) and type (varimax, promax, oblimin, etc.).
8. Interpret each model using a priori guidelines for acceptability.
9. Report the results of each decision step.

REFERENCES AND RESOURCES

Aiken, L. S., West, S. G., & Millsap, R. E. (2008). Doctoral training in statistics, measurement, and methodology in psychology. *American Psychologist, 63*(1), 32–50. https://doi.org/10.1037/0003-066X.63.1.32

Anderson, S. F. (2020). Misinterpreting p: The discrepancy between p values and the probability the null hypothesis is true, the influence of multiple testing, and implications for the replication crisis. *Psychological Methods, 25*(5), 596–609. https://doi.org/10.1037/met0000248

Anscombe, F. J. (1973). Graphs in statistical analysis. *The American Statistician, 27*(1), 17–21. https://doi.org/10.2307/2682899

Armstrong, J. S., & Soelberg, P. (1968). On the interpretation of factor analysis. *Psychological Bulletin, 70*(5), 361–364. https://doi.org/10.1037/h0026434

Auerswald, M., & Moshagen, M. (2019). How to determine the number of factors to retain in exploratory factor analysis: A comparison of extraction methods under realistic conditions. *Psychological Methods, 24*(4), 468–491. http://dx.doi.org/10.1037/met0000200

Bandalos, D. L. (2018). *Measurement theory and applications in the social sciences.* Guilford.

Bandalos, D. L., & Boehm-Kaufman, M. R. (2009). Four common misconceptions in exploratory factor analysis. In C. E. Lance & R. J. Vandenberg (Eds.), *Statistical and methodological myths and urban legends: Doctrine, verity and fable in the organizational and social sciences* (pp. 61–87). Routledge.

Bandalos, D. L., & Finney, S. J. (2019). Factor analysis: Exploratory and confirmatory. In G. R. Hancock, L. M. Stapleton, & R. O. Mueller (Eds.), *The reviewer's guide to quantitative methods in the social sciences* (2nd ed., pp. 98–122). Routledge.

Bandalos, D. L., & Gerstner, J. J. (2016). Using factor analysis in test construction. In K. Schweizer & C. DiStefano (Eds.), *Principles and methods of test construction: Standards and recent advances* (pp. 26–51). Hogrefe.

Baraldi, A. N., & Enders, C. K. (2013). Missing data methods. In T. D. Little (Ed.), *Oxford handbook of quantitative methods: Statistical analyses* (Vol. 2, pp. 635–664). Oxford University Press.

Barendse, M. T., Oort, F. J., & Timmerman, M. E. (2015). Using exploratory factor analysis to determine the dimensionality of discrete responses. *Structural Equation Modeling*, *22*(1), 87–101. https://doi.org/10.1080/10705511.2014.934850

Barrett, P. T. (2007). Structural equation modelling: Adjudging model fit. *Personality and Individual Differences*, *42*(5), 815–824. https://doi.org/10.1016/j.paid.2006.09.018

Barrett, P. T., & Kline, P. (1982). Factor extraction: An examination of three methods. *Personality Study and Group Behaviour*, *3*(1), 84–98.

Bartholomew, D. J. (1995). Spearman and the origin and development of factor analysis. *British Journal of Mathematical and Statistical Psychology*, *48*(2), 211–220. https://doi.org/10.1111/j.2044-8317.1995.tb01060.x

Bartlett, M. S. (1950). Tests of significance in factor analysis. *British Journal of Psychology*, *3*(2), 77–85. https://doi.org/10.1111/j.2044-8317.1950.tb00285.x

Basto, M., & Pereira, J. M. (2012). An SPSS R-menu for ordinal factor analysis. *Journal of Statistical Software*, *46*(4), 1–29. https://doi.org/10.18637/jss.v046.i04

Beaujean, A. A. (2013). Factor analysis using R. *Practical Assessment, Research & Evaluation*, *18*(4), 1–11. https://doi.org/10.7275/z8wr-4j42

Beavers, A. S., Lounsbury, J. W., Richards, J. K., Huck, S. W., Skolits, G. J., & Esquivel, S. L. (2012). Practical considerations for using exploratory factor analysis in educational research. *Practical Assessment, Research & Evaluation*, *18*(6), 1–13. https://doi.org/10.7275/qv2q-rk76

Bedeian, A. G., Sturman, M. C., & Streiner, D. L. (2009). Decimal dust, significant digits, and the search for stars. *Organizaitonal Research Methods*, *12*(4), 687–694. https://doi.org/10.1177/1094428108321153

Benjamin, D. J., & Berger, J. O. (2019). Three recommendations for improving the use of p-values. *The American Statistician*, *73*(S1), 186–191. https://doi.org/10.1080/000313 05.2018.1543135

Benson, J. (1998). Developing a strong program of construct validation: A test anxiety example. *Educational Measurement: Issues and Practice*, *17*(1), 10–22. https://doi.org/10.1111/j.1745-3992.1998.tb00616.x

Benson, J., & Nasser, F. (1998). On the use of factor analysis as a research tool. *Journal of Vocational Education Research*, *23*(1), 13–33.

Bentler, P. M. (2005). *EQS 6 structural equations program manual*. Multivariate Software.

Berk, R. (2011). Evidence-based versus junk-based evaluation research: Some lessons from 35 years of the evaluation review. *Evaluation Review*, *35*(3), 191–203. https://doi.org/10.1177/0193841X11419281

Bernstein, I. H., & Teng, G. (1989). Factoring items and factoring scales are different: Spurious evidence for multidimensionality due to item categorization. *Psychological Bulletin*, *105*(3), 467–477. https://doi.org/10.1037/0033-2909.105.3.467

Bishara, A. J., & Hittner, J. B. (2015). Reducing bias and error in the correlation coefficient due to nonnormality. *Educational and Psychological Measurement*, *75*(5), 785–804. https://doi.org/10.1177/0013164414557639

Bollen, K. A. (2002). Latent variables in psychology and the social sciences. *Annual Review of Psychology*, *53*(1), 605–634. https://doi.org/10.1146/annurev.psych.53.100901.135239

Bollen, K. A., & Barb, K. H. (1981). Pearson's r and coarsely categorized measures. *American Sociological Review*, *46*(2), 232–239. https://doi.org/10.2307/2094981

Box, G. E. P. (1976). Science and statistics. *Journal of the American Statistical Association*, *71*(356), 791–799. http://doi.org/10.1080/01621459.1976.10480949

Brannick, M. T. (1995). Critical comments on applying covariance structure modeling. *Journal of Organizational Behavior, 16*(3), 201–213. https://doi.org/10.1002/job.4030160303

Breckler, S. J. (1990). Applications of covariance structure modeling in psychology: Cause for concern? *Psychological Bulletin, 107*(2), 260–273. https://doi.org/10.1037/0033-2909.107.2.260

Briggs, N. E., & MacCallum, R. C. (2003). Recovery of weak common factors by maximum likelihood and ordinary least squares estimation. *Multivariate Behavioral Research, 38*(1), 25–56. https://doi.org/10.1207/S15327906MBR3801_2

Briggs, S. R., & Cheek, J. M. (1986). The role of factor analysis in the development and evaluation of personality scales. *Journal of Personality, 54*(1), 106–148. https://doi.org/10.1111/j.1467-6494.1986.tb00391.x

Brown, T. A. (2013). Latent variable measurement models. In T. D. Little (Ed.), *Oxford handbook of quantitative methods: Statistical analysis* (Vol. 2, pp. 257–280). Oxford University Press.

Brown, T. A. (2015). *Confirmatory factor analysis for applied research* (2nd ed.). Guilford.

Browne, M. W. (2001). An overview of analytic rotation in exploratory factor analysis. *Multivariate Behavioral Research, 36*(1), 111–150. https://doi.org/10.1207/S15327906MBR3601_05

Browne, M. W., & Cudeck, R. (1993). Alternative ways of assessing model fit. In K. A. Bollen & J. S. Long (Eds.), *Testing structural equation models* (pp. 136–162). Sage.

Brunner, M., Nagy, G., & Wilhelm, O. (2012). A tutorial on hierarchically structured constructs. *Journal of Personality, 80*(4), 796–846. https://doi.org/10.1111/j.1467-6494.2011.00749.x

Budaev, S. V. (2010). Using principal components and factor analysis in animal behaviour research: Caveats and guidelines. *Ethology, 116*(5), 472–480. https://doi.org/10.1111/j.1439-0310.2010.01758.x

Buja, A., & Eyuboglu, N. (1992). Remarks on parallel analysis. *Multivariate Behavioral Research, 27*(4), 509–540. https://doi.org/10.1207/s15327906mbr2704_2

Burnham, K. P., & Anderson, D. R. (2004). Multimodel inference: Understanding AIC and BIC in model selection. *Sociological Methods & Research, 33*(2), 261–304. https://doi.org/10.1177/0049124104268644

Burt, C. (1940). *The factors of the mind: An introduction to factor-analysis in psychology.* University of London Press.

Cain, M. K., Zhang, Z., & Yuan, K. H. (2017). Univariate and multivariate skewness and kurtosis for measuring nonnormality: Prevalence, influence, and estimation. *Behavior Research Methods, 49*(5), 1716–1735. https://doi.org/10.3758/s13428-016-0814-1

Canivez, G. L., & Watkins, M. W. (2010). Exploratory and higher-order factor analyses of the Wechsler adult intelligence scale-fourth edition (WAIS-IV) adolescent subsample. *School Psychology Quarterly, 25*(4), 223–235. https://doi.org/10.1037/a0022046

Canivez, G. L., Watkins, M. W., & Dombrowski, S. C. (2016). Factor structure of the Wechsler intelligence scale for children-fifth edition: Exploratory factor analysis with the 16 primary and secondary subtests. *Psychological Assessment, 28*(8), 975–986. https://doi.org/10.1037/pas0000238

Caron, P. O. (2019). Minimum average partial correlation and parallel analysis: The influence of oblique structures. *Communications in Statistics: Simulation and Computation, 48*(7), 2110–2117. https://doi.org/10.1080/03610918.2018.1433843

Carretta, T. R., & Ree, J. J. (2001). Pitfalls of ability research. *International Journal of Selection and Assessment, 9*(4), 325–335. https://doi.org/10.1111/1468-2389.00184

Carroll, J. B. (1961). The nature of the data, or how to choose a correlation coefficient. *Psychometrika, 26*(4), 347–372. https://doi.org/10.1007/BF02289768

Carroll, J. B. (1978). How shall we study individual differences in cognitive abilities? Methodological and theoretical perspectives. *Intelligence, 2*(2), 87–115. https://doi.org/10.1016/0160-2896(78)90002-8

Carroll, J. B. (1983). Studying individual differences in cognitive abilities: Through and beyond factor analysis. In R. F. Dillon & R. R. Schmeck (Eds.), *Individual differences in cognition* (pp. 1–33). Academic Press.

Carroll, J. B. (1985). Exploratory factor analysis: A tutorial. In D. K. Detterman (Ed.), *Current topics in human intelligence* (pp. 25–58). Ablex Publishing Company.

Carroll, J. B. (1993). *Human cognitive abilities: A survey of factor-analytic studies.* Cambridge University Press.

Carroll, J. B. (1995a). On methodology in the study of cognitive abilities. *Multivariate Behavioral Research, 30*(3), 429–452. https://doi.org/10.1207/s15327906mbr3003_6

Carroll, J. B. (1995b). Reflections on Stephen Jay Gould's "the mismeasure of man" (1981): A retrospective review. *Intelligence, 21*(2), 121–134. https://doi.org/10.1016/0160-2896(95)90022-5

Cattell, R. B. (1946). *The description and measurement of personality.* World Book.

Cattell, R. B. (1952). *Factor analysis: An introduction and manual for the psychologist and social scientist.* Greenwood Press.

Cattell, R. B. (1966). The scree test for the number of factors. *Multivariate Behavioral Research, 1*(2), 245–276. https://doi.org/10.1207/s15327906mbr0102_10

Cattell, R. B. (1978). *The scientific use of factor analysis in behavioral and life sciences.* Plenum Press.

Chen, F. F., West, S. G., & Sousa, K. H. (2006). A comparison of bifactor and second-order models of quality of life. *Multivariate Behavioral Research, 41*(2), 189–225.

Chen, S. F., Wang, S., & Chen, C. Y. (2012). A simulation study using EFA and CFA programs based on the impact of missing data on test dimensionality. *Expert Systems with Applications, 39*(4), 4026–4031. https://doi.org/10.1016/j.eswa.2011.09.085

Child, D. (2006). *The essentials of factor analysis* (3rd ed.). Continuum.

Cho, S. J., Li, F., & Bandalos, D. (2009). Accuracy of the parallel analysis procedure with polychoric correlations. *Educational and Psychological Measurement, 69*(5), 748–759. https://doi.org/10.1177/0013164409332229

Choi, J., Peters, M., & Mueller, R. O. (2010). Correlational analysis of ordinal data: From Pearson's *r* to Bayesian polychoric correlation. *Asia Pacific Education Review, 11*(4), 459–466. https://doi.org/10.1007/s12564-010-9096-y

Clark, D. A., & Bowles, R. P. (2018). Model fit and item factor analysis: Overfactoring, underfactoring, and a program to guide interpretation. *Multivariate Behavioral Research, 53*(4), 544–558. https://doi.org/10.1080/00273171.2018.1461058

Cliff, N. (1983). Some cautions concerning the application of causal modeling methods. *Multivariate Behavioral Research, 18*(1), 115–126. https://doi.org/10.1207/s15327906mbr1801_7

Clifton, J. D. W. (2020). Managing validity versus reliability trade-offs in scale-building decisions. *Psychological Methods, 25*(3), 259–270. https://doi.org/10.1037/met0000236

Collier, J. (2010). *Using SPSS syntax: A beginner's guide.* Sage.

Comrey, A. L. (1988). Factor-analytic methods of scale development in personality and clinical psychology. *Journal of Consulting and Clinical Psychology, 56*(5), 754–761. https://doi.org/10.1037//0022-006x.56.5.754

Comrey, A. L., & Lee, H. B. (1992). *A first course in factor analysis* (2nd ed.). Erlbaum.

Conway, J. M., & Huffcutt, A. I. (2003). A review and evaluation of exploratory factor analysis practices in organizational research. *Organizational Research Methods, 6*(2), 147–168. https://doi.org/10.1177/1094428103251541

Cooper, C. (2019). *Psychological testing: Theory and practice*. Routledge.

Costello, A. B., & Osborne, J. W. (2005). Best practices in exploratory factor analysis: Four recommendations for getting the most from your analysis. *Practical Assessment, Research & Evaluation, 10*(7), 1–9. https://doi.org/10.7275/jyj1-4868

Crawford, A. V., Green, S. B., Levy, R., Lo, W. J., Scott, L., Svetina, D., & Thompson, M. S. (2010). Evaluation of parallel analysis methods for determining the number of factors. *Educational and Psychological Measurement, 70*(6), 885–901. https://doi.org/10.1177/0013164410379332

Cribbie, R. A. (2000). Evaluating the importance of individual parameters in structural equation modeling: The need for type I error control. *Personality and Individual Differences, 29*(3), 567–577. https://doi.org/10.1016/S0191-8869(99)00219-6

Cronbach, L. J. (1951). Coefficient alpha and the internal structure of tests. *Psychometrika, 16*(3), 297–334. https://doi.org/10.1007/BF02310555

Cronk, B. C. (2020). *How to use SPSS: A step-by-step guide to analysis and interpretation* (11th ed.). Routledge.

Cudeck, R. (2000). Exploratory factor analysis. In H. E. A. Tinsley & S. D. Brown (Eds.), *Handbook of applied multivariate statistics and mathematical modeling* (pp. 265–296). Academic Press.

Curran, P. J. (2016). Methods for the detection of carelessly invalid responses in survey data. *Journal of Experimental Social Psychology, 66*, 4–19. https://doi.org/10.1016/j.jesp.2015.07.006

Curran, P. J., West, S. G., & Finch, J. F. (1996). The robustness of test statistics to nonnormality and specification error in confirmatory factor analysis. *Psychological Methods, 1*(1), 16–29. https://doi.org/10.1037/1082-989X.1.1.16

DeCarlo, L. T. (1997). On the meaning and use of kurtosis. *Psychological Methods, 2*(3), 292–307. https://doi.org/10.1037/1082-989X.2.3.292

DeSimone, J. A., Harms, P. D., & DeSimone, A. J. (2015). Best practice recommendations for data screening. *Journal of Organizational Behavior, 36*(2), 171–181. https://doi.org/10.1002/job.1962

DeVellis, R. F. (2017). *Scale development: Theory and applications* (4th ed.). Sage.

de Winter, J. C. F., & Dodou, D. (2012). Factor recovery by principal axis factoring and maximum likelihood factor analysis as a function of factor pattern and sample size. *Journal of Applied Statistics, 39*(4), 695–710. https://doi.org/10.1080/02664763.2011.610445

de Winter, J. C. F., Dodou, D., & Wieringa, P. A. (2009). Exploratory factor analysis with small sample sizes. *Multivariate Behavioral Research, 44*(2), 147–181. https://doi.org/10.1080/00273170902794206

de Winter, J. C. F., Gosling, S. D., & Potter, J. (2016). Comparing the Pearson and Spearman correlation coefficients across distributions and sample sizes: A tutorial using simulations and empirical data. *Psychological Methods, 21*(3), 273–290. https://doi.org/10.1037/met0000079

Digman, J. M. (1990). Personality structure: Emergence of the five-factor model. *Annual Review of Psychology, 41*, 417–440. https://doi.org/10.1146/annurev.ps.41.020190.002221

Dinno, A. (2009). Exploring the sensitivity of Horn's parallel analysis to the distributional form of random data. *Multivariate Behavioral Research, 44*(3), 362–388. https://doi.org/10.1080/00273170902938969

DiStefano, C. (2002). The impact of categorization with confirmatory factor analysis. *Structural Equation Modeling, 9*(3), 327–346. https://doi.org/10.1207/S153280 07SEM0903_2

DiStefano, C. (2016). Examining fit with structural equation models. In K. Schweizer & C. DiStefano (Eds.), *Principles and methods of test construction: Standards and recent advances* (pp. 166–193). Hogrefe.

DiStefano, C., & Hess, B. (2005). Using confirmatory factor analysis for construct validation: An empirical review. *Journal of Psychoeducational Assessment, 23*(3), 225–241. https://doi.org/10.1177/073428290502300303

DiStefano, C., Shi, D., & Morgan, G. B. (2020). Collapsing categories is often more advantageous than modeling sparse data: Investigations in the cfa framework. *Structural Equation Modeling.* https://doi.org/10.1080/10705511.2020.1803073

DiStefano, C., Zhu, M., & Mindrila, D. (2009). Understanding and using factor scores: Considerations for the applied researcher. *Practical Assessment, Research & Evaluation, 14*(20), 1–11. https://doi.org/10.7275/da8t-4g52

Dombrowski, S. C., Beaujean, A. A., McGill, R. J., Benson, N. F., & Schneider, W. J. (2019). Using exploratory bifactor analysis to understand the latent structure of multidimensional psychological measures: An example featuring the WISC-V. *Structural Equation Modeling, 26*(6), 847–860. https://doi.org/10.1080/10705511.2019.1622421

Dombrowski, S. C., Canivez, G. L., & Watkins, M. W. (2018). Factor structure of the 10 WISC-V primary subtests across four standardization age groups. *Contemporary School Psychology, 22*(1), 90–104. https://doi.org/10.1007/s40688-017-0125-2

Dunn, A. M., Heggestad, E. D., Shanock, L. R., & Theilgard, N. (2018). Intra-individual response variability as an indicator of insufficient effort responding: Comparison to other indicators and relationships with individual differences. *Journal of Business and Psychology, 33*(1), 105–121. https://doi.org/10.1007/s10869-016-9479-0

Dziuban, C. D., & Shirkey, E. S. (1974). When is a correlation matrix appropriate for factor analysis? Some decision rules. *Psychological Bulletin, 81*(6), 358–361. https://doi.org/10.1037/h0036316

Edwards, J. R., & Bagozzi, R. P. (2000). On the nature and direction of relationships between constructs and measures. *Psychological Methods, 5*(2), 155–174. https://doi.org/10.1037/1082-989x.5.2.155

Enders, C. K. (2017). Multiple imputation as a flexible tool for missing data handling in clinical research. *Behaviour Research and Therapy, 98*, 4–18. https://doi.org/10.1016/j.brat.2016.11.008

Epskamp, S., Maris, G., Waldorp, L. J., & Borsboom, D. (2018). Network psychometrics. In P. Iwing, T. Booth, & D. J. Hughes (Eds.), *The Wiley handbook of psychometric testing: A multidisciplinary reference on survey, scale and test development* (pp. 953–986). Wiley.

Fabrigar, L. R., & Wegener, D. T. (2012). *Exploratory factor analysis.* Oxford University Press.

Fabrigar, L. R., Wegener, D. T., MacCallum, R. C., & Strahan, E. J. (1999). Evaluating the use of exploratory factor analysis in psychological research. *Psychological Methods, 4*(3), 272–299. https://doi.org/10.1037/1082-989X.4.3.272

Fava, J. L., & Velicer, W. F. (1992). The effects of overextraction on factor and component analysis. *Multivariate Behavioral Research, 27*(3), 387–415. https://doi.org/10.1207/s15327906mbr2703_5

Fava, J. L., & Velicer, W. F. (1996). The effects of underextraction in factor and component analysis. *Educational and Psychological Measurement, 56*(6), 907–929. https://doi. org/10.1177/0013164496056006001

Feldt, L. S., & Brennan, R. L. (1993). Reliability. In R. L. Linn (Ed.), *Educational measurement* (3rd ed., pp. 105–146). Oryx Press.

Fernstad, S. J. (2019). To identify what is not there: A definition of missingness patterns and evaluation of missing value visualization. *Information Visualization, 18*(2), 230–250. https://doi.org/10.1177/1473871618785387

Ferrando, P. J., & Lorenzo-Seva, U. (2000). Unrestricted versus restricted factor analysis of multidimensional test items: Some aspects of the problem and some suggestions. *Psicológica, 21*(3), 301–323.

Ferrando, P. J., & Lorenzo-Seva, U. (2018). Assessing the quality and appropriateness of factor solutions and factor score estimates in exploratory item factor analysis. *Educational and Psychological Measurement, 78*(5), 762–780. https://doi.org/10.1177/00131 64417719308

Ferrando, P. J., Navarro-González, D., & Lorenzo-Seva, U. (2019). Assessing the quality and effectiveness of the factor score estimates in psychometric factor-analytic applications. *Methodology, 15*(3), 119–127. https://doi.org/10.1027/1614-2241/a000170

Feynman, R. P. (1974). Cargo cult science. *Engineering and Science, 37*(7), 10–13. http:// calteches.library.caltech.edu/51/1/ES37.7.1974.pdf

Field, A., Miles, J., & Field, Z. (2012). *Discovering statistics using R*. Sage.

Finch, W. H. (2006). Comparison of the performance of varimax and promax rotations: Factor structure recovery for dichotomous items. *Journal of Educational Measurement, 43*(1), 39–52. https://doi.org/10.1111/j.1745-3984.2006.00003.x

Finch, W. H. (2013). Exploratory factor analysis. In T. Teo (Ed.), *Handbook of quantitative methods for educational research* (pp. 167–186). Sense Publishers.

Finch, W. H. (2020a). *Exploratory factor analysis*. Sage.

Finch, W. H. (2020b). Using fit statistic differences to determine the optimal number of factors to retain in an exploratory factor analysis. *Educational and Psychological Measurement, 80*(2), 217–241. https://doi.org/10.1177/0013164419865769

Finney, S. J., & DiStefano, C. (2013). Nonnormal and categorical data in structural equation modeling. In G. R. Hancock & R. O. Mueller (Eds.), *Structural equation modeling: A second course* (2nd ed., pp. 439–492). Information Age Publishing.

Flake, J. K., & Fried, E. I. (2020). Measurement schmeasurement: Questionable measurement practices and how to avoid them. *PsyArXiv*. https://doi.org/10.31234/osf.io/ hs7wm

Flora, D. B. (2018). *Statistical methods for the social and behavioural sciences: A model-based approach*. Sage.

Flora, D. B., & Curran, P. J. (2004). An empirical evaluation of alternative methods of estimation for confirmatory factor analysis with ordinal data. *Psychological Methods, 9*(4), 466–491. https://doi.org/10.1037/1082-989X.9.4.466

Flora, D. B., & Flake, J. K. (2017). The purpose and practice of exploratory and confirmatory factor analysis in psychological research: Decisions for scale development and validation. *Canadian Journal of Behavioural Science, 49*(2), 78–88. https://doi.org/10.1037/ cbs0000069

Flora, D. B., LaBrish, C., & Chalmers, R. P. (2012). Old and new ideas for data screening and assumption testing for exploratory and confirmatory factor analysis. *Frontiers in Psychology, 3*(55), 1–21. https://doi.org/10.3389/fpsyg.2012.00055

Floyd, F. J., & Widaman, K. F. (1995). Factor analysis in the development and refinement of clinical assessment instruments. *Psychological Assessment, 7*(3), 286–299. https://doi.org/10.1037/1040-3590.7.3.286

Ford, J. K., MacCallum, R. C., & Tait, M. (1986). The application of exploratory factor analysis in applied psychology: A critical review and analysis. *Personnel Psychology, 39*(2), 291–314. https://doi.org/10.1111/j.1744-6570.1986.tb00583.x

Freedman, D. A. (1987). A rejoinder on models, metaphors, and fables. *Journal of Educational Statistics, 12*(2), 206–223. https://doi.org/10.3102/10769986012002206

French, J. W., Tucker, L. R., Newman, S. H., & Bobbitt, J. M. (1952). A factor analysis of aptitude and achievement entrance tests and course grades at the United States coast guard academy. *Journal of Educational Psychology, 43*(2), 65–80. https://doi.org/10.1037/h0054549

Garrido, L. E., Abad, F. J., & Ponsoda, V. (2011). Performance of Velicer's minimum average partial factor retention method with categorical variables. *Educational and Psychological Measurement, 71*(3), 551–570. https://doi.org/10.1177/0013164410389489

Garrido, L. E., Abad, F. J., & Ponsoda, V. (2013). A new look at Horn's parallel analysis with ordinal variables. *Psychological Methods, 18*(4), 454–474. https://doi.org/10.1037/a0030005

Garrido, L. E., Abad, F. J., & Ponsoda, V. (2016). Are fit indices really fit to estimate the number of factors with categorical variables? Some cautionary findings via Monte Carlo simulation. *Psychological Methods, 21*(1), 93–111. http://dx.doi.org/10.1037/met0000064

Garson, G. D. (2013). *Factor analysis.* Statistical Publishing Associates.

Gaskin, C. J., & Happell, B. (2014). Exploratory factor analysis: A review of recent evidence, an assessment of current practice, and recommendations for future use. *International Journal of Nursing Studies, 51*(3), 511–521. https://doi.org/10.1016/j.ijnurstu.2013.10.005

Gelman, A., & Loken, E. (2014). The statistical crisis in science. *American Scientist, 102*(6), 460–465. https://doi.org/10.1511/2014.111.460

George, D., & Mallery, P. (2020). *IBM SPSS statistics 26 step by step: A simple guide and reference* (16th ed.). Routledge.

Gerbing, D. W., & Hamilton, J. G. (1996). Viability of exploratory factor analysis as a precursor to confirmatory factor analysis. *Structural Equation Modeling, 3*(1), 62–72. https://doi.org/10.1080/10705519609540030

Gibson, T. O., Morrow, J. A., & Rocconi, L. M. (2020). A modernized heuristic approach to robust exploratory factor analysis. *Quantitative Methods in Psychology, 16*(4), 295–307. https://doi.org/10.20982/tqmp.16.4.p295

Gignac, G. E. (2007). Multi-factor modeling in individual differences research: Some recommendations and suggestions. *Personality and Individual Differences, 42*(1), 37–48. https://doi.org/10.1016/j.paid.2006.06.019

Gignac, G. E. (2008). Higher-order models versus direct hierarchical models: *g* as superordinate or breadth factor? *Psychology Science Quarterly, 50*(1), 21–43.

Gilman, R., Laughlin, J. E., & Huebner, E. S. (1999). Validation of the self-description questionnaire-II with an American sample. *School Psychology International, 20*(3), 300–307. https://doi.org/10.1177/0143034399203005

Giordano, C., & Waller, N. G. (2020). Recovering bifactor models: A comparison of seven methods. *Psychological Methods, 25*(2), 143–156. https://doi.org/10.1037/met0000227

Glorfeld, L. W. (1995). An improvement on Horn's parallel analysis methodology for selecting the correct number of factors to retain. *Educational and Psychological Measurement, 55*(3), 377–393. https://doi.org/10.1177/0013164495055003002

Goldberg, L. R., & Velicer, W. F. (2006). Principles of exploratory factor analysis. In S. Strack (Ed.), *Differentiating normal and abnormal personality* (2nd ed., pp. 209–237). Springer.

Golino, H. F., & Epskamp, S. (2017). Exploratory graph analysis: A new approach for estimating the number of dimensions in psychological research. *PlosOne, 12*(6), 1–26. https://doi.org/10.1371/journal.pone.0174035

Golino, H. F., Shi, D., Christensen, A. P., Garrido, L. E., Nieto, M. D., Sadana, R., & Martinez-Molina, A. (2020). Investigating the performance of exploratory graph analysis and traditional techniques to identify the number of latent factors: A simulation and tutorial. *Psychological Methods, 25*(3), 292–320. https://doi.org/10.1037/met0000255

Goodwin, L. D. (1999). The role of factor analysis in the estimation of construct validity. *Measurement in Physical Education and Exercise Science, 3*(2), 85–100. https://doi.org/10.1207/s15327841mpee0302_2

Goodwin, L. D., & Leech, N. L. (2006). Understanding correlation: Factors that affect the size of r. *Journal of Experimental Education, 74*(3), 251–266. https://doi.org/10.3200/JEXE.74.3.249-266

Gorsuch, R. L. (1983). *Factor analysis* (2nd ed.). Erlbaum.

Gorsuch, R. L. (1988). Exploratory factor analysis. In J. R. Nesselroade & R. B. Cattell (Eds.), *Handbook of multivariate experimental psychology* (2nd ed.). Plenum Press.

Gorsuch, R. L. (1990). Common factor analysis versus component analysis: Some well and little known facts. *Multivariate Behavioral Research, 25*(1), 33–39. https://doi.org/10.1207/s15327906mbr2501_3

Gorsuch, R. L. (1997). Exploratory factor analysis: Its role in item analysis. *Journal of Personality Assessment, 68*(3), 532–560. https://doi.org/10.1207/s15327752jpa6803_5

Gorsuch, R. L. (2003). Factor analysis. In J. A. Schinka & W. F. Velicer (Eds.), *Handbook of psychology: Research methods in psychology* (Vol. 2, pp. 143–164). Wiley.

Graham, J. M., Guthrie, A. C., & Thompson, B. (2003). Consequences of not interpreting structure coefficients in published CFA research: A reminder. *Structural Equation Modeling, 10*(1), 142–153. https://doi.org/10.1207/S15328007SEM1001_7

Green, S. B., & Salkind, N. J. (2017). *Using SPSS for Windows and Macintosh: Analyzing and understanding data* (8th ed.). Pearson.

Greenwald, A. G., Pratkanis, A. R., Leippe, M. R., & Baumgardner, M. H. (1986). Under what conditions does theory obstruct research progress? *Psychological Review, 93*(2), 216–229. https://doi.org/10.1037/0033-295X.93.2.216

Greer, T., Dunlap, W. P., Hunter, S. T., & Berman, M. E. (2006). Skew and internal consistency. *Journal of Applied Psychology, 91*(6), 1351–1358. https://doi.org/10.1037/0021-9010.91.6.1351

Greiff, S., & Heene, M. (2017). Why psychological assessment needs to start worrying about model fit. *European Journal of Psychological Assessment, 33*(5), 313–317. https://doi.org/10.1027/1015-5759/a000450

Grice, J. W. (2001). Computing and evaluating factor scores. *Psychological Methods, 6*(4), 430–450. https://doi.org/10.1037/1082-989X.6.4.430

Grieder, S., & Steiner, M. D. (2020). Algorithmic jingle jungle: A comparison of implementations of principal axis factoring and promax rotation in R and SPSS. *PsyArXiv*. https://psyarxiv.com/7hwrm

Guadagnoli, E., & Velicer, W. F. (1988). Relation of sample size to the stability of component patterns. *Psychological Bulletin, 103*(2), 265–275. https://doi.org/10.1037/0033-2909.103.2.265

Hägglund, G. (2001). Milestones in the history of factor analysis. In R. Cukeck, S. du Toit, & D. Sörbom (Eds.), *Structural equation modeling: Present and future* (pp. 11–38). Scientific Software International.

Hahs-Vaughn, D. L. (2017). *Applied multivariate statistical concepts.* Routledge.

Haig, B. D. (2018). *Method matters in psychology: Essays in applied philosophy of science.* Springer.

Hair, J. F., Black, W. C., Babin, B. J., & Anderson, R. E. (2019). *Multivariate data analysis* (8th ed.). Cengage Learning.

Hancock, G. R., & Liu, M. (2012). Bootstrapping standard errors and data-model fit statistics in structural equation modeling. In R. H. Hoyle (Ed.), *Handbook of structural equation modeling* (pp. 296–306). Guilford.

Hancock, G. R., & Schoonen, R. (2015). Structural equation modeling: Possibilities for language learning researchers. *Language Learning, 65*(S1), 160–184. https://doi.org/10.1111/lang.12116

Harman, H. H. (1976). *Modern factor analysis* (3rd ed.). University of Chicago Press.

Hattori, M., Zhang, G., & Preacher, K. J. (2017). Multiple local solutions and geomin rotation. *Multivariate Behavioral Research, 52*(6), 720–731. https://doi.org/10.1080/00273171.2017.1361312

Hayashi, K., Bentler, P. M., & Yuan, K. H. (2007). On the likelihood ratio test for the number of factors in exploratory factor analysis. *Structural Equation Modeling, 14*(3), 505–526. https://doi.org/10.1080/10705510701301891

Hayduk, L. A. (2014). Shame for disrespecting evidence: The personal consequences of insufficient respect for structural equation model testing. *BMC Medical Research Methodology, 14*(124), 1–24. https://doi.org/10.1186/1471-2288-14-124

Hayes, A. F. (2018). *Using SPSS: A little syntax guide.* www.afhayes.com

Hayes, A. F., & Coutts, J. J. (2020). Use omega rather than Cronbach's alpha for estimating reliability. But. . . . *Communication Methods and Measures, 14*(1), 1–24. https://doi.org/10.1080/19312458.2020.1718629

Hayton, J. C., Allen, D. G., & Scarpello, V. (2004). Factor retention decisions in exploratory factor analysis: A tutorial on parallel analysis. *Organizational Research Methods, 7*(2), 191–205. https://doi.org/10.1177/1094428104263675

Heene, M., Hilbert, S., Draxler, C., Ziegler, M., & Bühner, M. (2011). Masking misfit in confirmatory factor analysis by increasing variances: A cautionary note on the usefulness of cutoff values of fit indices. *Psychological Methods, 16*(3), 319–336. https://doi.org/10.1037/a0024917

Hendrickson, A. E., & White, P. O. (1964). Promax: A quick method for rotation to oblique simple structure. *British Journal of Mathematical Psychology, 17*(1), 65–70. https://doi.org/10.1111/j.2044-8317.1964.tb00244.x

Henson, R. K., Hull, D. M., & Williams, C. S. (2010). Methodology in our education research culture: Toward a stronger collective quantitative proficiency. *Educational Researcher, 39*(3), 229–240. https://doi.org/10.3102/0013189X10365102

Henson, R. K., & Roberts, J. K. (2006). Use of exploratory factor analysis in published research: Common errors and some comment on improved practice. *Educational and Psychological Measurement, 66*(3), 393–416. https://doi.org/10.1177/0013164405282485

Hetzel, R. D. (1996). A primer on factor analysis with comments on patterns of practice and reporting. In B. Thompson (Ed.), *Advances in social science methodology* (Vol. 4, pp. 175–206). JAI Press.

Heymans, M. W., & Eekhout, I. (2019). *Applied missing data analysis with SPSS and (R) studio.* https://bookdown.org/mwheymans/bookmi

Hoelzle, J. B., & Meyer, G. J. (2013). Exploratory factor analysis: Basics and beyond. In I. B. Weiner, J. A. Schinka, & W. F. Velicer (Eds.), *Handbook of psychology: Research methods in psychology* (Vol. 2, 2nd ed., pp. 164–188). Wiley.

Hogarty, K. Y., Hines, C. V., Kromrey, J. D., Ferron, J. M., & Mumford, K. R. (2005). The quality of factor solutions in exploratory factor analysis: The influence of sample size, communality, and overdetermination. *Educational and Psychological Measurement, 65*(2), 202–226. https://doi.org/10.1177/0013164404267287

Holgado-Tello, F. P., Chacón-Moscoso, S., Barbero-García, I., & Vila-Abad, E. (2010). Polychoric versus Pearson correlations in exploratory and confirmatory factor analysis of ordinal variables. *Quality & Quantity, 44*(1), 153–166. https://doi.org/10.1007/s11135-008-9190-y

Holzinger, K. J., & Harman, H. H. (1941). *Factor analysis; a synthesis of factorial methods.* University of Chicago Press.

Holzinger, K. J., & Swineford, F. (1937). The bi-factor method. *Psychometrika, 2*(1), 41–54. https://doi.org/10.1007/BF02287965

Holzinger, K. J., & Swineford, F. (1939). *A study in factor analysis: The stability of a bifactor solution.* Supplementary Educational Monograph No. 48. University of Chicago Press.

Hopwood, C. J., & Donnellan, M. B. (2010). How should the internal structure of personality inventories be evaluated? *Personality and Social Psychology Review, 14*(3), 332–346. https://doi.org/10.1177/1088868310361240

Horn, J. L. (1965). A rationale and test for the number of factors in factor analysis. *Psychometrika, 30*(2), 179–185. https://doi.org/10.1007/BF02289447

Howard, M. C. (2016). A review of exploratory factor analysis decisions and overview of current practices: What we are doing and how can we improve? *International Journal of Human-Computer Interaction, 32*(1), 51–62. https://doi.org/10.1080/10447318.2015.1087664

Hoyle, R. H. (2000). Confirmatory factor analysis. In H. E. A. Tinsley & S. D. Brown (Eds.), *Handbook of multivariate statistics and mathematical modeling* (pp. 465–497). Academic Press.

Hoyle, R. H., & Duvall, J. L. (2004). Determining the number of factors in exploratory and confirmatory factor analysis. In D. Kaplan (Ed.), *The Sage handbook of quantitative methodology for the social sciences* (pp. 301–315). Sage.

Hu, L., & Bentler, P. M. (1999). Cutoff criteria for fit indexes in covariance structure analysis: Conventional criteria versus new alternatives. *Structural Equation Modeling, 6*(1), 1–55. https://doi.org/10.1080/10705519909540118

Humphreys, L. G. (1982). The hierarchical factor model and general intelligence. In N. Hirschberg & L. G. Humphreys (Eds.), *Multivariate applications in the social sciences* (pp. 223–239). Erlbaum.

Hunsley, J., & Mash, E. J. (2007). Evidence-based assessment. *Annual Review of Clinical Psychology, 3*(1), 29–51. https://doi.org/10.1146/annurev.clinpsy.3.022806.091419

Hurley, A. E., Scandura, T. A., Schriesheim, C. A., Brannick, M. T., Seers, A., Vandenberg, R. J., & Williams, L. J. (1997). Exploratory and confirmatory factor analysis: Guidelines, issues, and alternatives. *Journal of Organizational Behavior, 18*(6), 667–683. http://doi.org/cg5sf7

Hussey, I., & Hughes, S. (2020). Hidden invalidity among 15 commonly used measures in social and personality psychology. *Advances in Methods and Practices in Psychological Science, 3*(2), 166–184. https://doi.org/10.1177/2515245919882903

Hutchinson, S. R. (1998). The stability of post hoc model modifications in confirmatory factor analysis models. *Journal of Experimental Education, 66*(4), 361–380. https://doi.org/10.1080/00220979809601406

IBM. (2020). *IBM SPSS statistics.* www.ibm.com/products/spss-statistics

Izquierdo, I., Olea, J., & Abad, F. J. (2014). Exploratory factor analysis in validation studies: Uses and recommendations. *Psicothema, 26*(3), 395–400. https://doi.org/10.7334/psicothema2013.349

Jebb, A. T., Parrigon, S., & Woo, S. E. (2017). Exploratory data analysis as a foundation of inductive research. *Human Resource Management Review, 27*(2), 265–276. https://doi.org/10.1016/j.hrmr.2016.08.003

Jennrich, R. I., & Bentler, P. M. (2011). Exploratory bi-factor analysis. *Psychometrika, 76*(4), 537–549. https://doi.org/10.1007/s11336-011-9218-4

Jennrich, R. I., & Sampson, P. F. (1966). Rotation for simple loading. *Psychometrika, 31*(3), 313–323. https://doi.org/10.1007/BF02289465

Johnson, R. L., & Morgan, G. B. (2016). *Survey scales: A guide to development, analysis, and reporting.* Guilford.

Kahn, J. H. (2006). Factor analysis in counseling psychology research, training, and practice: Principles, advances, and applications. *Counseling Psychologist, 34*(5), 684–718. https://doi.org/10.1177/0011000006286347

Kaiser, H. F. (1958). The varimax criterion for analytic rotation in factor analysis. *Psychometrika, 23*(3), 187–200. https://doi.org/10.1007/BF02289233

Kaiser, H. F. (1974). An index of factorial simplicity. *Psychometrika, 39*(1), 31–36. https://doi.org/10.1007/BF02291575

Kanyongo, G. Y. (2005). Determining the correct number of components to extract from a principal components analysis: A Monte Carlo study of the accuracy of the scree plot. *Journal of Modern Applied Statistical Methods, 4*(1), 120–133. https://doi.org/10.22237/jmasm/1114906380

Kline, P. (1991). *Intelligence: The psychometric view.* Routledge.

Kline, P. (1994). *An easy guide to factor analysis.* Routledge.

Kline, P. (2000). *A psychometrics primer.* Free Association Books.

Kline, R. B. (2012). Assumptions in structural equation modeling. In R. Hoyle (Ed.), *Handbook of structural equation modeling* (pp. 111–125). Guilford.

Kline, R. B. (2013). Exploratory and confirmatory factor analysis. In Y. Petscher, C. Schatschneider, & D. L. Compton (Eds.), *Applied quantitative analysis in education and the social sciences* (pp. 171–207). Routledge.

Koul, A., Becchio, C., & Cavallo, A. (2018). Cross-validation approaches for replicability in psychology. *Frontiers in Psychology, 9*(1117), 1–4. https://doi.org/10.3389/fpsyg.2018.01117

Lai, K., & Green, S. B. (2016). The problem with having two watches: Assessment of fit when RMSEA and CFI disagree. *Multivariate Behavioral Research, 51*(2–3), 220–239. https://doi.org/10.1080/00273171.2015.1134306

Larsen, K. R., & Bong, C. H. (2016). A tool for addressing construct identity in literature reviews and meta-analyses. *MIS Quarterly, 40*(3), 529–551. https://doi.org/10.25300/MISQ/2016/40.3.01

Lawley, D. N., & Maxwell, A. E. (1963). *Factor analysis as a statistical method.* Butterworth.

Lawrence, F. R., & Hancock, G. R. (1999). Conditions affecting integrity of a factor solution under varying degrees of overextraction. *Educational and Psychological Measurement, 59*(4), 549–579. https://doi.org/10.1177/00131649921970026

Le, H., Schmidt, F. L., Harter, J. K., & Lauver, K. J. (2010). The problem of empirical redundancy of constructs in organizational research: An empirical investigation. *Organizational Behavior and Human Decision Processes, 112*(2), 112–125. https://doi.org/10.1016/j.obhdp.2010.02.003

Lee, C. T., Zhang, G., & Edwards, M. C. (2012). Ordinary least squares estimation of parameters in exploratory factor analysis with ordinal data. *Multivariate Behavioral Research, 47*(2), 314–339. https://doi.org/10.1080/00273171.2012.658340

Lee, K., & Ashton, M. C. (2007). Factor analysis in personality research. In R. W. Robins, R. C. Fraley, & R. F. Krueger (Eds.), *Handbook of research methods in personality psychology* (pp. 424–443). Guilford.

Leech, N. L., & Goodwin, L. D. (2008). Building a methodological foundation: Doctoral-level methods courses in colleges of education. *Research in the Schools, 15*(1), 1–8.

Lei, P. W., & Wu, Q. (2012). Estimation in structural equation modeling. In R. H. Hoyle (Ed.), *Handbook of structural equation modeling* (pp. 164–180). Guilford.

Lester, P. E., & Bishop, L. K. (2000). Factor analysis. In P. E. Lester & L. K. Bishop (Eds.), *Handbook of tests and measurement in education and the social sciences* (2nd ed., pp. 27–45). Scarecrow Press.

Leys, C., Klein, O., Dominicy, Y., & Ley, C. (2018). Detecting multivariate outliers: Use a robust variant of the Mahalanobis distance. *Journal of Experimental Social Psychology, 74*, 150–156. https://doi.org/10.1016/j.jesp.2017.09.011

Likert, R. (1932). A technique for the measurement of attitudes. *Archives of Psychology, 22*(140), 1–55.

Lim, S., & Jahng, S. (2019). Determining the number of factors using parallel analysis and its recent variants. *Psychological Methods, 24*(4), 452–467. https://doi.org/10.1037/met0000230

Little, T. D., Lindenberger, U., & Nesselroade, J. R. (1999). On selecting indicators for multivariate measurement and modeling with latent variables: When "good" indicators are bad and "bad" indicators are good. *Psychological Methods, 4*(2), 192–211. https://doi.org/10.1037/1082-989X.4.2.192

Little, T. D., Wang, E. W., & Gorrall, B. K. (2017). VIII: The past, present, and future of developmental methodology. *Monographs of the Society for Research in Child Development, 82*(2), 122–139. https://doi.org/10.1111/mono.12302

Liu, Y., Zumbo, B. D., & Wu, A. D. (2012). A demonstration of the impact of outliers on the decisions about the number of factors in exploratory factor analysis. *Educational and Psychological Measurement, 72*(2), 181–199. https://doi.org/10.1177/0013164411410878

Lloret, S., Ferreres, A., Hernández, A., & Tomás, I. (2017). The exploratory factor analysis of items: Guided analysis based on empirical data and software. *Anales de Psicologia, 33*(2), 417–432. https://doi.org/10.6018/analesps.33.2.270211

Lorenzo-Seva, U., & Ferrando, P. J. (2015). POLYMAT-C: A comprehensive SPSS program for computing the polychoric correlation matrix. *Behavior Research Methods, 47*(3), 884–889. https://doi.org/10.3758/s13428-014-0511-x

Lorenzo-Seva, U., & Ferrando, P. J. (2019). A general approach for fitting pure exploratory bifactor models. *Multivariate Behavioral Research, 54*(1), 15–30. https://doi.org/10.1080/00273171.2018.1484339

Lorenzo-Seva, U., & Ferrando, P. J. (2020). Not positive definite correlation matrices in exploratory item factor analysis: Causes, consequences and a proposed solution. *Structural Equation Modeling.* https://doi.org/10.1080/10705511.2020.1735393

Lorenzo-Seva, U., Timmerman, M. E., & Kiers, H. A. L. (2011). The hull method for selecting the number of common factors. *Multivariate Behavioral Research, 46*(2), 340–364. https://doi.org/10.1080/00273171.2011.564527

Lozano, L. M., García-Cueto, E., & Muñiz, J. (2008). Effect of the number of response categories on the reliability and validity of rating scales. *Methodology*, *4*(2), 73–79. https://doi.org/10.1027/1614-2241.4.2.73

Lubinski, D., & Dawis, R. V. (1992). Aptitudes, skills, and proficiencies. In M. D. Dunnette & L. M. Hough (Eds.), *Handbook of industrial and organizational psychology* (Vol. 3, 2nd ed., pp. 1–59). Consulting Psychology Press.

MacCallum, R. C. (2003). Working with imperfect models. *Multivariate Behavioral Research*, *38*(1), 113–139. https://doi.org/10.1207/S15327906MBR3801_5

MacCallum, R. C. (2009). Factor analysis. In R. E. Millsap & A. Maydeu-Olivares (Eds.), *Sage handbook of quantitative methods in psychology* (pp. 123–147). Sage.

MacCallum, R. C., & Austin, J. T. (2000). Applications of structural equation modeling in psychological research. *Annual Review of Psychology*, *51*(1), 201–226. https://doi.org/10.1146/annurev.psych.51.1.201

MacCallum, R. C., Browne, M. W., & Cai, L. (2007). Factor analysis models as approximations. In R. Cudeck & R. C. MacCallum (Eds.), *Factor analysis at 100: Historical developments and future directions* (pp. 153–175). Erlbaum.

MacCallum, R. C., Roznowski, M., & Necowitz, L. B. (1992). Model modifications in covariance structure analysis: The problem of capitalization on chance. *Psychological Bulletin*, *111*(3), 490–504. https://doi.org/10.1037/0033-2909.111.3.490

MacCallum, R. C., Widaman, K. F., Preacher, K. J., & Hong, S. (2001). Sample size in factor analysis: The role of model error. *Multivariate Behavioral Research*, *36*(4), 611–637. https://doi.org/10.1207/S15327906MBR3604_06

MacCallum, R. C., Widaman, K. F., Zhang, S., & Hong, S. (1999). Sample size in factor analysis. *Psychological Methods*, *4*(1), 84–99. https://doi.org/10.1037/1082-989X.4.1.84

Malone, P. S., & Lubansky, J. B. (2012). Preparing data for structural equation modeling: Doing your homework. In R. H. Hoyle (Ed.), *Handbook of structural equation modeling* (pp. 263–276). Guilford.

Mansolf, M., & Reise, S. P. (2015). Local minima in exploratory bifactor analysis. *Multivariate Behavioral Research*, *50*(6), 738. https://doi.org/10.1080/00273171.2015.1121127

Mansolf, M., & Reise, S. P. (2016). Exploratory bifactor analysis: The Schmid-Leiman orthogonalization and Jennrich-Bentler analytic rotations. *Multivariate Behavioral Research*, *51*(5), 698–717. https://doi.org/10.1080/00273171.2016.1215898

Mardia, K. V. (1970). Measures of multivariate skewness and kurtosis with applications. *Biometrika*, *57*(3), 519–530. https://doi.org/10.1093/biomet/57.3.519

Marsh, H. W. (1990). *Self-description questionnaire—II manual*. University of Western Sydney, Macarthur.

Marsh, H. W., Muthen, B., Asparouhov, T., Ludtke, O., Robitzsch, A., Morin, A. J. S., & Trautwein, U. (2009). Exploratory structural equation modeling, integrating CFA and EFA: Application to students' evaluations of university teaching. *Structural Equation Modeling*, *16*(3), 439–476. https://doi.org/10.1080/10705510903008220

Matsunaga, M. (2010). How to factor-analyze your data right: Do's, don'ts, and how-to's. *International Journal of Psychological Research*, *3*(1), 97–110. https://doi.org/10.21500/20112084.854

Maydeu-Olivares, A. (2017). Assessing the size of model misfit in structural equation models. *Psychometrika*, *82*(3), 533–558. https://doi.org/10.1007/s11336-016-9552-7

McArdle, J. J. (2011). Some ethical issues in factor analysis. In A. T. Panter & S. K. Sterba (Eds.), *Handbook of ethics in quantitative methodology* (pp. 313–339). Routledge.

McClain, A. L. (1996). Hierarchical analytic methods that yield different perspectives on dynamics: Aids to interpretation. In B. Thompson (Ed.), *Advances in social science methodology* (Vol. 4, pp. 229–240). JAI Press.

McCoach, D. B., Gable, R. K., & Madura, J. P. (2013). *Instrument development in the affective domain: School and corporate applications.* Springer.

McCroskey, J. C., & Young, T. J. (1979). The use and abuse of factor analysis in communication research. *Human Communication Research, 5*(4), 375–382. https://doi.org/10.1111/j.1468-2958.1979.tb00651.x

McDonald, R. P. (1985). *Factor analysis and related methods.* Erlbaum.

McDonald, R. P. (1999). *Test theory: A unified approach.* Erlbaum.

McDonald, R. P. (2010). Structural models and the art of approximation. *Perspectives on Psychological Science, 5*(6), 675–686. https://doi.org/10.1177/1745691610388766

Meehl, P. E. (1990). Why summaries of research on psychological theories are often uninterpretable. *Psychological Reports, 66*(1), 195–244. https://doi.org/10.2466/pr0.1990.66.1.195

Meehl, P. E. (2006). The power of quantitative thinking. In N. G. Waller, L. J. Yonce, W. M. Grove, D. Faust, & M. F. Lenzenweger (Eds.), *A Paul Meehl reader: Essays on the practice of scientific psychology* (pp. 433–444). Erlbaum.

Mertler, C. A., & Vannatta, R. A. (2001). *Advanced and multivariate statistical methods: Practical application and interpretation.* Pyrczak Publishing.

Messick, S. (1995). Validity of psychological assessment. *American Psychologist, 50*(9), 741–749. https://doi.org/10.1037/0003-066X.50.9.741

Molina, J., Servera, M., & Burns, G. L. (2020). Structure of ADHD/ODD symptoms in Spanish preschool children: Dangers of confirmatory factor analysis for evaluation of rating scales. *Assessment, 27*(8), 1748–1757. https://doi.org/10.1177/1073191119839140

Morin, A. J. S., Arens, A. K., Tran, A., & Caci, H. (2016). Exploring sources of construct-relevant multidimensionality in psychiatric measurement: A tutorial and illustration using the composite scale of morningness. *International Journal of Methods in Psychiatric Research, 25*(4), 277–288. https://doi.org/10.1002/mpr.1485

Morin, A. J. S., Myers, N. D., & Lee, S. (2020). Modern factor analytic techniques. In G. Tenenbaum & R. C. Eklund (Eds.), *Handbook of sport psychology* (4th ed., pp. 1044–1073). Wiley.

Morrison, J. T. (2009). Evaluating factor analysis decisions for scale design in communication research. *Communication Methods and Measures, 3*(4), 195–215. https://doi.org/10.1080/19312450903378917

Mucherah, W., & Finch, H. (2010). The construct validity of the self description questionnaire on high school students in Kenya. *International Journal of Testing, 10*(2), 166–184. https://doi.org/10.1080/15305051003739904

Mueller, R. O., & Hancock, G. R. (2019). Structural equation modeling. In G. R. Hancock, L. M. Stapleton, & R. O. Mueller (Eds.), *The reviewer's guide to quantitative methods in the social sciences* (2nd ed., pp. 445–456). Routledge.

Mulaik, S. A. (1987). A brief history of the philosophical foundations of exploratory factor analysis. *Multivariate Behavioral Research, 22*(3), 267–305. https://doi.org/10.1207/s15327906mbr2203_3

Mulaik, S. A. (2010). *Foundations of factor analysis* (2nd ed.). Chapman & Hall, CRC.

Mulaik, S. A. (2018). Fundamentals of common factor analysis. In R. Irwing, T. Booth, & D. J. Hughes (Eds.), *The Wiley handbook of psychometric testing: A multidisciplinary reference on survey, scale and test development* (pp. 211–251). Wiley.

Mundfrom, D. J., Shaw, D. G., & Ke, T. L. (2005). Minimum sample size recommendations for conducting factor analyses. *International Journal of Testing, 5*(2), 159–168. https://doi.org/10.1207/s15327574ijt0502_4

Murphy, K. R., & Aguinis, H. (2019). HARKing: How badly can cherry-picking and question trolling produce bias in published results? *Journal of Business and Psychology*, *34*(1), 1–17. https://doi.org/10.1007/s10869-017-9524-7

Mvududu, N. H., & Sink, C. A. (2013). Factor analysis in counseling research and practice. *Counseling Outcome Research and Evaluation*, *4*(2), 75–98. https://doi.org/10.1177/2150137813494766

Nasser, F., Benson, J., & Wisenbaker, J. (2002). The performance of regression-based variations of the visual scree for determining the number of common factors. *Educational and Psychological Measurement*, *62*(3), 397–419. https://doi.org/10.1177/0016440 2062003001

Nesselroade, J. R. (1994). Exploratory factor analysis with latent variables and the study of processes of development and change. In A. von Eye & C. C. Clogg (Eds.), *Latent variables analysis: Applications for developmental research* (pp. 131–154). Sage.

Newman, D. A. (2014). Missing data: Five practical guidelines. *Organizational Research Methods*, *17*(4), 372–411. https://doi.org/10.1177/1094428114548590

Nichols, J. Q. V. A., Shoulberg, E. K., Garner, A. A., Hoza, B., Burt, K. B., Murray-Close, D., & Arnold, L. E. (2017). Exploration of the factor structure of ADHD in adolescence through self, parent, and teacher reports of symptomatology. *Journal of Abnormal Child Psychology*, *45*(3), 625–641. https://doi.org/10.1007/s10802-016-0183-3

Norman, G. R., & Streiner, D. L. (2014). *Biostatistics: The bare essentials* (4th ed.). People's Medical Publishing.

Norris, M., & Lecavalier, L. (2010). Evaluating the use of exploratory factor analysis in developmental disability psychological research. *Journal of Autism and Developmental Disorders*, *40*(1), 8–20. https://doi.org/10.1007/s10803-009-0816-2

Nunnally, J. C., & Bernstein, I. H. (1994). *Psychometric theory* (3rd ed.). McGraw-Hill.

O'Connor, B. P. (2000). SPSS and SAS programs for determining the number of components using parallel analysis and Velicer's MAP test. *Behavior Research Methods, Instruments, & Computers*, *32*(3), 396–402. https://doi.org/10.3758/BF03200807

Onwuegbuzie, A. J., & Daniel, L. G. (2002). Uses and misuses of the correlation coefficient. *Research in the Schools*, *9*(1), 73–90.

Open Science Collaboration. (2015). Estimating the reproducibility of psychological science. *Science*, *349*(6251), 1–8. https://doi.org/10.1126/science.aac4716

Orcan, F. (2018). Exploratory and confirmatory factor analysis: Which one to use first? *Journal of Measurement and Evaluation in Education and Psychology*, *9*(4), 414–421. https://doi.org/10.21031/epod.394323

Osborne, J. W. (2014). *Best practices in exploratory factor analysis*. CreateSpace Independent Publishing.

Osborne, J. W., & Banjanovic, E. S. (2016). *Exploratory factor analysis with SAS*. SAS Institute.

Osborne, J. W., Costello, A. B., & Kellow, J. T. (2007). Best practices in exploratory factor analysis. In J. W. Osborne (Ed.), *Best practices in quantitative methods* (pp. 86–99). Sage.

Osborne, J. W., & Fitzpatrick, D. C. (2012). Replication analysis in exploratory factor analysis: What it is and why it makes your analysis better. *Practical Assessment, Research & Evaluation*, *17*(15), 1–8. https://doi.org/10.7275/h0bd-4d11

Panter, A. T., Swygert, K. A., Dahlstrom, W. G., & Tanaka, J. S. (1997). Factor analytic approaches to personality item-level data. *Journal of Personality Assessment*, *68*(3), 561–589. https://doi.org/10.1207/s15327752jpa6803_6

Park, H. S., Dailey, R., & Lemus, D. (2002). The use of exploratory factor analysis and principal components analysis in communication research. *Human Communication Research, 28*(4), 562–577. https://doi.org/10.1111/j.1468-2958.2002.tb00824.x

Pearson, R. H., & Mundfrom, D. J. (2010). Recommended sample size for conducting exploratory factor analysis on dichotomous data. *Journal of Modern Applied Statistical Methods, 9*(2), 359–368. https://doi.org/10.22237/jmasm/1288584240

Peres-Neto, P., Jackson, D., & Somers, K. (2005). How many principal components? Stopping rules for determining the number of non-trivial axes revisited. *Computational Statistics Data Analysis, 49*(4), 974–997. https://doi.org/10.1016/j.csda.2004.06.015

Peterson, C. (2017). Exploratory factor analysis and theory generation in psychology. *Review of Philosophy and Psychology, 8*(3), 519–540. https://doi.org/10.1007/s13164-016-0325-0

Peterson, R. A. (2000). A meta-analysis of variance accounted for and factor loadings in exploratory factor analysis. *Marketing Letters, 11*(3), 261–275. https://doi.org/10.1023/A:1008191211004

Pett, M. A., Lackey, N. R., & Sullivan, J. J. (2003). *Making sense of factor analysis.* Sage.

Pituch, K. A., & Stevens, J. P. (2016). *Applied multivariate statistics for the social sciences* (6th ed.). Routledge.

Platt, J. R. (1964). Strong inference. *Science, 146*(3642), 347–353. https://doi.org/10.1126/science.146.3642.347

Plonsky, L., & Gonulal, T. (2015). Methodological synthesis in quantitative L2 research: A review of reviews and a case study of exploratory factor analysis. *Language Learning, 65*(S1), 9–36. https://doi.org/10.1111/lang.12111

Podsakoff, P. M., MacKenzie, S. B., & Podsakoff, N. P. (2012). Sources of method bias in social science research and recommendations on how to control it. *Annual Review of Psychology, 63*(1), 539–569. https://doi.org/10.1146/annurev-psych-120710-100452

Popper, K. (2002). *Conjectures and refutations: The growth of scientific knowledge.* Routledge.

Preacher, K. J., & MacCallum, R. C. (2003). Repairing Tom Swift's electric factor analysis machine. *Understanding Statistics, 2*(1), 13–43. https://doi.org/10.1207/S15328031US0201_02

Preacher, K. J., & Merkle, E. C. (2012). The problem of model selection uncertainty in structural equation modeling. *Psychological Methods, 17*(1), 1–14. https://doi.org/10.1037/a0026804

Preacher, K. J., Zhang, G., Kim, C., & Mels, G. (2013). Choosing the optimal number of factors in exploratory factor analysis: A model selection perspective. *Multivariate Behavioral Research, 48*(1), 28–56. https://doi.org/10.1080/00273171.2012.710386

Puth, M. T., Neuhäuser, M., & Ruxton, G. D. (2015). Effective use of Spearman's and Kendall's correlation coefficients for association between two measured traits. *Animal Behaviour, 102*, 77–84. https://doi.org/10.1016/j.anbehav.2015.01.010

Raîche, G., Walls, T. A., Magis, D., Riopel, M., & Blais, J. G. (2013). Non-graphical solutions for Cattell's scree test. *Methodology, 9*(1), 23–29. https://doi.org/10.1027/1614-2241/a000051

Ramlall, I. (2017). *Applied structural equation modelling for researchers and practitioners.* Emerald Group Publishing.

R Core Team. (2020). *R: A language and environment for statistical computing.* R Foundation for Statistical Computing.

Reddy, M. V. (2020). *Statistical methods in psychiatry research and SPSS* (2nd ed.). Apple Academic Press.

Reio, T. G., & Shuck, B. (2015). Exploratory factor analysis: Implications for theory, research, and practice. *Advances in Developing Human Resources, 17*(1), 12–25. https://doi.org/10.1177/1523422314559804

Reise, S. P. (2012). The rediscovery of bifactor measurement models. *Multivariate Behavioral Research, 47*(5), 667–696. https://doi.org/10.1080/00273171.2012.715555

Reise, S. P., Bonifay, W., & Haviland, M. G. (2018). Bifactor modelling and the evaluation of scale scores. In P. Irwing, T. Booth, & D. J. Hughes (Eds.), *The Wiley handbook of psychometric testing: A multidisciplinary reference on survey, scale and test development* (pp. 677–707). Wiley.

Reise, S. P., Moore, T. M., & Haviland, M. G. (2010). Bifactor models and rotations: Exploring the extent to which multidimensional data yield univocal scale scores. *Journal of Personality Assessment, 92*(6), 544–559. https://doi.org/10.1080/00223891.2010.496477

Reise, S. P., Waller, N. G., & Comrey, A. L. (2000). Factor analysis and scale revision. *Psychological Assessment, 12*(3), 287–297. https://doi.org/10.1037/1040-3590.12.3.287

Rencher, A. C., & Christensen, W. F. (2012). *Methods of multivariate analysis* (3rd ed.). Wiley.

Revelle, W. (2016). *An introduction to psychometric theory with applications in R.* http://personality-project.org/r/book/

Revelle, W., & Rocklin, T. (1979). Very simple structure—alternative procedure for estimating the optimal number of interpretable factors. *Multivariate Behavioral Research, 14*(4), 403–414. https://doi.org/10.1207/s15327906mbr1404_2

Rhemtulla, M., Brosseau-Liard, P. E., & Savalei, V. (2012). When can categorical variables be treated as continuous? A comparison of continuous and categorical SEM estimation methods under suboptimal conditions. *Psychological Methods, 17*(3), 354–373. https://doi.org/10.1037/a0029315

Rhemtulla, M., van Bork, R., & Borsboom, D. (2020). Worse than measurement error: Consequences of inappropriate latent variable measurement models. *Psychological Methods, 25*(1), 30–45. https://doi.org/10.1037/met0000220

Rigdon, E. E., Becker, J. M., & Sarstedt, M. (2019). Factor indeterminacy as metrological uncertainty: Implications for advancing psychological measurement. *Multivariate Behavioral Research, 54*(3), 429–443. https://doi.org/10.1080/00273171.2018.1535420

Roberson, R. B., Elliott, T. R., Chang, J. E., & Hill, J. N. (2014). Exploratory factor analysis in rehabilitation psychology: A content analysis. *Rehabilitation Psychology, 59*(4), 429–438. https://doi.org/10.1037/a0037899

Roberts, S., & Pashler, H. (2000). How persuasive is a good fit? A comment on theory testing. *Psychological Review, 107*(2), 358–367. https://doi.org/10.1037/0033-295X.107.2.358

Rodriguez, A., Reise, S. P., & Haviland, M. G. (2016). Applying bifactor statistical indices in the evaluation of psychological measures. *Journal of Personality Assessment, 98*(3), 223–237. https://doi.org/10.1080/00223891.2015.1089249

Ropovik, I. (2015). A cautionary note on testing latent variable models. *Frontiers in Psychology, 6*(1715), 1–8. https://doi.org/10.3389/fpsyg.2015.01715

Roth, P. L. (1994). Missing data: A conceptual review for applied psychologists. *Personnel Psychology, 47*(3), 537–560. https://doi.org/10.1111/j.1744-6570.1994.tb01736.x

Rouquette, A., & Falissard, B. (2011). Sample size requirements for the validation of psychiatric scales. *International Journal of Methods in Psychiatric Research, 20*(4), 235–249. https://doi.org/10.1002/mpr.352

Rubin, D. B. (1976). Inference and missing data. *Biometrika, 63*(3), 581–592. https://doi.org/10.1093/biomet/63.3.581

Rubin, M. (2017). When does HARKing hurt? Identifying when different types of undisclosed post hoc hypothesizing harm scientific progress. *Review of General Psychology*, *21*(4), 308–320. https://doi.org/10.1037/gpr0000128

Rummel, R. J. (1967). Understanding factor analysis. *Journal of Conflict Resolution*, *11*(4), 444–480. https://doi.org/10.1177/002200276701100405

Rummel, R. J. (1970). *Applied factor analysis*. Northwestern University Press.

Ruscio, J., & Roche, B. (2012). Determining the number of factors to retain in an exploratory factor analysis using comparison data of known factorial structure. *Psychological Assessment*, *24*(2), 282–292. https://doi.org/10.1037/a0025697

Russell, D. W. (2002). In search of underlying dimensions: The use (and abuse) of factor analysis in personality and social psychology bulletin. *Personality and Social Psychology Bulletin*, *28*(12), 1629–1646. https://doi.org/10.1177/014616702237645

Sakaluk, J. K., & Short, S. D. (2017). A methodological review of exploratory factor analysis in sexuality research: Used practices, best practices, and data analysis resources. *Journal of Sex Research*, *54*(1), 1–9. https://doi.org/10.1080/00224499.2015.1137538

Saris, W. E., Satorra, A., & van der Veld, W. M. (2009). Testing structural equation models or detection of misspecifications? *Structural Equation Modeling*, *16*(4), 561–582. https://doi.org/10.1080/10705510903203433

Sass, D. A. (2010). Factor loading estimation error and stability using exploratory factor analysis. *Educational and Psychological Measurement*, *70*(4), 557–577. https://doi.org/10.1177/0013164409355695

Sass, D. A., & Schmitt, T. A. (2010). A comparative investigation of rotation criteria within exploratory factor analysis. *Multivariate Behavioral Research*, *45*(1), 73–103. https://doi.org/10.1080/00273170903504810

Savalei, V. (2012). The relationship between root mean square error of approximation and model misspecification in confirmatory factor analysis models. *Educational and Psychological Measurement*, *72*(6), 910–932. https://doi.org/10.1177/0013164412452564

Schmid, J., & Leiman, J. M. (1957). The development of hierarchical factor solutions. *Psychometrika*, *22*(1), 53–61. https://doi.org/10.1007/BF02289209

Schmitt, T. A. (2011). Current methodological considerations in exploratory and confirmatory factor analysis. *Journal of Psychoeducational Assessment*, *29*(4), 304–321. https://doi.org/10.1177/0734282911406653

Schmitt, T. A., & Sass, D. A. (2011). Rotation criteria and hypothesis testing for exploratory factor analysis: Implications for factor pattern loadings and interfactor correlations. *Educational and Psychological Measurement*, *71*(1), 95–113. https://doi.org/10.1177/0013164410387348

Schmitt, T. A., Sass, D. A., Chappelle, W., & Thompson, W. (2018). Selecting the "best" factor structure and moving measurement validation forward: An illustration. *Journal of Personality Assessment*, *100*(4), 345–362. https://doi.org/10.1080/00223891.2018.1449116

Schönbrodt, F. D., & Perugini, M. (2013). At what sample size do correlations stabilize? *Journal of Research in Personality*, *47*(5), 609–612. https://doi.org/10.1016/j.jrp.2013.05.009

Schumacker, R. E., & Lomax, R. G. (2004). *A beginner's guide to structural equation modeling* (2nd ed.). Erlbaum.

Schwarz, G. (1978). Estimating the dimension of a model. *Annals of Statistics*, *6*(2), 461–464. https://doi.org/10.1214/aos/1176344136

Selbom, M., & Tellegen, A. (2019). Factor analysis in psychological assessment research: Common pitfalls and recommendations. *Psychological Assessment*, *31*(12), 1428–1441. https://doi.org/10.1037/pas0000623

Shaffer, J. A., DeGeest, D., & Li, A. (2016). Tackling the problem of construct proliferation: A guide to assessing the discriminant validity of conceptually related constructs. *Organizational Research Methods, 19*(1), 80–110. https://doi.org/10.1177/1094428115598239

Shi, D., & Maydeu-Olivares, A. (2020). The effect of estimation methods on SEM fit indices. *Educational and Psychological Measurement, 80*(3), 421–445. https://doi.org/10.1177/0013164419885164

Simmons, J. P., Nelson, L. D., & Simonsohn, U. (2011). False-positive psychology: Undisclosed flexibility in data collection and analysis allows presenting anything as significant. *Psychological Science, 22*(11), 1359–1366. https://doi.org/10.1177/0956797611417632

Simms, L. J., & Watson, D. (2007). The construct validation approach to personality scale construction. In R. W. Roberts, R. C. Fraley, & R. F. Krueger (Eds.), *Handbook of research methods in personality psychology* (pp. 240–258). Guilford.

Spearman, C. (1904). "General intelligence," objectively determined and measured. *American Journal of Psychology, 15*(2), 201–293. https://doi.org/10.1037/11491-006

Spector, P. E., Van Katwyk, P. T., Brannick, M. T., & Chen, P. Y. (1997). When two factors don't reflect two constructs: How item characteristics can produce artifactual factors. *Journal of Management, 23*(5), 659–677. https://doi.org/10.1177/014920639702300503

Spurgeon, S. L. (2017). Evaluating the unintended consequences of assessment practices: Construct irrelevance and construct underrepresentation. *Measurement and Evaluation in Counseling and Development, 50*(4), 275–281. https://doi.org/10.1080/07481756.2017.1339563

Steiger, J. H. (1990). Structural model evaluation and modification: An interval estimation approach. *Multivariate Behavioral Research, 25*(2), 173–180. https://doi.org/10.1207/s15327906mbr2502_4

Steiger, J. H. (2001). Driving fast in reverse: The relationship between software development, theory, and education in structural equation modeling. *Journal of the American Statistical Association, 96*(453), 331–338. https://doi.org/10.1198/016214501750332893

Stevens, S. S. (1946). On the theory of scales of measurement. *Science, 103*(2684), 677–680. https://doi.org/10.1126/science.103.2684.677

Stewart, D. W. (1981). The application and misapplication of factor analysis in marketing research. *Journal of Marketing Research, 18*(1), 51–62. https://doi.org/10.1177/002224378101800105

Stewart, D. W. (2001). Factor analysis. *Journal of Consumer Psychology, 10*(1–2), 75–82. https://onlinelibrary.wiley.com/doi/10.1207/S15327663JCP1001%262_07

Streiner, D. L. (1994). Figuring out factors: The use and misuse of factor analysis. *Canadian Journal of Psychiatry, 39*(3), 135–140. https://doi.org/10.1177/070674379403900303

Streiner, D. L. (1998). Factors affecting reliability of interpretations of scree plots. *Psychological Reports, 83*(2), 687–694. https://doi.org/10.2466/pr0.1998.83.2.687

Streiner, D. L. (2018). Commentary no. 26: Dealing with outliers. *Journal of Clinical Psychopharmacology, 38*(3), 170–171. https://doi.org/10.1097/jcp.0000000000000865

Tabachnick, B. G., & Fidell, L. S. (2019). *Using multivariate statistics* (7th ed.). Pearson.

Tarka, P. (2018). An overview of structural equation modeling: Its beginnings, historical development, usefulness and controversies in the social sciences. *Quality & Quantity, 52*(1), 313–354. https://doi.org/10.1007/s11135-017-0469-8

Tataryn, D. J., Wood, J. M., & Gorsuch, R. L. (1999). Setting the value of k in promax: A Monte Carlo study. *Educational and Psychological Measurement, 59*(3), 384–391. https://doi.org/10.1177/00131649921969938

te Grotenhuis, M., & Visscher, C. (2014). *How to use SPSS syntax: An overview of common commands.* Sage.

Themessl-Huber, M. (2014). Evaluation of the X2-statistic and different fit-indices under misspecified number of factors in confirmatory factor analysis. *Psychological Test and Assessment Modeling, 56*(3), 219–236.

Thompson, B. (2004). *Exploratory and confirmatory factor analysis: Understanding concepts and applications.* American Psychological Association.

Thomson, G. (1950). *The factorial analysis of human ability* (4th ed.). University of London Press.

Thurstone, L. L. (1931). Multiple factor analysis. *Psychological Review, 38*(5), 406–427. https://doi.org/10.1037/h0069792

Thurstone, L. L. (1935). *The vectors of mind: Multiple-factor analysis for the isolation of primary traits.* University of Chicago Press.

Thurstone, L. L. (1937). Current misuse of the factorial methods. *Psychometrika, 2*(2), 73–76. https://doi.org/10.1007/BF02288060

Thurstone, L. L. (1940). Current issues in factor analysis. *Psychological Bulletin, 37*(4), 189–236. https://doi.org/10.1037/h0059402

Thurstone, L. L. (1947). *Multiple factor analysis.* University of Chicago Press.

Tinsley, H. E. A., & Tinsley, D. J. (1987). Uses of factor analysis in counseling psychology research. *Journal of Counseling Psychology, 34*(4), 414–424. https://doi.org/10.1037/0022-0167.34.4.414

Tomarken, A. J., & Waller, N. G. (2003). Potential problems with "well fitting" models. *Journal of Abnormal Psychology, 112*(4), 578–598. https://doi.org/10.1037/0021-843X.112.4.578

Tomarken, A. J., & Waller, N. G. (2005). Structural equation modeling: Strengths, limitations, and misconceptions. *Annual Review of Clinical Psychology, 1*(1), 31–65. https://doi.org/10.1146/annurev.clinpsy.1.102803.144239

Tukey, J. W. (1980). We need both exploratory and confirmatory. *American Statistician, 34*(1), 23–25. https://doi.org/10.1080/00031305.1980.10482706

van der Eijk, C., & Rose, J. (2015). Risky business: Factor analysis of survey data—assessing the probability of incorrect dimensionalisation. *PLoS One, 10*(3), e0118900. https://doi.org/10.1371/journal.pone.0118900

Velicer, W. F. (1976). Determining the number of components from the matrix of partial correlations. *Psychometrika, 41*(3), 321–327. https://doi.org/10.1007/BF02293557

Velicer, W. F., Eaton, C. A., & Fava, J. L. (2000). Construct explication through factor or component analysis: A review and evaluation of alternative procedures for determining the number of factors or components. In R. D. Goffin & E. Helmes (Eds.), *Problems and solutions in human assessment: Honoring Douglas N. Jackson at seventy* (pp. 41–71). Kluwer Academic Publishers.

Velicer, W. F., & Fava, J. L. (1998). Effects of variable and subject sampling on factor pattern recovery. *Psychological Methods, 3*(2), 231–251. https://doi.org/10.1037/1082-989X.3.2.231

Velicer, W. F., & Jackson, D. N. (1990). Component analysis versus common factor analysis: Some issues in selecting an appropriate procedure. *Multivariate Behavioral Research, 25*(1), 1–28. https://doi.org/10.1207/s15327906mbr2501_1

Vernon, P. E. (1961). *The structure of human abilities* (2nd ed.). Methuen.

Wainer, H. (1976). Estimating coefficients in linear models: It don't make no nevermind. *Psychological Bulletin, 83*(2), 213–217. https://doi.org/10.1037/0033-2909.83.2.213

Walkey, F., & Welch, G. (2010). *Demystifying factor analysis: How it works and how to use it.* Xlibris.

Walsh, B. D. (1996). A note on factors that attenuate the correlation coefficient and its analogs. In B. Thompson (Ed.), *Advances in social science methodology* (Vol. 4, pp. 21–31). JAI Press.

Wang, L. L., Watts, A. S., Anderson, R. A., & Little, T. D. (2013). Common fallacies in quantitative research methodology. In T. D. Little (Ed.), *Oxford handbook of quantitative methods: Statistical analysis* (Vol. 2, pp. 718–758). Oxford University Press.

Warne, R. T., & Burningham, C. (2019). Spearman's *g* found in 31 non-Western nations: Strong evidence that *g* is a universal phenomenon. *Psychological Bulletin, 145*(3), 237–272. http://dx.doi.org/10.1037/bul0000184

Warner, R. M. (2007). *Applied statistics: From bivariate through multivariate techniques.* Sage.

Wasserstein, R. L., & Lazar, N. A. (2016). The ASA's statement on *p*-values: Context, process, and purpose. *The American Statistician, 70*(2), 129–133. https://doi.org/10.10 80/00031305.2016.1154108

Watkins, M. W. (2006). Orthogonal higher-order structure of the Wechsler intelligence scale for children—fourth edition. *Psychological Assessment, 18*(1), 123–125. https:// doi.org/10.1037/1040-3590.18.1.123

Watkins, M. W. (2009). Errors in diagnostic decision making and clinical judgment. In T. B. Gutkin & C. R. Reynolds (Eds.), *Handbook of school psychology* (4th ed., pp. 210–229). Wiley.

Watkins, M. W. (2017). The reliability of multidimensional neuropsychological measures: From alpha to omega. *The Clinical Neuropsychologist, 31*(6–7), 1113–1126. https://doi. org/10.1080/13854046.2017.1317364

Watkins, M. W. (2018). Exploratory factor analysis: A guide to best practice. *Journal of Black Psychology, 44*(3), 219–246. https://doi.org/10.1177/0095798418771807

Watkins, M. W., & Browning, L. J. (2015). The Baylor revision of the motivation to read survey (B-MRS). *Research and Practice in the Schools, 3*(1), 37–50.

Watkins, M. W., & Canivez, G. L. (2021). Assessing the psychometric utility of IQ scores: A tutorial using the Wechsler intelligence scale for children—fifth edition. *School Psychology Review.* https://doi.org/10.1080/2372966X.2020.1816804

Watkins, M. W., Greenawalt, C. G., & Marcell, C. M. (2002). Factor structure of the Wechsler intelligence scale for children—third edition among gifted students. *Educational and Psychological Measurement, 62*(1), 164–172. https://doi. org/10.1177/0013164402062001011

Watson, J. C. (2017). Establishing evidence for internal structure using exploratory factor analysis. *Measurement and Evaluation in Counseling and Development, 50*(4), 232–238. https://doi.org/10.1080/07481756.2017.1336931

Weaver, B., & Maxwell, H. (2014). Exploratory factor analysis and reliability analysis with missing data: A simple method for SPSS users. *Quantitative Methods for Psychology, 10*(2), 143–152. https://doi.org/10.20982/tqmp.10.2.p143

Wegener, D. T., & Fabrigar, L. R. (2000). Analysis and design for nonexperimental data. In H. T. Reis & C. M. Judd (Eds.), *Handbook of research methods in social and personality psychology* (pp. 412–450). Cambridge University Press.

Widaman, K. F. (1993). Common factor analysis versus principal component analysis: Differential bias in representing model parameters? *Multivariate Behavioral Research, 28*(3), 263–311. https://doi.org/10.1207/s15327906mbr2803_1

Widaman, K. F. (2012). Exploratory factor analysis and confirmatory factor analysis. In H. Cooper (Ed.), *APA handbook of research methods in psychology: Data analysis and research publication* (Vol. 3, pp. 361–389). American Psychological Association.

Widaman, K. F. (2018). On common factor and principal component representations of data: Implications for theory and for confirmatory replications. *Structural Equation Modeling, 25*(6), 829–847. https://doi.org/10.1080/10705511.2018.1478730

Williams, B., Onsman, A., & Brown, T. (2010). Exploratory factor analysis: A five-step guide for novices. *Journal of Emergency Primary Health Care, 8*(3), 1–13. https://doi.org/10.33151/ajp.8.3.93

Wolf, E. J., Harrington, K. M., Clark, S. L., & Miller, M. W. (2013). Sample size requirements for structural equation models: An evaluation of power, bias, and solution propriety. *Educational and Psychological Measurement, 73*(6), 913–934. https://doi.org/10.1177/0013164413495237

Wolff, H. G., & Preising, K. (2005). Exploring item and higher order factor structure with the Schmid-Leiman solution: Syntax codes for SPSS and SAS. *Behavior Research Methods, 37*(1), 48–58. https://doi.org/10.3758/BF03206397

Wood, J. M., Tataryn, D. J., & Gorsuch, R. L. (1996). Effects of under- and overextraction on principal axis factor analysis with varimax rotation. *Psychological Methods, 1*(4), 254–265. https://doi.org/10.1037/1082-989X.1.4.354

Woods, C. M. (2006). Careless responding to reverse-worded items: Implications for confirmatory factor analysis. *Journal of Psychopathology and Behavioral Assessment, 28*(3), 189–194. https://doi.org/10.1007/s10862-005-9004-7

Worthington, R. L., & Whittaker, T. A. (2006). Scale development research: A content analysis and recommendations for best practices. *Counseling Psychologist, 34*(6), 806–838. https://doi.org/10.1177/0011000006288127

Wothke, W. (1993). Nonpositive definite matrices in structural modeling. In K. A. Bollen & J. S. Long (Eds.), *Testing structural equation models* (pp. 256–293). Sage.

Xia, Y., & Yang, Y. (2019). RMSEA, CFI, and TLI in structural equation modeling with ordered categorical data: The story they tell depends on the estimation methods. *Behavior Research Methods, 51*(1), 409–428. https://doi.org/10.3758/s13428-018-1055-2

Xiao, C., Bruner, D. W., Dai, T., Guo, Y., & Hanlon, A. (2019). A comparison of missing-data imputation techniques in exploratory factor analysis. *Journal of Nursing Measurement, 27*(2), 313–334. https://doi.org/10.1891/1061-3749.27.2.313

Ximénez, C. (2009). Recovery of weak factor loadings in confirmatory factor analysis under conditions of model misspecification. *Behavior Research Methods, 41*(4), 1038–1052. https://doi.org/10.3758/BRM.41.4.1038

Yakovitz, S., & Szidarovszky, F. (1986). *An introduction to numerical computation.* Palgrave Macmillan.

Yuan, K. H. (2005). Fit indices versus test statistics. *Multivariate Behavioral Research, 40*(1), 115–148. https://doi.org/10.1207/s15327906mbr4001_5

Zhang, G. (2014). Estimating standard errors in exploratory factor analysis. *Multivariate Behavioral Research, 49*(4), 339–353. https://doi.org/10.1080/00273171.2014.908271

Zhang, G., & Browne, M. W. (2006). Bootstrap fit testing, confidence intervals, and standard error estimation in the factor analysis of polychoric correlation matrices. *Behaviormetrika, 33*(1), 61–74. https://doi.org/10.2333/bhmk.33.61

Zhang, G., & Preacher, K. J. (2015). Factor rotation and standard errors in exploratory factor analysis. *Journal of Educational and Behavioral Statistics, 40*(6), 579–603. https://doi.org/10.3102/1076998615606098

Zinbarg, R. E., Revelle, W., Yovel, I., & Li, W. (2005). Cronbach's α, Revelle's β, and Mcdonald's ωh: Their relations with each other and two alternative conceptualizations of reliability. *Psychometrika, 70*(1), 123–133. https://doi.org/10.1007/s11336-003-0974-7

Zoski, K. W., & Jurs, S. (1996). An objective counterpart to the visual scree test for factor analysis: The standard error scree. *Educational and Psychological Measurement, 56*(3), 443–451. https://doi.org/10.1177/0013164496056003006

Zwick, W. R., & Velicer, W. F. (1986). A comparison of five rules for determining the number of components to retain. *Psychological Bulletin, 99*(3), 432–442. https://doi.org/10.1037/0033-2909.99.3.432

Zygmont, C., & Smith, M. R. (2014). Robust factor analysis in the presence of normality violations, missing data, and outliers: Empirical questions and possible solutions. *Tutorial in Quantitative Methods for Psychology, 10*(1), 40–55. https://doi.org/10.20982/tqmp.10.1.p040

INDEX